THE MAIDEN VOYAGE

by Geoffrey Marcus

BEFORE THE LAMPS WENT OUT

THE
MAIDEN VOYAGE

A COMPLETE AND DOCUMENTED ACCOUNT
OF THE 'TITANIC' DISASTER

GEOFFREY MARCUS

All royalties from the sale of
this book are being donated to
the **RNCI**.

UNWIN
PAPERBACKS

LONDON SYDNEY WELLINGTON

First published in Great Britain by George Allen & Unwin in 1969
First published in paperback by Unwin® Paperbacks, an imprint of
Unwin Hyman Limited, in 1988

All Royalties from the sale of this book will be donated to the RNLI

Unwin Hyman Limited
15–17 Broadwick Street, London W1V 1FP

Allen & Unwin Australia Pty Ltd
8 Napier Street, North Sydney, NSW 2060, Australia

Allen & Unwin New Zealand Pty Ltd with the Port Nicholson Press
60 Cambridge Terrace, Wellington, New Zealand

ISBN 0 04 440263 5

A CIP catalogue record is available from The British Library

Printed and bound in Great Britain by Cox & Wyman Ltd, Reading

Preface

On a certain June morning the Cunard liner, *Scotia*, on her homeward passage, lay for a while with her engines stopped in mid-Atlantic. The weather was fine and the sea calm, with a gentle swell. Most of the crew who were not on duty had mustered on the after deck before a small casket covered with a blue ensign. The Master, Captain R. O. Venn, accompanied by the assembled officers and men, recited Psalm 23, *The Lord is my Shepherd*, and after this took the casket to the side and scattered the ashes contained in it on the water. The service ended with a few short prayers. Afterwards an entry was made in the ship's log, which was duly signed by the Master and Mate.

M.V. *Scotia*, New York to Southampton, June 12th, 1967, at 0938, Lat. 41° 46' N., Long. 50° 14' W., the Cremated remains of the late Commander J. G. Boxhall were scattered on the sea during a brief ceremony.

It was in accordance with a wish he had expressed towards the end of his life that the ashes of the former Fourth Officer of the *Titanic*, Joseph Grove Boxhall, were thus cast upon the waters over the position where, two miles below, the wreck lies on the ocean bed, off the Grand Banks of Newfoundland. He was the last surviving officer of a disaster which, at the time, had appalled the world and was accounted 'the most terrible shipwreck in history'. Now they are all gone, these officers: Lightoller, Lowe, Pitman, Boxhall. . . .

The spectacle of the giant liner, ablaze with lights from stem to stern, shearing through the calm, black waters of the ice-track on that cold, starlit night of more than half a century ago, is one of the most poignant and dramatic memories of the old world which passed away for ever with the outbreak of the First World War. Almost immediately a luxuriant growth of legend and myth sprang up which bade fair to submerge the true facts of the affair altogether. For weeks the newspapers on both sides of the ocean were full of it. In the last few decades it has inspired a whole series of plays and films, books by the score, and several hundreds—if not, indeed, thousands—of articles.

Nevertheless, the present writer makes no apology for adding to what would appear to be a more than ample coverage. Though the *Titanic* disaster belongs essentially to the realm of nautical history it has scarcely even been mentioned in a maritime history. Though it demands, above all things, a strictly factual and objective approach, no comprehensive, detailed, documented account of the affair has yet appeared.

Nor has the present writer any scruples about bringing into the open certain inconvenient and embarassing truths which, in the judgment of some, had better remain buried in oblivion. 'Our national evil,' declared G. K. Chesterton, writing of these matters soon after the catastrophe, '. . . is to hush everything up; it is to damp everything down; it is to leave every great affair unfinished, to leave every enormous question unanswered.' That is, indeed, fair comment on what happened in this country in the aftermath of the disaster. At the Official Inquiry a good many awkward truths *were* hushed up, and a number of very important questions left unanswered.

Not the least significant of the lessons taught us by the affair is the efficacy of planned, official prevarication. The Official Lie may truly be said to take an unconscionable time in dying . . . that is, if it ever does die. No competent historian who has investigated the matter can have any doubts as to the origin of the German Corpse Factory legend of 1917. Yet no admission has ever been forthcoming from the British authorities that the whole story was a deliberate fabrication on their part, for political ends; and to this day millions of people probably believe in the truth of the story. Official prevarication is sometimes resorted to for far less weighty considerations. During the last war the present writer was an interested spectator of an unedifying manœuvre to cover up a rather serious breach of the regulations by a Naval chaplain. The official version of what happened (see Hansard, Vol. 403, col. 2393–4) was utterly and completely untrue; it had to be, to accomplish its purpose: yet it was connived at, probably by the Naval authorities, and certainly by the Church authorities. As *John Bull* observed of the opening gambit of officialdom following the *Titanic* disaster, '*What* a game it is!'

It was with the object of clearing away some of the cloaking camouflage erected at the time by the vested interests concerned, and getting at something like the real truth of the matter, that this book was conceived.

Acknowledgments

My grateful thanks are due to the following (a number of whom, it may be said, were actors in the drama, as well as eye-witnesses of the scenes narrated) for the kind assistance they have given me during the preparation of this book: Mrs Nancy Bayliss; Miss Nancy Blair; Mr Gus Cohen; Captain A. G. Course; Mr John P. Eaton; Captain A. R. B. Gillespie; Mr Walter J. Gray, formerly of the Marconi Company; Mrs Sylvia Lightoller; Mr Stanley T. Lord; Mr W. Maconachie, of Marconi Marine; Miss Margaret Moody; Miss Margaret Murdoch; Captain F. T. O'Brien; Professor A. Temple Patterson; Mrs Emily Richards; Mr Alfred Rowe; Miss Edith Russell; Mr H. F. Smith, formerly of Marconi Marine and Editor of the *Wireless World*; Captain Sir Ivan Thompson; Mr H. O. Wilde.

I am greatly indebted to the late Commander J. G. Boxhall, R.D., R.N.R., who, on an autumn night several years ago, related for my benefit the story of the *Titanic* disaster as it had concerned him, the Fourth Officer. It was a most moving and memorable experience; for the Commander narrated the final scenes of the tragedy in great detail, exactly as if it had all happened only the week before. I am similarly indebted to the late Captain Albert E. Smith for drawing my attention to the part played by his ship, the S.S. *Rappahannock*, on the night of the disaster, and to the late Captain Arthur Gadd, O.B.E., Senior Trinity House Pilot, for describing the spectacle at the Ocean Dock, Southampton, shortly before the *Titanic* sailed.

I have to thank The Times Newspapers Ltd for permitting me to quote at length from *The Times* Law Reports; to Her Majesty's Stationery Office for allowing me to make extensive excerpts from the transcript of evidence given at the British Inquiry into the loss of the *Titanic*; to Messrs Angus & Robertson Ltd. for permitting me to quote from *Tramps and Ladies*, by the late Captain Sir James Bisset; and to Captain A. G.

Acknowledgments

Course for letting me make use of his account of Commander Boxhall's funeral in his journal, *The Cape Horner*.

I have also to thank Mr T. R. Hemming, Mrs Sylvia Lightoller, and Mrs Sheila MacDonald who have been kind enough to lend me photographs to be reproduced in my book.

My thanks are due also to The Syren and Shipping Ltd. and Marconi Marine for permitting me to reproduce contemporary photographs in their possession; and similarly to the Editors of the *Mariner's Mirror* and *Sunday Telegraph* for allowing me to make use of material which has already appeared in those journals.

Contents

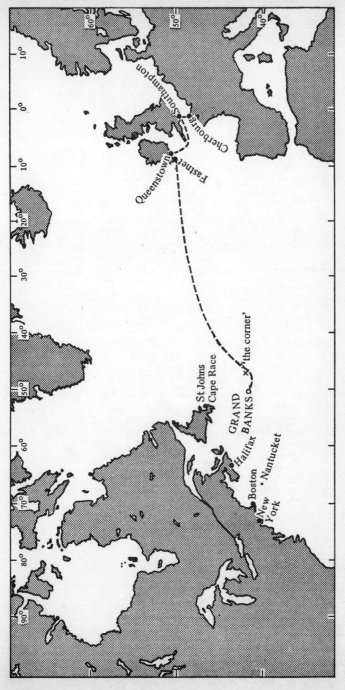

The track of the *Titanic*

Chapter 1

The Boat Train

At 9.30 on Wednesday, April 10th, 1912, Waterloo Station was clear of the busy early morning traffic. Successive trainloads of City men—from Wandsworth, Wimbledon, and Raynes Park, from Kingston and Surbiton, from Shepperton, Feltham, and Hounslow, from the Windsor loop, from Twickenham and Hampton Court, from Barnes and Richmond, from Morden, Ewell, Epsom, and Leatherhead—had swarmed out on to the platforms, streamed across the wide concourse, and crowded out through the various exits. The magnates of the City and senior civil servants were still coming in from outlying districts like Twickenham, Kingston, and Hampton Court; and there were a fair number of silk hats to be seen among all that bobbing procession of trilbies and bowlers. A good many women, too, were hastening, with difficulty, in their hobble skirts, towards the exits. The largest railway terminus in London, Waterloo handled almost the heaviest suburban traffic in the world. It has been estimated that by ten o'clock one hundred trains would bring in about 50,000 passengers each day.

The station was then in the throes of reconstruction. A great roof of glass and steel, supported by giant pillars, spanned the roads and platforms from one to six, after which followed the old drab and dreary conglomeration of Victorian structures which, throughout the years, had become the target of many a music-hall jest—there were tales of passengers who got lost looking for trains, and trains which got lost looking for passengers (*vide* Jerome K. Jerome's *Three Men in a Boat*); the whole place was bathed in rather smoky sunshine and exuded a distinctive odour, 'an all-pervading smell, a compound of empty loose-lid milk-churns, horses, Welsh coal and oil lamps, the London and South-Western smell'.[1] The posters displayed outside the station bookstalls announced the principal items of the day's news: 'The Seddon Petition', 'Bonar Law in Belfast', 'Great Ulster Demonstration', 'End of the Coal Strike', 'Lloyd George and the Budget'.

Over on Platform 12 little groups of men and women stood chatting by the White Star Line Boat Train which was shortly to depart for Southampton. Occasionally porters wheeling their trolleys and other passers-by turned their heads at the sound of the nasal transatlantic accents and somewhat unfamiliar dress of most of these 'toffs'. Curious glances were directed at the tall figure of John Jacob Astor, reputed to be one of the richest men in the world ('Worth £30 millions, they say . . . £30 *millions!*'), the circumstances of whose recent divorce and remarriage had evoked countless scandalized columns in the American press and a fair amount of interested comment in the British. Presently one or two press photographers came over and snapped the great man. John Jacob Astor faced the cameras with equanimity; he was used to being 'snapped'.

As the minute-hand on the big dial approached the quarter to the hour, the groups standing about the platform began to break up as the passengers took their places in the train. Presently the guard fluttered his green flag; and, with a warning whistle, the White Star Line Boat Train began slowly to glide down the platform.

The multi-millionaire who had just settled himself in his seat was the great-grandson of the first John Jacob Astor, a poor Swabian peasant who had emigrated to the United States in 1783, amassed a fortune in the fur trade, and died, in 1848, with the bulk of his vast wealth invested in real estate in New York. Thereafter the Astor millions had increased and multiplied. The present John Jacob Astor had been not unjustly described as 'the world's greatest monument to unearned increment'. None of Lloyd George's detested dukes did so little for so much. The Astor estates embraced some of the most scandalous slum property on earth. 'He knew what he wanted and how to get it,' summed up the Astors' old family lawyer, Joseph Choate, who went on to praise his 'inexhaustible energy all through his life, which he lived in his own way, not in your way or mine, but his'.[2] By devious ways he had got himself appointed inspector-general in the Cuban campaign of 1899–

1901, and afterwards liked to show himself in his resplendent colonel's uniform at State functions. At his great mansion at Newport Astor had a garage with eighteen cars in it. His pleasure was to hurtle down the country lanes around the estate in a new racing car. Attired in engineer's overalls, he had driven a locomotive drawing a private coach filled exclusively with millionaires.

Astor's divorce in 1909 had been followed two years later by his marriage to Madeline Force, then a girl of eighteen, who was actually younger than his son Vincent. In the year 1911 divorce was not regarded as something which could be taken for granted. Astor and his young bride found it advisable to winter abroad. They were now returning from Egypt and Paris, with a number of burning questions still undecided. Would Astor be able to regain his old position in New York society? Would Madeline ever be permitted to succeed to the throne left vacant by the death of Astor's mother, Caroline?

Elsewhere in the long line of first class coaches, with their rich upholstery of dark blue broadcloth and profusion of gold braid, were men whose names were household words; men who controlled vast industrial, commercial, and financial concerns: on board the Boat Train that day were some of the finest business brains in America.

Benjamin Guggenheim was the leading member of a family of Swiss origin whose immense fortunes were founded on mining and smelting, with an important stake also in banking and the manufacture of machinery. The father, Meyer Guggenheim, had emigrated to America in 1847. It is said that for a time he sold shoe-laces in the streets of Philadelphia. He carefully trained his seven sons in commercial methods and organization and gradually built up one of the most closely knit family businesses which the United States had ever seen. His son Benjamin was responsible for the vast expansion of the American smelting industry; with the result that the family ultimately relinquished their other interests and devoted their whole capital and energies to smelting. The Guggenheim interests were closely associated with those of J. Pierpont Morgan. Isidor Straus was an elderly Bavarian Jew who in his early years had emigrated to the United States and gained a

fortune in commerce and banking. In partnership with R. H.
Macy he had built up the great department store known by
that name. He had also sat in Congress and had been the
valued counsellor and friend of President Cleveland. He was
returning with his wife from a winter holiday at Cap Martin
on the Riviera. George Widener was the son and right-hand
man of the great tramway magnate, P. A. B. Widener, a man
of obscure and humble origin, who had become the wealthiest
man in Philadelphia and dwelt in a magnificent mansion hung
with many of the world's finest paintings, including Rembrandt's
'Mill', recently purchased from Lord Lansdowne. Widener and
his wife had visited London on their way home from the
Riviera to purchase part of their daughter's trousseau for her
coming wedding. Accompanying them was their son Harry,
then twenty-seven years old, who was closely associated with
the family business interests and was, besides, an ardent
student and collector of rare books, the friend of A. S. Rosenbach
and Bernard Quaritch; within the last five years he had
established himself among the most eminent book collectors
of his day.

Among the other Americans in the train was Major Archibald
Butt, military aide to President Taft. Butt had led a full and
adventurous life as a soldier, news correspondent, novelist, and
diplomat. He was a man whose kindness and charm had
endeared him to all. (An old negro had once remarked of
Archie Butt as he passed him in the street on his way to the White
House, 'Dere goes de man what's de highest wid de mighty and
de lowest wid de lowly of any man in dis city!')[3] Butt was
returning to Washington after a sojourn in Italy which had
included a mission to the Vatican on behalf of President Taft.
He was accompanied by his friend, Francis Millet, a well-
known artist and author who was also an accomplished racon-
teur. Among the best of Millet's paintings were historical
subjects which were popular on both sides of the Atlantic, such
as 'Wandering Thoughts', 'Between Two Fires', and 'At the
Inn'. Millet was a born adventurer who had served as a drummer
boy in the American Civil War and had since wandered all over
the world. He had been through both the Russo-Turkish War
and the Spanish-American War as a war correspondent. He is

supposed to have said that if he could choose the manner of his death it would be first to live his life to the fullest degree and then to die in battle. Millet now lived quietly in England, at a beautiful house at Broadway in the Cotswolds, and looked like dying in his bed.

Another soldier on board the train was Colonel Archibald Gracie of the Seventh Regiment, an amateur military historian of comfortable private means, who for several years had been chiefly engaged in writing a book about one of the later campaigns of the American Civil War, entitled *The Truth about Chickamauga*. This work had just been published, and the Colonel was enjoying a much-needed rest. The stage was represented by Henry Burkhardt Harris, a well-nourished individual of forty-six, who was prominent in the New York theatrical world and had a number of plays running in the metropolis and on tour. He was returning with a British play which he hoped would be a success on Broadway. Henry Sleeper Harper, of the great publishing family of that name, was also on board the train.

Taken all in all, these Americans travelling in the Boat Train to Southampton might be considered a fairly representative cross-section of the community which had nurtured them. It was the final phase of what Mark Twain, in a revealing phrase, had characterized as 'the Gilded Age'. In that hectic and often ruthless scramble for wealth not a few had amassed fortunes such as the world had never known before. Generally speaking, American plutocracy knew more about making money than spending it. The exuberance of some of the parties they had got up in the early part of this century had excited adverse comment even at home. 'They have given,' Caroline Astor had observed severely, 'entertainments which belonged under a circus tent rather than in a gentlewoman's house.' Of late they had been spending much of their time in Europe—particularly in London.

More and more the leisured classes of the United States felt themselves drawn towards the greatest city in the world, where, increasingly at home among a kindred people, they discovered what America could never give them—the impressive ceremonial which had grown up around the ancient monarchy, the companionship of men and women whose names were written in history, the order, grace, and elegance of a mature civilization. Fresh in their memories was the wonderful London Season of 1911, which had witnessed, among other notable events, the coronation of King George V and Queen Mary, the stormy passage of the Parliament Bill, the first arrival in this country of Diagilev Russian Ballet led by Anna Pavlova, the conclusion of the long run of *The Arcadians* at the Adelphi Theatre, and the first performances of *The Count of Luxemburg* and *The Quaker Girl*. They recalled those fashionable gatherings in the early evening by Stanhope Gate in Hyde Park, and the long procession of motor-cars and carriages pouring down Park Lane past the great houses with their green sunblinds and window-boxes overflowing with scarlet and pink geraniums. The drama of politics added zest to life. Party passion rose higher just then than at any time since Gladstone's Home Rule Bill. The country seemed to be on the brink of a social and economic revolution, and at times it sounded like civil war gathering up. But, outside political circles, the ordinary life of the country went on as usual.

From the opening night at the Royal Opera House, Covent Garden, in April, to Cowes Regatta in July, the various events of the Season had become almost as familiar to the rich of the United States as they were to their English friends and connections (the recent spate of international marriages had greatly assisted this *rapprochement*).

In this final phase of 'the Gilded Age' American society was dominated by a circle of immensely wealthy families who thought and spoke and acted as if the world had been made for them. They used their riches to acquire magnificent mansions in New York, Newport, Palm Beach, and elsewhere; they crossed the ocean in the palatial ferries provided for them by the White Star, Cunard, and Hamburg-Amerika Lines; they travelled about the Continent in trains-de-luxe several hundred feet long. They would reside at hotels like Claridge's and the Savoy in London; Hotel de Crillon, the Maurice, and the Ritz in Paris; the Adlon in Berlin; the Carlton in Cannes, and the Riviera Palace in Monte Carlo, 'the Most Luxurious Hotel in the World', as the advertisements claimed. World-famous yachts like Cornelius Vanderbilt's *Northern Star* and J. Pierpont Morgan's *Corsair* might be seen at Cowes and Kiel in company with the Royal Yacht *Victoria and Albert* and the German Emperor's *Hohenzollern*. Lapped in the accumulated treasures of the long peace and drugged by the widely accepted doctrine of universal and inevitable progress, the favoured few were rapidly losing touch with reality and existing almost in a dream-world of their own.

The Boat Train swept on through suburban station after suburban station, from which the City men in their thousands had departed a couple of hours earlier, absorbed in their newspapers or laying them aside to discuss Lloyd George's Budget, the great Coal Strike (a million miners out since March 1st and millions of other men and women idle through the stoppage of coal supplies), the Home Rule Bill, the Insurance Act, the Stock Exchange boom, the spectacular production of Sir Herbert Tree's *Othello* at His Majesty's, Grahame White's recent accident while flying in a gale at Hendon, the fiasco of the Oxford and Cambridge Boat Race (both boats had actually *sunk*), the approaching eclipse of the sun, and the state of their gardens. Later on many of their wives and daughters would be following them up to town, to spend an agreeable afternoon in the West End, shopping, or just looking at the shop windows. Wednesday was also the day for going to see a matinée, such as the very popular period play running at the New Theatre, *Sweet Nell of Old Drury*, with Fred Terry as Charles II—as the hero of romantic drama not Lewis Waller himself had a more ardent and devoted following than Fred Terry. Other favourite matinées that day were Arnold Bennett's *Milestones* at the Royalty, Bernard Shaw's *Man and Superman* at the Criterion, and *Bunty Pulls the Strings* at the Haymarket. George Robey was playing at the Palladium, and Harry Lauder at the Tivoli.

The eyes of the American rich, when they chanced to turn to the window, roved uncomprehendingly over the quiet tree-lined streets and lanes, and gardens full of crocuses, daffodils, and narcissi, of the outer suburbs. Spring had come early that year. Already the hedgerows were in leaf. There was a fine show of flowering cherries. Soon the rattle of mowing-machines

23

would be heard, and the white-aproned Nannies and their charges would be strolling under the spreading almond blossom.

It was a pleasant, peaceful, orderly existence; withal a trifle humdrum. Always the same unvarying round, apart from the annual holiday in the country or by the sea, day in, day out, throughout the year. The same faces in the daily train to the City: the same colleagues at the office: the same greetings and jests exchanged. The lives of the women folk were, if possible, even more narrow and restricted than those of the men. Queen Alexandra's Day was an occasion, and the advent of the summer and winter sales something to be talked about for days. It was a world utterly removed from that of John Jacob Astor and his fellows. . . .

Soon they were out in the open country; slate roofs gave place to thatch, and streets and pavements and lamp-posts to woods and fields and hedgerows. The train steamed on past Woking and across the wide, rolling moors of north-west Surrey; a country of rough grass and heather and deep belts of woodland, where the vivid green of spruces alternated with the feathery tops of birches and the yellowish green of oaks, interspersed with pine-crested knolls, sandy swells, boggy hollows, and lakes, with the long ridge of the Hog's Back looming along the southern horizon. All this time the ground had been gradually rising; but after reaching the high grassy plateau beyond Basingstoke the long downward incline to Eastleigh and the coast began and the train roared through the deep chalk cuttings and short tunnels of the Hampshire Downs at something over seventy miles an hour.

Presently the Boat Train entered a long avenue of tall leafless beeches, and down into a deep cutting, then raced on past Winchester—a fleeting glimpse of walled gardens, spring elms, mellowed red roof-tiles, and the old grey cathedral in its close— and out into the open country again. The long downward incline continued. For several more miles the track was flanked by the Itchen, a famous trout stream, flowing southward through wide green water-meadows to the sea. Around were the fertile farmlands of the coastal plain. The quiet lanes which wandered through that trim and ordered landscape had changed but little since the days of Constable and Jane Austen. Most of the traffic was still horse-drawn. There still stood the immemorial grouping of manor-house, church, and encircling cottages. The lives of a large part of the local population were governed, as were those of their fathers before them, by the unchanging rhythm of the farming year. There was established, almost as if part of nature's law, a secure, stable, quietly permanent hierarchical structure of society which would have seemed wholly incomprehensible to the American plutocracy looking out on that sun-bathed countryside.

At the end of the eighty-mile run from Waterloo, the Boat Train steamed slowly through Terminus Station, and then, while the traffic was held up and an official flagged the train across Canute Road, glided a few hundred yards further on and finally drew up beside the platform running parallel with the quay. Beyond lay the great deep-water dock lately enlarged for the accommodation of the two huge liners built for the White Star Line; and around was the complex of quays, cranes, sheds, gantries, railway tracks, sidings, and harbour offices of one of the principal ports of Europe. The wind blew fresh and salty from the Solent. It was bright April weather, rather cold. As the passengers, crowding out of the sheds, gazed eagerly up at the latest addition to the White Star fleet, whose name was on everyone's lips, there were spontaneous exclamations of awe and admiration.

The new liner lay at her berth in the Ocean Dock, with three monstrous plumes of greyish smoke curling upwards from her tall funnels; her enormous hull completely dwarfing all the other shipping in the port. The Blue Peter flew at her fore yardarm. At her mainmast flew the house-flag of the White Star Line, and at her foremast the Stars and Stripes, the country of her destination; and on her bows, inscribed in letters of gold, was the name *TITANIC*.

Chapter 2

Sailing Day

The principal Southampton hotels were crowded the previous night with passengers and their friends who had come down from London to see them off. At the South-Western Hotel, which stood just across the road from the long line of shipping offices, warehouses, and other harbour buildings, a young London schoolmaster named Lawrence Beesley, who was going out to visit his brother in America, watched, as he sat at breakfast, the long straggling procession of firemen, trimmers, greasers, stewards, and others which from very early in the morning had been slowly making its way through the streets of dockland to join the new ship.[1] Hour after hour an apparently endless stream of people, both passengers and crew, filed across the gangways. From time to time a peremptory blast came from the ship's siren, warning all and sundry within a three-mile radius that it was sailing day. The deep, echoing vibrations scattered the seabirds, made all the windows rattle, and eventually died away beyond the Bargate. Huge electric cranes dealt swiftly and dexterously with mounds of luggage. The last of the stores were being taken on board.

Also staying at the South-Western Hotel was Thomas Andrews, a managing director of Harland and Wolff, the great shipbuilding firm which had built the *Olympic*, the *Titanic*, and all the other ships of the White Star fleet. Andrews, a master of everything relating to the construction and equipment of modern steamships, had been closely associated with his uncle and chief, Lord Pirrie, in the design of the *Titanic*, and in earlier years had supervised the construction of the *Baltic* and *Oceanic*. During the previous week Andrews had toiled early and late to get the mammoth liner ready for sailing day. On the 9th he had written home to Belfast: 'The *Titanic* is now about complete and will I think do the Old Firm credit tomorrow when we sail.'[2] On the 10th he went on board at 6.30 a.m., and for nearly six hours moved about the great vessel as she lay ready to depart, searching, viewing, weighing, and considering. The result of this final inspection satisfied Andrews. The *Titanic* was good—very good indeed. She would, he felt, always be remembered as one of the finest achievements of Harland and Wolff. Eight men from the Island Yard, including the chief draughtsman, were to sail in her to deal with any necessary alterations and repairs. Later in the morning he said goodbye to his secretary and the other officials. His last instructions to the former were, 'Remember now and keep Mrs Andrews informed of any news of the vessel'.[3] He seemed in excellent health and spirits.

J. Bruce Ismay, Chairman of the White Star Line, was also staying at the same hotel with his wife and three children. He was a strikingly handsome man, well over six feet in height; of strong carriage, very dark, of swarthy complexion, and always well turned out. The family had motored down to Southampton from their London house the day before. Today was a proud occasion for Ismay. He was sailing in the largest and most luxuriously appointed vessel in the world, in which were incorporated the improvements he had suggested after travelling last year in the *Olympic*. He was comfortably conscious of having 'gone one better' than his great German rival, Albert Ballin, of the Hamburg-Amerika Line. Thirteen years earlier he had succeeded his father, Thomas Henry Ismay, the founder of the family fortunes. If the former had not inherited his father's business acumen in full measure, he was admirably fitted to carry on his work. Under his leadership the White Star Line had advanced from strength to strength. In the last few years its profits had soared. It now bade fair to outstrip the rival Cunard Company. Ismay was a strict disciplinarian and ruthlessly enforced his views on managers and heads of departments. At the headquarters of the Line, 30 James Street, Liverpool, he bore the reputation of being an autocrat whose slightest wish was law. Ismay was not a particularly agreeable character; he was respected rather than liked; but he was a shrewd and able man.[4]

The Ismays went on board immediately after breakfast and

explored the giant liner with the air of proprietors: as, indeed, they were. They went everywhere, from the gymnasium and miniature golf course on the Boat Deck to the Turkish Baths, squash rackets court, and swimming pool far below on G Deck. For the Ismay children the crowded morning they spent in going all over the largest vessel in the world made a perfect beginning to the motoring holiday in the western counties to which they were proceeding with their mother as soon as the *Titanic* had sailed.

Meanwhile a good many passengers who arrived early were engaged in displaying the wonders of the *Titanic* to the friends who had come to see them off. They passed in through the first class entrance and past the Purser's office and inquiry office. They went up and down the grand staircase, or else used one of the electric lifts. They trooped along corridors and alleyways. They looked into the gymnasium on the Boat Deck, and some of them were encouraged by the instructor to mount the electric 'horse' and 'camel', while he switched on the little motor which activated their mechanism. They sauntered past the line of white-painted lifeboats hanging in the davits[5]— anachronisms, these, some people may have thought; since the *Titanic*, as everyone knew, was unsinkable.

Some of them paused for a moment to gaze at the great clock, with its two bronze figures symbolizing Honour and Glory crowning Time, set high up under the glass and wrought-iron dome at the head of the grand staircase, before going down to A Deck, where they inspected the reading and writing-room, the lounge, the palm court, and the first class smoking-room. Forward of this were state-rooms, which also took up most of B and C Decks. At the after end of B Deck they admired the restaurant, Louis Seize in design, with its fawn-coloured walnut panelling and large bay windows hung with silk curtains, where passengers might dine *à la carte*. On the deck outside it was the Café Parisien, which had the appearance of a pleasant sunlit verandah with its trellis-work entwined with climbing-plants and comfortable wicker chairs grouped around small tables. On C Deck was the well-appointed second class library, and, aft, the third class smoking-room and lounge. On D Deck was the first class dining saloon—an immense room, capable of seating more than 550 people, with recessed bays where family and other parties could dine together in semi-privacy, with white panelling and a coved and moulded ceiling. It was approached through a spacious reception room with delicately carved white panelling in the Jacobean style and a deep-piled, richly coloured carpet. Further aft, and separated from it by their respective galleys and pantries, was the second class dining saloon, which extended, like that of the first class, the whole breadth of the ship, and would seat 400 people. Two decks below, on F Deck, in the centre of the ship, was the third class dining room, with its gallery and pantry. On G Deck was the squash rackets court, measuring 30 feet by 20 feet, with a gallery for spectators; aft was a swimming-bath, measuring 33 feet by 17 feet, and still further aft were the Turkish Baths.[6]

The two 'millionaire suites' on B Deck in particular caught the imagination of the public. A contemporary writer waxed lyrical as he dilated on the glories of one of these private suites, which would cost, at the height of the season, £870 for the single crossing—a tremendous sum for those days.

There is a complete habitation with bed-rooms, sitting-room, bath-room, and service-room complete. Twin bedsteads, perfect examples of Empire or Louis Seize, symbolize the romance to which the most extravagant luxury in the world is but a minister. Instead of ports there are windows—windows that look straight out on to the blue sea, as might the windows of a castle on a cliff. Instead of stoves or radiators there are open grates, where fires of sea-coal are burning brightly. Every suite is a different style, and each and all are designed and furnished by artists; and the love and repose of millionaires can be celebrated in the surroundings of Adam and Hepplewhite, or Louis Quatorze or the Empire, according to their tastes. And for the hire of each of these theatres the millionaire must pay some two hundred guineas a day, with the privilege of being quite alone, cut off from the common herd who are only paying perhaps five-and-twenty pounds a day, and with the privilege, if he chooses, of seeing nothing at all that has to do with a ship, not even the sea.[7]

In short, the immense structure of decks amidships, comprising about two-thirds of the total length of the ship, was devoted almost entirely to the accommodation of the first class passengers. With the exception of the officers' quarters on the

Boat Deck, the second class smoking-room at the after end of B Deck, and the second class library and third class lounge and smoking-room on C Deck, in this superstructure were situated all the most magnificent and luxuriously appointed accommodation in the ship. The object of the Company was to satisfy the American *penchant* for travelling in the most extravagant comfort and luxury imaginable, and in this it could be regarded as wholly successful. Nothing was forgotten. There was a special lounge for the first class ladies' maids and gentlemen's gentlemen. There were special quarters even for the first class dogs. The dominant impression which those looking over the liner received was one of vastness: the immense proportions of the public rooms, the broad and lofty corridors, and the wide companionways and spacious landings were all suggestive of a palace rather than a ship. Her Second Officer has related that it took him a fortnight to find his way with any certainty from one part of the ship to another by the shortest route.

The *Titanic* had a gross tonnage of 46,328 tons. She measured 882 feet in length and her maximum width was 92 feet. She was driven by quadruple expansion engines operating the wing propellers, and a low pressure turbine operating the centre screw. The boiler rooms and coal bunkers were situated below the third class dining-room, from which they were separated by a heavy steel deck. Aft of these were the two engine-rooms; the forward and larger of the two containing the reciprocating machinery, and the after and smaller the turbine engine. The *Titanic* had a cellular double bottom throughout her entire length, but not a double skin, as had the *Mauretania* and *Lusitania*, which meant a considerable saving of expense; she was divided into sixteen watertight compartments.

Everything to do with the vessel was on a gigantic scale. Her boilers were large enough 'to pass a double-decker tramcar.' Her centre anchor, which it took a team of strong horses to drag on a wooden trolley, weighed over 15 tons. Her enormous rudder weighed 100 tons; its length was considerably greater than that of a cricket-pitch. Her centre screw weighed 22 tons, and each of her wing screws 38 tons. When the *Titanic* arrived in the Hudson River, New Yorkers were told, they would see a ship that was more than four city blocks long, and which, if stood on end, would be 181.7 feet higher than the Singer Building.[8] 'The *Titanic*,' declared *Engineering*, 'was the product of the fullest experience, alike in design and construction, one of the premier ship-owning companies and one of the most scientific and practical shipbuilding organizations in the world. She embodied all that judgment and knowledge could devise to make her immune from all disaster.'[9] It has been said during the week while the leviathan lay in the Ocean Dock one of the seamen observed complacently, 'God Himself could not sink this ship'.

The entry into service of the *Titanic* marked a milestone in the fierce competition among the leading shipping lines of Great Britain, Germany, and France for the cream of the North Atlantic passenger traffic. It was the ambition of the White Star Line to operate the largest and finest ships on this route. Their object was spacious and comfortable accommodation rather than speed. With the completion in 1899 of the *Oceanic* and in the years following of the *Celtic, Cedric, Baltic,* and *Adriatic,* they were by all accounts in a strong position compared with their Cunard rivals, who at this time operated, like themselves, out of Liverpool. Then, in 1907, the Cunard Line produced the *Mauretania* and *Lusitania,* which were not only the largest (31,000 tons), but also the fastest, vessels afloat. The challenge was at once taken up by the White Star Line, which had lately gained an important advantage by re-routing their principal vessels from Southampton, via Cherbourg, to New York. It was at this stage that the formation, under the aegis of J. Pierpont Morgan, of a huge combine of shipping lines, known as the International Mercantile Marine Company, culminating in the adherence of the White Star Line, provided the finances for the construction of a new type of mammoth liner; the first of which, the *Olympic*, was laid down in 1908.

The *Olympic*, which provided spacious and luxurious accommodation on a scale never before attempted, was an immediate and unqualified success. She was acclaimed as 'the largest and finest product of the stupendous skill of the first maritime nation of the world'. 'The *Olympic* is a marvel!' Ismay cabled home triumphantly to his wife after accompanying her on her maiden voyage.[10] The advent of the *Olympic* ushered in the era of floating palaces. She became, in fact, so extremely popular with the rich, particularly with the American rich, that there was not enough first class accommodation to meet the demand. As soon as the *Olympic* was launched, the keel of the *Titanic* was laid (1909). The *Titanic* was built from the same plans as the *Olympic*, with only minor modifications. A third giant liner was to follow, to complete the service. On May 30th, 1911, Morgan paid a special visit to Belfast to witness the launching of the *Titanic* and was shown the suite he was to occupy when she went into service.[11] The *Olympic* and *Titanic* were beyond compare the largest, the most comfortable, and the most luxurious vessels that had ever put to sea. At last, the pundits could reflect with satisfaction, we had stolen a march on our formidable naval and commercial rivals across the North Sea.

'The ultimate object of the White Star Line,' the *Southampton Times* declared, 'is to have a weekly service of mammoth steamers from Southampton, and apparently they are to be challenged at every step by the Germans. For once in a way, however, the Germans have been bested, and the White Star Line can take to themselves the credit of having done something practical whilst the Germans were holding their hands. The present score is two to nil.'

It is always to be remembered that the demand for the ultra-expensive and luxurious accommodation available in these two huge liners was transatlantic rather than British. It represented in fact what the plutocracy of the United States wanted and was prepared to pay for. The Grand Hotel type of express steamship was certainly not to everyone's taste. Thus the late Captain Sir James Bisset relates a revealing conversation between a couple of old seamen in a Liverpool public-house.

'She'll be a floating palace.'

'Floating boarding-house, you mean. Not like going to sea at all!'

'But think of all the work and wages—a thousand men working for two years building her.'

'That's in Belfast, not here. A waste of money.'

'And think of all the work for her people. She'll carry a crew of a thousand—seamen, firemen, trimmers, stewards.'

'They'd be better on shore. She's so big, she'll bump into summat.'

'She's unsinkable.'

'My eye and Betty Martin! No ship's unsinkable.'[12]

After being put through her trials in Belfast Lough the *Titanic* came round to Southampton, arriving in Ocean Dock at midnight on April 3rd. During the next few days the Board of Trade surveys were carried out. Lifeboats and other life-saving equipment were tested and passed. Distress rockets, blue flares, and other 'fireworks' were inspected and approved. 'The Board of Trade Surveyor,' observed Lightoller, in his usual breezy style, 'Captain Clark, certainly lived up to his reputation of being the best cursed B.O.T. representative in the South of England at that time. Many small details, that another surveyor would have taken in his stride accepting the statement of the officer concerned, was not good enough for Clark. He must see everything, and himself check every item that concerned the survey. He would not accept anyone's word as sufficient—and got heartily cursed in consequence.'[13]

While the *Titanic* was at Southampton a good deal of confusion was caused by a re-shuffle among the senior officers. At the last moment the Captain had asked for a more experienced Chief Officer than the one they had given him. He wanted H. T. Wilde, who had been his Chief in the *Olympic*. The Company consented and Wilde was appointed, just for this one voyage, to the *Titanic*. W. M. Murdoch, who had been Chief Officer, was relegated to First, and C. H. Lightoller, hitherto First, took over the duties of Second. David Blair, formerly Second, was dropped out. The other officers remained the same. As for the crew, most of them had only joined the *Titanic* the week before and were completely lost on board so large a ship. Quite a number were entire strangers to one another. It would be some time before they all 'shook down'.

Apart from the confusion resulting from this re-shuffle among the watchkeeping officers, there was a certain amount of heart-burning and disappointment. Hitherto Murdoch's promotion in the Line had been satisfactorily regular and rapid; he had apparently been going straight to the top: his relegation at the last moment to the post of First Officer—after he had confidently reckoned on being Chief—was a severe disappointment. Lightoller was similarly put out at not getting the expected 'step up'—he had already been First of the *Oceanic*. Blair, too, was discomfited at thus suddenly losing a coveted berth and at having to pack his belongings and leave the ship, to which he hoped eventually to return. 'This is a marvellous ship,' he wrote to his sister-in-law, 'and I feel *very* disappointed I am not to make the first voyage.'[14]

The junior officers also had their grievances. Lowe, as he afterwards declared, was a total stranger in the ship and also to the run, 'I was a stranger to everybody on board'. The youngest of them all, the Sixth Officer, regarded his transference from the *Oceanic* to the *Titanic* with mixed feelings. James Moody had thoroughly enjoyed his time in the *Oceanic* and was loth to leave her; nor had he gained any increase in pay or promotion by his present appointment. Davy Blair, his friend and mentor in the *Oceanic*, would not be with them, more was the pity—but two or three of the other officers from that liner would, as well as Jack Phillips, the senior wireless operator, and several of the quartermasters; and at last, Moody might reflect with satisfaction, he had got a room to himself (though it was only about the size of a cupboard, he told his sister).[15]

'At last sailing day arrived,' declared Lightoller, 'and from end to end the ship, which for days had been like a nest of bees, now resembled a hive about to swarm.'[16]

All was bustle, hurry, and activity. Directing operations, now here, now there, seemingly in several places at once, was 'Big Neck' Nichols, the Bo'sun, who, together with the Chief Officer, had been all over the ship in the past few days. The final preparations were made. The Marine Superintendent went round examining hatches, derricks, davits, fenders, windlasses, and winches. Everything was in order.

An hour or so before noon the great ship was swarming with people—the various members of the crew, shore officials, contractors, tradesmen, technicians, messengers, visitors of all kinds, and the friends of the passengers, besides a large number of the passengers themselves. Then the Boat Train steamed slowly alongside the quay with several hundred more passengers and a party of newspapermen.

At the heart of the ensuing turmoil was the Purser's office. It was here that most of the ship's business was done; it was here that the ship's books were kept. The Purser was responsible, with his two assistants, for the smooth and efficient running of an organization which employed a staff of several hundreds. Just now, as the passengers streamed across the gangways, his work was redoubled.

Among the *Titanic's* few English first class passengers who stepped out on to the platform that morning was the famous journalist, W. T. Stead, whose total wealth amounted to no more than an insignificant fraction of that possessed by the American plutocrats. Nevertheless, it is likely that Stead in his day had exercised greater political and social power than any of them and had been on intimate terms with some of the highest in the land. At school he had been known as the boy 'with the hardest shins', and throughout his checkered career Stead had need of all his native toughness. 'He was,' T. P. O'Connor declared, 'a Peter the Hermit preaching the Crusades out of his time.' Editor during its most influential era of the *Pall Mall Gazette*, and later of the *Review of Reviews*, he had greatly extended the scope of the special article and signed contribution. He had been the first to introduce the interview into the British press. It was Stead who in the 'eighties had roused the government and nation with his articles on 'The Truth about the Navy', and started an agitation which led up to the Naval Defence Act; whose influence had been largely responsible for the dispatch of General Gordon to the Sudan and for the peaceful settlement of the Penjedh crisis; whose spectacular campaign exposing the white slave trade, 'The Maiden Tribute of Modern Babylon', was instrumental in securing the passage of the Criminal Law Amendment; whose powerful advocacy had swelled the Navy Estimates in 1893 and thereby put a period to Gladstone's last premiership. From the Bulgarian atrocities to the Boer War there was no writer in England who exercised an ascendancy comparable with Stead's. 'He was very nearly a great man,' was the later verdict of *Truth*, 'and certainly a most extraordinary one.' This

35

indefatigable old warrior was now in his sixty-fourth year; his best days were past and over, and his obsession with spiritualism was becoming rather an embarrassment to his friends (he was allegedly in regular communication with a 'guide' called Julia); but Stead was still a power to be reckoned with.

Stead informed one of the newspapermen that he had no previous intention of making the voyage, but that he was going out in response to President Taft's personal invitation to speak at the great peace conference which was to be held at the Carnegie Hall, New York, on April 21st. It was exactly the sort of occasion which might have been expected to attract the old crusader—half charlatan, half genius. Among the other speakers at this conference were to be the British Ambassador, James Bryce, Williams Jennings Bryan, and Booker Washington.

Two other notable Englishmen in the first class should be mentioned here. Henry Forbes Julian was one of the leading metallurgists of his day, whose researches had resulted in greatly improved processes for recovering gold and silver from ores. Christopher Head was a former Mayor of Chelsea and a well-known member of Lloyd's. He had practised for years as a barrister before devoting his main energies to the family firm. He was making the present passage in search of statistical and meteorological information regarding hurricanes and earth-quakes, in which branch of insurance he specialized. Modest and unassuming, liked and trusted by a wide circle, Head belonged essentially to the upper middle class world of that era, to outward appearance so solidly and securely entrenched, which Galsworthy has immortalized in *The Forsyte Saga*.

It had happened that a number of important passengers cancelled their passage at the last moment. J. Pierpont Morgan, who meant to have sailed in the new liner on her maiden voyage, had been obliged to abandon the project to take the cure at Aix. Her designer, Lord Pirrie, had also arranged to sail in the *Titanic*, but had been prevented by his doctor's orders. The American Ambassador in Paris had been forced to change his plans owing to a delay in the arrival of his successor. Norman Craig, a well-known barrister and M.P., had booked his passage, and then decided after all not to go. Henry Clay Frick, one of Andrew Carnegie's leading henchmen, had also cancelled his passage. Several other people in different walks of life had done likewise. There is no doubt that a certain amount of prejudice existed against maiden voyages at this time. It had been much the same in the case of the *Olympic*.

It is not generally known that the most celebrated wireless operator in the world, Jack Binns,[17] who had served for two years in the *Adriatic* under the present master of the *Titanic*, narrowly missed sailing in her on her maiden voyage. Binns, who had lately left the Marconi Marine to take up work on a New York newspaper, was eager to get to America as soon as possible. He felt he could not wait until the *Titanic's* sailing day, April 10th, and crossed in the *Minnesota* instead.

To some of the passengers, particularly those who came from some quiet country place or far-off fishing village, the sheer size of the new liner came as something of a shock. Her side was like a cliff. The topmost deck rose nearly 75 feet above the water; her four great funnels towered 70 feet above the boat deck; and her tall, tapering masts rose high above the funnels. 'I'm not going in that ship,' protested a Cornishwoman in dismay to her married daughter. 'It's *too* big!'

At the head of the gangway the surgeon was swiftly and expertly scrutinizing each steerage passenger before allowing him or her to pass. The American immigration laws were strict; some of the immigrants from the Mediterranean countries were carefully examined for traces of trachoma, by having their eyelids turned back to disclose the tell-tale spots. Those afflicted with this highly infectious disease were promptly sent back on shore.

A contemporary writer has thus depicted the scene as steerage passengers embarked in one of these ocean liners. The proceedings were managed with admirable smoothness and efficiency. No time at all was lost in marshalling the people towards and across the gangway; the emigrants were dealt with by the surgeons as expeditiously as possible, and all the time the procession was kept moving.

Once on board, too, it is astonishing how quickly the stewards direct the passengers to their quarters. No sooner are the passengers past the medical men at the head of the gangway, than they are taken care of.

'Single men this way, please,' a steward reiterated incessantly. 'Ticket number so and so, thank you. Straight along the passage. You will find a steward a little further on who will direct you.'

That steward is probably standing near the head of a staircase. 'Go down the stairs and turn to the left. Here you, sir, you to the right. You all together? All from the same town, eh? Yes, to the right, I'll see you again by and by.' And so on, directing them to their quarters where other stewards are in attendance to see that each man is shown his cabin and berth with as little delay as possible. The tickets are numbered to correspond with the numbers of the berths, and thanks to this arrangement and the careful direction of the stewards, the early arrivals are soon on deck again watching other passengers arrive.[18]

Compared with the average steerage accommodation in bygone days, the quarters provided for the third class on board the *Titanic* had improved out of all recognition. They were well ventilated, well heated, and brightly lit by electricity. The third class dining saloon was situated where the vessel's motion was least felt. The third class also had their own smoking-room, general room, and enclosed promenade, provided with chairs and tables, which could be used in any weather. The berths were clean and comfortable. The food was good, if it was plain; and there was plenty of it. All this cost only a few pounds for the trip. It was wonderful value for the money. It was good business for the Company, too. Great liners could not live by millionaires alone. Without the continually increasing and lucrative emigrant traffic, in fact, it would have been economically impossible to operate these mammoth luxury liners.

A maiden voyage is always an exciting event at Southampton. On the morning of April 10th, 1912, the sun shone down upon a lively and bustling scene. A good many of the relations and friends of the crew (nearly all of whom were Southampton men) had come down to see them off. Family parties were much in evidence; for large numbers of small boys and girls had accompanied their elders to the docks. Not only the adjoining quays, but also the decks of the *Oceanic* and *New York*, were thronged with eager sightseers. Many of the men and boys had climbed on to goods trucks and other vehicles in order to get a good view.

The new liner had been in the papers for weeks. She was 'the Biggest Ship in the World', 'the Wonder Ship', 'the Ship of Luxuries'. The elegance and luxury of her first class accommodation had become almost legendary in Southampton. In hotels, restaurants, clubs, public houses, buses, and trams, and even in schools, the talk was of her immense dimensions, her strength and power, and her 'unsinkability'. It had been remarked that while her sister ship, the *Olympic*, was all that could be desired, the *Titanic* was—well, something even beyond that! 'They're breaking all records this time,' was the rumour that had gone round the town. It was confidently anticipated that the great vessel was going to create the biggest stir that British shipping circles had ever known.[19]

In the Master's room abaft the bridge, filled just then with a blue haze of cigar smoke, Captain Edward J. Smith, familiarly and affectionately known throughout the shipping world as 'E.J.', was entertaining his guests on sailing day. Most of the fret and bustle of the morning were over. The Master's report to the Company had been made out and signed. '*I herewith report this ship loaded and ready for sea. The engines and boilers are in good order for the voyage, and all charts and sailing directions up-to-date.—Your obedient servant, Edward J. Smith.*'

A big, broad-shouldered, grey-bearded man of fifty-nine, 'E.J.' was generally regarded as the *beau ideal* of a Western Ocean Mail Boat commander. His personality radiated authority, tact, good humour, and confidence. He had a pleasant, quiet voice and a ready smile. A natural leader and a fine seaman, Captain Smith was popular alike with officers and men. 'I had been with him many years, off and on,' declared one of his officers, 'in the mail boats, *Majestic*, mainly, and it was an education to see him con his own ship up through the intricate channels entering New York at full speed. One particularly bad corner, known as the South-West Spit, used to make us fairly flush with pride as he swung her round, judging his distances to a nicety; she heeling over to the helm with only a matter of feet to spare between each end of the ship and the banks.' 'Though I believe he's an awful stickler for discipline,' the youthful Sixth Officer confided to his sister, 'he's popular with everbody.' 'This crew knew him to be a good, kind-hearted man,' a steward related; 'and we looked upon him as a sort of father'. Captain Smith had commanded no less than seventeen of the Company's ships, including the *Oceanic* and *Olympic*. His career had been one of uninterrupted success. He was now Commodore of the Line. After thirty-two years in the Company's service he was nearing his retirement. The coming voyage, in command of the largest vessel in the world, was to be the crown of his career. 'Daddy Haddock,' wrote the Sixth Officer irreverently, 'is going to the *Olympic* until old "E.J." retires on his old age pension from the *Titanic....*'[20] 'He was a man in whom we had entire and absolute confidence,' J. Bruce Ismay, the Chairman of the Line, was later to testify.

Well before sailing time, the Pilot, George Bowyer, was seen coming along the quay. As he stepped on board the officer at the head of the gangway gave an order to the quartermaster, who telephoned to the bridge; and the pilot's flag was immediately run up. Bowyer went up to report to the Master, and to exchange the latest shipping gossip with the officials, agents, and others assembled in his room. 'Uncle George,' as he was known to everyone in the port, was a tough old character who had been at sea since the age of twelve. The Bowyers had been pilots at Southampton for generations (a Bowyer brought ships in and out of the port as far back as the Napoleonic Wars). 'Uncle George' had been a Trinity House Pilot for more than thirty years and always piloted the Company's ships.[21]

After passing the time of day with the others, George Bowyer made his excuses and went out on the bridge, to see that all were on their stations: the Chief Officer on the forecastle head in charge of moorings; the Second Officer assisting him and seeing to the springs at the after end of the forecastle head and passing on orders from the bridge; the First Officer right aft in charge of the moorings there; the Third Officer on the docking bridge forward of the First Officer's station, assisting him and passing on orders from the bridge; the Fourth Officer on the navigating bridge working the telegraph in accordance with the Pilot's and Master's instructions, and logging the times of movements; the Fifth Officer also on the bridge, working the telephones; the Sixth Officer at the gangway. The Bo'sun and his party were assembled on the forecastle head to attend to the mooring ropes and tugboats' hawsers; and another party, led by the Bo'sun's Mate, were stationed in the stern for the same purpose. Down on the quay the Marine Superintendent was waiting with his gang—some fifteen forward, some fifteen aft—to handle the great ropes.[22]

Shortly before noon, several deep reverberating notes of warning from the liner's siren gave notice of her impending departure. The final messages and farewells were exchanged. The friends of the passengers, the newspapermen, and the other visitors from the shore began to leave. Last of all the shore staff and harbour officials left the ship. Expectancy among the spectators quickened as the tugs moved into position. The *Titanic's* promenade decks were crowded with passengers gazing down at the throng below.

Just before the last gangway was removed a crowd of firemen hurried along the quay with bundles of luggage slung over their shoulders, with the evident intention of joining the ship. (Some of these had slipped ashore after the morning muster for a final drink.) But an official stationed at the shore end of the gangway refused to permit them to come on board. Waving them all peremptorily back, he remained obdurate, despite their pleas and explanations; and at last the gangway was hauled ashore.[23]

'Gangway's lowered,' was reported to the bridge; and 'E.J.' came out on the port wing and gazed down to see for himself.

'Make fast the tugs!' The Pilot's order was quickly passed by telephone by the Fifth Officer to the officers in charge on the forecastle head and right aft. Shortly after came the reply. 'Tugs are all fast.'

There was a sudden jingle of bells, and a murmur went round—'*She's off*'. A tremor ran through the immense hull as far below the great engines began to turn over. Hundreds of hats and handkerchiefs were waved from the quay and from the ship. Up forward, a number of firemen and others yelled vociferously from port-holes; one of them was waving an old cloth cap and playing a mouth-organ. The crowds ashore raised a cheer. There came a swift response from those on board. The Ismay children stood with their mother gazing up at the tall figure of J. Bruce Ismay on the promenade deck high above. Elated as a boy at being on board 'the biggest ship in the world',

W. T. Stead was waving to his wife among the people below. Even the most blasé traveller among the passengers experienced at that moment something of the authentic thrill and exhilaration of the start of an Atlantic crossing. *They were off!*

A chorus of shouts mingled with a sudden rattle of winches: the great ropes hissed as they coiled around the drum-heads.

The Pilot was giving his orders: 'Let go the stern ropes. . . . Let go the head rope. . . .' Then, as the tugs started to pull off: 'Let go the back spring. . . . Tow her off aft. . . .' The chasm between the quay and the ship's cliff-like side imperceptibly widened as, inch by inch, the tugs pulled her off the quay. 'Let go your after tug.'

A long pause.

'Slow ahead!'

The Fourth Officer moved the handle of the telegraph. There was the answering clang of a bell in the depths below: the two huge screws began to revolve: the *Titanic* was under way. Very gradually and very slowly, hardly seeming to move at first, the giant liner glided away from the quay, and, with her escort of tugs, crept towards the entrance of the dock.[24]

Chapter 3

Vanity Fair Afloat

As the *Titanic* slowly cleared the dock a good many from among the crowd of spectators broke away and kept pace with her along the quay. In the next few moments they were to witness what might easily have been a disastrous accident.

Two liners, the *New York* and the *Oceanic*, were lying moored alongside each other just outside the entrance. As the bows of the *Titanic* came level with those of the *New York*, the swift displacement of an immense volume of water in such a restricted area set up a powerful suction which, combined with the effect of an offshore breeze, dragged the *New York*, with irresistible force, away from her berth. The sudden strain snapped her mooring lines: long coils of heavy ropes were flung high into the air, and the crowd of onlookers scattered in alarm: a 60-foot gangway plunged heavily into the water, and the vessel began to swing outward from the quay. Both Captain Smith and his Pilot had apparently underestimated the effect of moving the mammoth liner in a confined space. On board the *New York* there was a sudden frenzied shouting of orders, with seamen rushing to and fro and lowering mats over the side in readiness for the impending collision.

But her Master had at once stopped the *Titanic's* engines—and only just in time; for, as she glided through the water, the *New York's* stern cleared her port quarter by a matter of inches. Then a couple of tugs which had actually cast off and were following in her wake came round her stern and made fast to the *New York*, hauling her back to the quay.

The *Titanic* slowly went ahead again. But as she passed the *Oceanic* the smaller vessel strained at her mooring lines with such force that she heeled over several degrees as she strove to follow the *Titanic*. The alarmed officials on the quay hurriedly jumped backwards over the straining ropes and ordered the crowds to stand further back. It was not in fact until the great liner had turned the corner into the river that the strain on the ropes at last relaxed, and the *Oceanic* swung slowly back into her proper berth.[1]

As the *Titanic* steamed down the river the collision which had been so narrowly averted was the topic of every conversation. A number of people recalled the collision between the *Olympic* and the cruiser *Hawke* only the previous summer, and the suction theory then successfully advanced by the Admiralty in the law courts. Among certain of the passengers and such of the crew as were heard to discuss it the incident was regarded with not a little misgiving. Thus, as she stood looking down over the side, Mrs Harris, wife of the American impresario, found herself suddenly addressed by a stranger.

'This is a bad omen,' he told her, in serious tones; and he added, 'Do you love life?'

'I love it,' she replied simply.

'Then get off this ship at Cherbourg,' he urged her, 'if we get that far. That's what I'm going to do.'

Mrs Harris laughed it off, and quoted the many confident assertions that had been made concerning the 'unsinkability' of the *Titanic*. She never saw the man again. He probably carried out his intention of getting off the ship at Cherbourg. But she was to remember that conversation many years after.[2]

Everyone on the bridge felt they could breathe freely again when at last they were well clear of the docks and steaming down Southampton Water. For a few moments they had been very near indeed to a serious accident, and they all knew it. On a previous voyage Captain Smith had informed Bowyer that he was getting used to the huge proportions of the *Olympic*; clearly, however, there was still much to be learned about the management of these mammoth liners. The Captain's gaze turned occasionally to the stocky, bearded figure of the Pilot, in whom he had complete confidence. On the blackest night, and with the trickiest tide, one could always rely on 'Uncle George'.[3]

Under the supervision of the Bo'sun, the seamen had been hard at work preparing for sea: the mooring ropes had all been stowed away, and everything secured and tidied up generally.

With the docks and Netley Hospital on her port quarter and the sandy beaches and the beautiful New Forest country away to starboard, the great ship proceeded at half-speed down Southampton Water; then she suddenly slowed down to negotiate the awkward turn to starboard round Calshot Spit, and entered the Thorn Channel, then a comparatively narrow and shallow passage, where the greatest skill and judgment were required. A few minutes ahead lay the still more difficult right-angled turn to port round the West Bramble buoy into the deep channel leading past Cowes roads (this was invariably used by the larger ships entering or leaving Southampton) and so on to Spithead and the Nab.

'In piloting,' said Bowyer truly, many years afterwards, 'there is always something to be learned'. Rounding the West Bramble was a hazardous manœuvre for so large a ship, especially with the flood making and a westerly wind—it had been fouled more than once, and it was here that the disastrous collision between the *Hawke* and *Olympic* had occurred. But 'Uncle George' was not easily rattled. Five years before he had brought in the then largest ship in the world, the *Adriatic*, in a dead low spring tide, with barely two feet of water to spare. As he stood by the helmsman, the Pilot's keen gaze measured the distance to the West Bramble and the set of the tide; and then, with a quick glance at certain marks ashore, he gave his orders to the wheel and the engine-room. At a point about two-thirds of the distance between the North Thorn buoy and the West Bramble, the helm was put hard-a-starboard.[4] The ship's speed was reduced to only a few knots as she rounded the West Bramble, and, leaving Egypt Point astern, steadied on a course that would take her clear of the Ryde Middle Bank.

Rapidly gathering way again, the *Titanic* steamed past the green lawns of the Royal Yacht Squadron at West Cowes, where telescopes and binoculars were levelled at the great liner, and past the promenade, where men, women, and children lined the railings to see her go by. Cowes front was, and is, a favourite rendezvous for viewing the great ships entering or leaving Southampton. Here, close in with the land, where the *Titanic* straightened out after rounding the Bramble for running down the channel to Spithead and the Nab, the beauty and symmetry of her lines could be seen to the best advantage. There was not the large throng who had watched the departure of the *Olympic* on her maiden voyage the previous year; for that was in June, when there were a good many holiday-makers on the island. Nor was the weather, cold and gusty as it was, suitable for sitting or standing about in the open, or for children's paddling—it was a day rather for kites and skipping-ropes. But the forty or fifty people who were strolling on the front watched her with eager admiration; a small boy tugging impatiently at his mother's skirts in his anxiety to get as near the water's edge as possible. Seated in a boat out in the roads, in readiness to take a photograph, was a local pharmacist who had recently given evidence in connection with the *Hawke's* collision with the *Olympic*. 'E.J.' on the bridge high above, recognizing the photographer, saluted him with four blasts of the liner's siren (more than half a century afterwards Mr Frank Beken well remembers the incident).

Now the intricate S-shaped channel leading out of Southampton was safely astern, there was a general feeling of relief among the officers; and tension was relaxed. The *Titanic* swept on past Osborne Bay with its low sea wall and encircling woodlands in their fresh spring foliage; past the historic anchorage at Spithead, where she dipped her ensign to a number of destroyers which seemed dwarfed to insignificance by her tremendous proportions; past Ryde with its long pier running out beyond the spit and its white-walled houses rising, tier on tier, up the hillside; past Lloyd's signal station at the north-eastern corner of the island, where the look-out viewed her through his telescope and presently made an entry in his log. A few hardy parties playing on the sands followed her with their eyes. In years to come they would murmur, 'I saw the *Titanic* that day!' In one of the villas on the eastward side of the island a young medical student ran upstairs and craned out of his bedroom window to see her stand proudly out into the Channel. Even at that distance she looked enormous. High up on the cliffs of the Wight or across the water on the low sandy shores of Selsey Bill the coastguards on their rounds would pause and point their telescopes at the great vessel.

As she approached the Nab Lightship, the liner slowed down

to drop the Pilot. With a parting handshake, a few words of farewell, and good wishes for the voyage, 'Uncle George' climbed down into the waiting cutter. He did not doubt that, in a fortnight or so, they would see the *Titanic* back again in Southampton. . . .[5]

Presently the engine-room telegraph signalled 'Full speed ahead'; and the great ship, under way again, swept out into the Channel, heading for Cherbourg. The gold band along her black hull glistened in the sunlight. On the promenade decks the stewards were hard at work setting out chairs. The orchestra was playing in the immense dining saloon as the first class passengers sat down to luncheon. It was remarked that amidst the strains of gay music and the cheerful hum of conversation the low throb of the ship's engines was scarcely audible. The bright sunshine and cold bracing wind had given most people a good appetite. It seemed an auspicious start to the maiden voyage. The misgivings aroused by the contretemps outside Ocean Dock were by this time almost forgotten.

Away to starboard lay the fast receding shore of the Isle of Wight, with its bays and headlands, its beaches and sands, its valleys, woods, chines, and meadows, and its trim watering-places: Culver Cliff, white in the sunlight; then Sandown Bay and the high brown cliffs beyond Shanklin Chine; Sandown and Shanklin, with their piers and promenades; the grey shoulder of Dunnose, the spring woods of the Undercliff backed by the distant escarpment, and the high downs above; then Ventnor Bay and Woody Point, and, finally, St Catherine's Head and a vista of lofty chalk cliffs to the westward gradually sinking beneath the horizon.

A few hours later came the shuffle and rattle of tea trays as the stewards trod expertly to and fro across the deep-piled carpet. It was expected that they would reach Cherbourg in the early evening. A good many passengers spent most of the time between meals trying to find their way about the ship. Even with the aid of the little guide books thoughtfully supplied by the Company and all the illuminated signs it was a daunting experience to face the seemingly endless stretches of promenade decks and corridors and companionways. But, despite the difficulties, people were anxious to visit the squash rackets court, the swimming pool, the children's playroom, the gymnasium, the Café Parisien, and all the other wonders of the giant ship.

While the passengers were enjoying themselves, Thomas Andrews and his men moved methodically about the ship, working from deck to deck, from room to room, and from job to job, executing minor alterations and putting things right generally. Back again in his state-room, which was becoming crammed with plans and blueprints of every description, he sat absorbedly over his diagrams and calculations.[6]

Down in the Turkish Baths on G Deck the masseuse, Maud Slocombe, was diligently disinterring from odd corners empty beer bottles and other sundries left behind by the builders. . . .[7]

Meanwhile there had been concern among some of the crew at an omission which was destined to have infinitely more serious consequences than the 'bad omen' that had created such perturbation at Southampton. There were no glasses in the crow's nest. Shortly after 'Uncle George' had taken his departure, one of the look-out men, George Symons, went along to the officers' quarters on the Boat Deck to make inquiries. Lightoller, recognizing his voice, came out of his room, saying:

'What is it, Symons?'

'We have no look-out glasses in the crow's nest,' was the answer.

'All right,' acknowledged Lightoller; and he went along to see the First Officer, who replied that he knew all about it and would deal with the matter.

'Symons, there are none,' Lightoller presently told the look-out. The latter returned to the foc's'le and informed the others. There followed a long and indignant argument among the look-outs, who could not understand why they could not have the glasses, which had invariably been supplied to them in the *Oceanic*, which had been kept in a special box in the port after corner of the crow's nest of the *Titanic* during the passage from Belfast to Southampton, and which now, unaccountably, were to be withheld from them.[8]

What had apparently happened was this: on leaving Belfast a pair of glasses had been provided for the men in the crow's nest by Blair, then Second Officer. But when Blair had later been replaced by Lightoller, the former before leaving the ship had given instructions for these glasses to be taken out of the crow's nest and locked up in his cabin. The difficulty about the glasses, in fact, appears to have been part of the general muddle and confusion resulting from the re-shuffle of the senior officers at Southampton.

As the sun sank towards the western horizon the coast of France came in sight—a distant cliff crowned with some white buildings, a lighthouse set on a headland, the long breakwater sheltering the entrance to Cherbourg roads, and the low, sandy shore of Cape de la Hogue, with the high plateau of the Cotentin looming in the background. The *Titanic* lay that evening in the roadstead in the deepening dusk. There was a hasty transference of passengers and mails from the two White Star tenders, *Nomadic* and *Traffic*, which had come alongside; after which the liner's engines sprang into action again, as she headed for Queenstown, and the lights of Cherbourg faded in the distance.

The *Titanic* had now taken on board practically her full complement of first class passengers. A few more were expected at Queenstown, but these were only a handful. The first class was predominantly American. Some of the wealthiest and most influential families in the United States were represented in the *Titanic's* passenger list.

Charles Melville Hays, who was making the crossing as Ismay's guest, was a prominent figure in the American railway world. Born in Rock Island, Illinois, in 1856, he had started life as a humble railway clerk in St. Louis, Missouri. Later he had entered the service of the Canadian Grand Trunk Railroad, forging steadily ahead until, in 1910, he became President and had almost seen his dream accomplished of a great railroad stretching from the Atlantic to the Pacific coast. By his long and arduous labours Hays had made himself a master of the whole complicated business of railway management. He had recently been studying hotel business in Europe. John B. Thayer, President of the Pennsylvanian Railroad, like Charles Hays, had started life at the bottom of the ladder. Washington Roebling, the president and director of John A. Roebling's Sons, had supervised the construction of Brooklyn Bridge, then one of the engineering wonders of the world. There was Washington Dodge, the banker, whose wife was a well-known figure in New York society; Arthur Ryerson, the steel entrepreneur; and, besides these magnates of the business world, a number of other notables, such as Clarence Moore, a prominent social figure and sportsman, James Clinch Smith, a past master of the 'dead pan' type of humour, whose house in Paris was much frequented by American visitors to France, and Jaques Futrelle, the author of a great many short stories of the mystery *genre*, who had been acclaimed as the American Conan Doyle.

The passengers who came on board the *Titanic* that evening also included one who was, perhaps, the most original and picturesque personality of them all. This was Mrs J. J. Brown, of Denver, Colerado, the wife of the manager of a Leadville gold mine who had 'struck it rich' in 1894 and had thereafter prospered exceedingly. She was a middle-aged matron of Irish extraction, Amazonian proportions, and superabundant vitality. When the Brown family went to live on Capitol Hill, Denver, among the bankers and mine-owners, Maggie Brown's all-consuming desire was to be accepted by the neighbours. As was to be expected, the élite of Denver mercilessly snubbed her. Even the lesser fry who came to her parties used to sneer at their hostess. 'The newly minted gentlemen,' writes Richard O'Connor, 'had worked with pick and shovel on arrival, and their ladies had bent over their washboards; but all that was crammed into a forgotten attic of the past.'[9] Maggie Brown's command of the English language and spelling were alike uncertain; and as the result of an unlucky letter she had published in a local weekly she became known far and wide as the 'Hand Made of the Lord'. Mrs J. J. Brown was a phenomenon which only Ireland and the Middle West could have produced; imagination boggles at the thought of Maggie Brown in a sedate English drawing-room, but harks back rather to such fierce warrior females of Erin as Ineen Dubh O'Donnell and Graine O'Malley. In the West of Ireland vernacular, she would have been styled 'a powerful woman'.

It was Maggie Brown's delight to entertain lavishly and often, while her husband generally took refuge in the furnace room.

Relations between the two became increasingly strained; there were furious quarrels, and finally they separated. James Joseph Brown spent much of his time in the mining camps of Arizona, while Maggie usually resided in Newport, with frequent trips to Europe—once she had been round the world. If the élite of Denver failed to appreciate Maggie, those of Newport did. With her dynamic personality and flamboyant attire, Maggie was a character. The wild Irish tomboy with flaming red hair who ran away from home with her brothers had become a woman of the world. She would fascinate her friends and acquaintances with stories of her experiences, real or imaginary—more often the latter; for Maggie was an incorrigible romancer. In moments of crisis she would swear 'like a pit-boss'. Maggie was well known to the pursers and stewards of the great transatlantic liners. She had made the eastward passage in the *Olympic*; and at the last moment she had settled to return in the *Titanic* on her maiden voyage, after spending part of the winter in Egypt with the Astors.[10]

Among the few British passengers who boarded the ship at Cherbourg were Sir Cosmo and Lady Duff-Gordon. The lady, who had founded the fashionable and highly successful dress-making firm of 'Madame Lucile', which attracted a large clientele from among the wealthiest American families, was, perhaps, better known than her husband. The rise of 'Lucile' from small beginnings had been meteoric. Virtually single-handed at the outset, she now employed a staff of at least a thousand, and had branches in London, Paris, and New York. She had been the first to introduce the mannequin to London; and an aura of glamour and romance surrounded 'Lucile's' girls (one of whom had lately married into the peerage), like the chorus at the Gaiety. As befitted a sister of Elinor Glyn, there was nothing that 'Lucile' did not know about managing the press; though, generally speaking, her style was far more restrained than that of her famous red-haired, green-eyed sister. On the present occasion the Duff-Gordons were travelling *incognito* as Mr and Mrs Morgan.

Among the other British passengers who embarked at Cherbourg was the Countess of Rothes, who was going out to join her husband on his fruit farm in British Columbia.

The seasonal exodus of rank and fashion from the south of France had begun a week or so earlier, and people were now on their way home to their respective capitals. Special trains made up of the finest and most luxurious rolling stock in the world carried them swiftly and smoothly to Rome, Paris, Vienna, Berlin, and St Petersburg. Behind them were weeks and months passed at one of the favourite resorts on the Riviera: Monte Carlo, Mentone, Nice, or Cannes. This lovely coast, with its genial winter climate, had, in recent years, become the playground of Europe. The sandy coves and rocky promontories, the white villas by the shore looking out on the dark blue waters of the Mediterranean, the aloes and cypresses, the vines and olive groves, the purple mists in the shadow of the mountains, cast a lifelong spell on all who knew them. The regular visits of Queen Victoria had done much to popularize the Riviera, which was visited more and more every year. J. P. Vanderbilt had been at Monte Carlo earlier in 1912, and A. J. Balfour had spent a long holiday at Cannes. Puccini's *A Girl of the Golden West* had just been put on for the first time in Monte Carlo.

In Paris the hotels were full of people returning from the South. Some of those on their way to America spent a few days there. The young chestnut foliage in the Champs Elysées and the Avenue du Bois de Boulogne was looking its best in the radiant spring sunshine. There was a revival of Messager's *Les Deux Pigeons*, a new revue at the Folies Bergères, and a blood-curdling melodrama at the Grand Guignol. Finally, at 9.40 that morning, April 10th, the *Titanic* contingent was carried off from the City of Light in one of the *Trains Transatlantiques* which ran between Paris and Cherbourg.

All this was part of the luxurious cosmopolitan life to which the very rich on both sides of the ocean had become accustomed. Many of the first class ladies and gentlemen had with them their own personal maids and valets; and the amount of luggage they brought on board was staggering. Mrs Charlotte Drake Cardeza was accompanied by no less than fourteen trunks, four suitcases, and three crates of baggage.[11] 'I had in my cabin,' related a certain Gallic lady, 'jewels worth £4,000, as well as many trunks of dresses and hats. One does not come from Paris and buy one's clothes in America. That is understood, is it not?'[12]

'We reached here in nice time,' Andrews wrote to his wife in Ireland, 'and took on board quite a number of passengers. The two little tenders looked well, you will remember we built them about a year ago. We expect to arrive at Queenstown about 10.30 a.m. tomorrow. The weather is fine and everything shaping for a good voyage. I have a seat at the Doctor's table.'[13]

As at Southampton, the newspapermen were warmly welcomed on board and shown all over the ship. (The White Star Line believed in cultivating the press). Like Sheba's Queen at the court of King Solomon, the French journalists might well declare that, in comparison between what they had heard and read about the new liner, and what they now beheld with their own eyes, the half had not been told them. They were carried from deck to deck in the swift electric lifts. They trod the acres of deep, soft carpets. They admired the kaleidoscope of colour and movement under the great tapestry in the reception room. They saw the squash rackets court, the swimming pool, the restaurant, the Café Parisien, the tailor's and hairdresser's shops, and all the other marvels of this floating palace. When their articles appeared on the morrow they would be generously garnished with superlatives and hyperboles. The maiden voyage had indeed begun in a blaze of publicity.[14]

The Company had spared no pains to make the voyage a memorable experience in the lives of their wealthy patrons. With 'E.J.' as Master, Joseph Bell as Chief Engineer, McElroy as Purser, and O'Loughlin as Surgeon, the team that they had picked was an outstanding one. They had taken the best men out of the finest ships in their fleet to give the new liner a first-rate start in her career of service.

That first night at sea the old experienced travellers among the passengers quickly made themselves at home in the new liner, which was so very like, and yet in certain respects a distinct improvement on, the *Olympic*. There was the pleasure of renewing their acquaintance with Mr McElroy and old Dr O'Loughlin—the Senior Purser and the Senior Surgeon respectively of the White Star Line. Sometimes as they took possession of their state-rooms they were fortunate enough to find that they had been assigned their own particular steward from a former voyage. Now they really felt at home! There was the excitement of reunions, both expected and unexpected, with other passengers, and much interested conjecture as to who was on board. Then, as soon as maybe, they would stroll into the dining saloon or restaurant, and later into the palm court or smoking-room, in hopes, perhaps, of a glimpse of John Jacob Astor and Madeline.

After dinner, as the *Titanic* swept out across the darkened Channel, the ship's orchestra played on A Deck while the passengers took their coffee and liqueurs and chatted with one another, sitting round the little tables under the palms. Old friendships were renewed, and new ones formed, during this first night of the voyage. Similarly in the smoking-room the usual coteries began to establish themselves, often under the aegis of some well-known personality like W. T. Stead, Frank Millet, or Archie Butt. There was a lot of talk in these congenial surroundings on this and other nights, during the last hour or so before midnight. It was worth hearing, too; for many of those present had led full and interesting lives.

Later on, as the concert was drawing to a close, the gay and happy throng began to disperse, passing up and down the two main staircases, pausing in the foyers for a final chat, and taking leave of one another in the corridors on their way to bed.

This was the first of several such memorable nights on board the new liner. The *Titanic* was proclaimed a tremendous success. The elegance and luxury of the private cabins, the size and magnificence of the public rooms, the White Star Line's high standards of personal service, had created a most favourable impression. The rich and distinguished of two continents who had elected to make the crossing in her could congratulate themselves on the wisdom of their choice. She was indeed a ship worthy of the galaxy of millionaires who had booked their passage in her; she had more than fulfilled everyone's expectations. If the British continued to favour the *Mauretania* and *Lusitania*, the 'Wonder Ship' of the White Star Line was assuredly more to the taste of the plutocracy of the New World.

'The ship,' wrote Stead admiringly, 'is a monstrous floating Babylon.'[15]

Late in the forenoon of Thursday, April 11th, the *Titanic* came within sight of the Irish coast. First the look-outs up in the crow's nest, then the officers on the bridge, and shortly after the passengers on the promenade decks and at the windows of the public rooms, saw the distant grey mountains of Cork rise slowly out of the sea.

It was another fine April day, but rather too cold for sitting out on deck. The sea was calm, with a long gentle swell setting in from the west. Some of the first class passengers found an admirable vantage-point in the warmth and comfort of the great bow window at the forward end of the writing-room to watch the sun shining on the green hill-slopes and rugged grey cliffs between Ballycotton Bay and the Old Head of Kinsale which were steadily growing nearer and clearer. It was a high, bold, rocky coast of shallow coves and sandy beaches enclosed by lofty headlands, their summits sometimes crowned by a ruined signal-tower or an ancient castle. As the ship stood in to the land, it was possible to see the fort and flagstaff on the eastern side of the harbour entrance and the remarkable double wall running down the face of the hill to the sea, and a similar fort and flagstaff behind a ruined church on the opposite headland. For the first time for many hours the *Titanic's* engines slowed and slowed as she approached the Daunt light-vessel, moored a few miles to the southward of Queenstown, to take on board her Pilot. Then she ran on again, and, with the sounding-line dropping continually, steamed slowly in through the Heads, rounded the low-lying Roche's Point with its lighthouse and signal-towers, and finally anchored two miles off the land.

Chapter 4

Last Sight of Land

For the last two hours and more the crowds assembled on the headlands on either side of the entrance to Cork Harbour had been waiting and watching for the liner's arrival. Most of them were from Queenstown and the surrounding countryside, but some had walked or driven out from as far away as Cork City. From the moment a slowly swelling smoke-cloud had appeared above the distant horizon there was an eager hum of comment and conjecture.

Presently the liner was lying off Roche's Point, and the two tenders, *Ireland* and *America*, steaming out from the White Star Line jetty in Queenstown, had gone alongside. The gangways were quickly attached and passengers, mails, and luggage rapidly transferred to the liner. There were altogether 130 passengers and nearly 1,400 sacks of mail. As at Southampton and Cherbourg, the local press was welcomed on board and escorted over the liner; and 'E.J.' and the Purser posed for their photographs. No less than their British and French colleagues, the Irish newspaper men showed themselves profoundly impressed by her size and magnificence. Meanwhile a fleet of bumboats had come alongside; a number of their owners were allowed to cross the gangway, and for an hour or so part of one of the promenade decks was turned into an improvised market for the sale of Irish linen and laces; John Jacob Astor paid $800 for a single article.[1]

The great majority of the passengers who embarked at Queenstown were emigrants, travelling steerage, for the most part young men and girls. They came from all over the island, but more especially from the south and west, from small farms and quiet country towns where the dullness and monotony of everyday life was broken only by an occasional festivity like Puck Fair or St Patrick's Day, drawn by the lure of the New

World and the hope of opportunities which were unlikely ever to be vouchsafed to them in their own country. They trooped on board in small parties of relatives and friends, well over a hundred of them—Buckleys, Dalys, Foleys, Flynns, Kellys, McCoys, Morans, Murphys, O'Briens, O'Connors, Ryans, and many others.

Queenstown, it has been said, 'is a wound which Ireland cannot stanch; and from it pours a constant stream of her best and her youngest blood'. For well over a hundred years this stream had been pouring overseas to swell the population of North America, more especially of the United States. It was a cruel, but imperative, uprooting; for the truth was, there was nothing for them at home. With mingled grief and hope they would set out on the great adventure of their lives, bound for the land of opportunity—in all probability never to behold Ireland again. With a handful of dollars in their pockets, they would plunge into the fiercely competitive life of the New World. A few, a very few, would make their fortunes over there; and, in course of time, merge with the American middle and upper classes. The great majority would toil hard for meagre wages to the end of their days, thankful if only they had a roof over their heads and food for themselves and their children. In recent years, however, things had improved, and they were often able to send home a few pounds each Christmas to their parents in the Old Country.

At Queenstown, it is related, there occurred another 'bad omen'. As one of the tenders was coming alongside the *Titanic*, some of the passengers saw a fireman's head, black with coal dust, suddenly shoot up on top of one of the huge funnels—a dummy one, which was used for ventilation—which towered above the Boat Deck. The man had climbed up inside the funnel to give everybody a surprise. But, in some cases, the joke went the wrong way. An American lady confided to Beesley, in all good faith, that she saw the fireman's head herself, and attributed the loss of the *Titanic* to this apparition.[2]

There also occurred something that may not have been due to superstition at all, but to a deep-seated and wholly justified misgiving at all the bragging and boasting that had gone on in connection with these mammoth liners and at the increasing risks that were being taken by the crack steamships on the North Atlantic run. Whatever the cause may have been, the rumour persisted that the *Titanic* was unlucky. On this day, the 11th, a young fireman named John Coffey was struck with sudden foreboding and deserted his ship. (He signed on in the *Mauretania* on the following Sunday.) He was not the only member of the ship's company to experience this uneasiness. 'I still don't like this ship,' the Chief Officer wrote to his sister before the call at Queenstown; '... I have a queer feeling about it.'[3]

Scarcely had the last hundred sacks of mail been transferred from tender to liner than the siren of the *Titanic* and the whistle of the tenders gave warning to her shore visitors that their time was up. Soon after the tenders cast off, the gangways were raised, and the bumboats were ordered to stand clear; and then the anchor was hove up and the *Titanic* throbbed to life as the great screws began to revolve, and she turned slowly through a quarter-circle until she was heading once again to the westward. In her wake hovered and circled myriads of hungry seabirds, alert for the garbage shot from her waste pipes. Soon the grey terraced houses of Queenstown and the slender tapering spire of St Colman's Cathedral were left astern. The last that could be seen of Queenstown was a little white house built on the hill to the south of the town.[4]

Now that all the bustle and excitement of embarkation was behind them and they had time for reflection, some of the Irish passengers in the steerage stood silently gazing down from their promenade deck at the ever-lengthening trail of foam astern, and thought with aching hearts of the hills of home and of the scent of turf smoke in the twilight and of some small, white-walled farmstead which, as they well knew, they were unlikely ever to see again.

It was about this time that two of the look-outs, George Hogg and Alfred Evans, asked the Second Officer, 'Where is our glasses, sir?' Lightoller made some indeterminate response which the two did not quite catch—'Get them later', or something of the sort. It would seem that Hogg was very anxious to have these glasses, and had asked for them repeatedly.[5]

Most of the first class passengers knew very little about the coast that they were skirting; but they were enjoying luxurious conditions of travel such as their forbears had never dreamed of. They reclined in soft-cushioned chairs under the vine-covered trellis in the verandah café, or strolled about the glass-sheltered promenade decks, while, across a smooth, sunlit sea, the south coast of Ireland unrolled itself mile by mile.

The black hull of the Daunt light-vessel was well astern as they ran down the bold and rugged shore west of Cork Harbour; past the rocky islets called the Sovereigns with their teeming colonies of seabirds; past the Old Head of Kinsale—a massive projecting headland, bounded by high precipitous cliffs, on which stood a lighthouse, with an old signal-tower and a ruined castle behind it; past the cliffs and rocks of Court-macsherry Bay, the Seven Heads, a long stretch of sands, and Galley Head rising out of the sea like an island on the starboard bow; past the pinnacled Stags, the bluff, bold promontory of Toe Head, and then the rocky, flat-topped Kedge Island. From now onward the coast was high, barren, and rocky. From time to time there might be seen a trim white coastguard station, surrounded by well-kept gardens and flanked by a tall flagstaff from which floated the Union Jack; or a ruined signal-tower on a lofty headland—relic of the Napoleonic Wars. Where the cliffs came down low there were glimpses of the interior, where sunlight and shadow chased one another across the distant checkerwork of fields and pastures; there were scattered farmsteads, a few fishermen's cottages beside a cove, and an occasional church or chapel. But for the most part the prospect was one of lonely, grassy hill-slopes, glens overgrown with bracken and heather, brambly thickets, stretches of flaming furze, and gaunt grey cliffs with the groundswell foaming on the rocky prongs below.

There were many who saw the *Titanic* that day as, steaming within four or five miles of the rugged coast, she drove on to the westward. Sure, she was a beauty! To the end of their lives some of them would remember the splendid spectacle of the great liner, with her black hull and white upper works gleaming in the sunlight, sweeping on proudly past the headlands of the west. Little groups of people gathered outside a coastguard station, some crabbers pulling out to their lobster-pots, women standing in cottage doorways, fishermen drying their nets on some harbour wall, children strolling home from school, boys trudging beside well-laden donkeys, a dispensary doctor on his rounds, the look-outs on watch in Lloyd's signal stations, loungers and longshoremen in every fishing cove between Kinsale and Crookhaven—paused for a moment from their various occupations and followed her, admiringly, with their eyes.

About tea-time the slim circular tower of the Fastnet was sighted; and, before nightfall hid the coast of Ireland from their view, there was vouchsafed that magical vision of far-off shadowy mountain-ranges, headlands, sea-loughs, and islands which, in clear weather, is the departing traveller's last sight of the Old World. To the northward rose up the bold, precipitous shores of Cape Clear Island with the westering sun shining down on its small walled fields and thatched white cottages; away beyond was an archipelago of isles and rocks, ringed and streaked with foam; and in the background, the distant outline of Mizen Head and Dursey Island, and, further off still, the pinnacled peaks of the Skelligs and the faint grey curve of the Kerry mountains.

A few of the passengers were still gazing silently at that glorious prospect and the flock of seagulls following astern when presently the sunset faded into twilight, the Tearaght light began to gleam across the water far away to the eastward, and the bugle-call sounded for dinner.

From the Fastnet the *Titanic* followed the usual outward-bound track for mail steamers to the Nantucket light vessel. This was the Great Circle course from the Fastnet to what was called 'the corner', or turning-point, in the vicinity of lat. 42° N. and long. 47° W., and from thence by rhumb line to Sandy Hook.

A word of explanation is necessary here. On a Mercator chart (presenting as it does a distorted impression of the earth's surface) the rhumb, or straight course line, is apparently the shortest distance between any two points. On a globe, however, the shortest distance between any two points is the arc of a Great Circle, or *orthodromic curve*, which, if carried round the globe, would divide it into two equal portions, and whose plane would always pass through the centre. It can be demonstrated by experiments with lengths of fine silk thread and pins that the straight line on the chart is in fact a circuitous route when laid down a globe. The only exception to this is where a straight line on the chart happens to coincide either with the equator or with a meridian, since both of these are Great Circles in themselves. For short distances these considerations are of small consequence, and the Mercator chart is the one commonly used at sea. For the North Atlantic crossing, however, it is a very different matter.

On a Mercator chart the ship's track is represented by a rhumb line which cuts each meridian at the same angle. On a globe, owing to the convergence of the meridians towards the poles, the Great Circle does not cut each meridian at the same angle. A Great Circle track between any two points on a Mercator chart is therefore represented by a curve. As steering a vessel along a Great Circle would entail continual alterations of course, convenient points must be selected along the curve and the vessel steered from one to the other along the rhumbs, or straight lines, joining them. In Great Circle sailing frequent alterations of course are necessary so that the vessel's track may coincide as nearly as possible with the Great Circle. Great Circle sailing is principally of use between places in high latitudes, where it allows of considerable saving of distance. It is to be observed that there are disadvantages as well in Great Circle sailing; but these will be dealt with in their proper place.

The track to be followed by the *Titanic* on her passage to New York was laid off by the commander on the large chart spread out on the table in the navigating room. Her true course when she took her departure from the Fastnet on that evening, Thursday, April 11th, was S. 68° W. The weather was fine and clear, with moderate winds from the west-south-west.[6]

The white-painted Marconi office abaft the officers' quarters on the boat deck represented something even more modern and more marvellous in the eyes of the average passenger than the navigational instruments on the bridge.

As early as 1864 Clerk Maxwell had deduced mathematically the existence of electro-magnetic waves in an imponderable medium called the ether. About twenty years later the German scientist Hertz established the truth of Clerk Maxwell's theory by experiment. But it was not until towards the turn of the century that the investigations of the brilliant young Italian physicist, Guglielmo Marconi, laid the foundations of a practical system of wireless telegraphy. The importance of the Marconi system was that it *worked*. The development of an effective aerial-earth system had for the first time made long-distance wireless communications possible.[7] In 1901 wireless signals traversed the Atlantic. This event created a world-wide sensation, for it had hitherto been generally believed that the curvature of the earth's surface would be an insuperable obstacle to the transmission of wireless signals above a distance of 200 miles. In 1902 Marconi patented the magnetic detector and a few years later developed and patented the horizontal directional aerial.

The *Titanic's* wireless station—known to the outside world by her call-sign, MGY—consisted of three separate compartments. In the first were contained the receiver, operating table, and control gear, in the second was the transmitting apparatus, and the third, entered through a doorway, was the sleeping cabin. Her radio equipment, it was claimed, was the most modern and most powerful possessed by any merchant vessel afloat with the exception of the *Olympic*. Its day-time range was from 250 to 400 miles, and at night it occasionally spanned a distance of 2,000 miles. The aerial was of the twin T type supported by two masts 200 feet high stepped 600 feet part; its mean height was about 170 feet. The earth connection was made by an insulated cable clamped to the hull of the vessel.[8]

The receiver embodied the standard Marconi magnetic, or *hysteresis*, detector, activated by clockwork, which, during the last ten years or so, had largely replaced the early coherer, 'the Father Adam of all receivers'.[9] The great advantage of the magnetic detector was that it was robust and reliable (even if the clockwork should fail it could still be operated by turning a handle), and could be permanently connected to the transmitting aerial, thus dispensing with all mechanical change-over switching gear between transmitter and receiver, and permitting the same aerial to be used both for transmitting and receiving. A serious disadvantage of this type of detector was that it gave rather weak signals.[10]

The magnetic detector was used in conjunction with the Marconi multiple tuner covering all wave-lengths between 300 and 2500 metres, and calibrated so that it could be pre-set to any given frequency. The multiple tuner embodied three circuits—the Stand-by, Intermediate, and Detector. In the Stand-by position, the aerial circuit was directly connected with the magnetic detector. This afforded broad tuning. In theory, as soon as the signal was picked up the other two circuits—the Intermediate and Detector—were switched in, which were supposed greatly to increase the selectivity. In practice, however, the Stand-by circuit only was used, because experience had shown that by switching in the other circuits there was a serious loss of signal strength without any adequate gain in selectivity.

The transmitter—a rotary disc discharger—was powered by a 5 kilowatt motor generator fed from the 110-volt D.C. ship's lighting system. MGY could also in an emergency utilize the oil-engine set erected on the Boat Deck; and a battery of accumulators was installed as a stand-by.

Wireless had already proved its worth at sea. The first merchant vessel to carry a radio installation was the *Kaiser Wilhelm de Grosse* in 1900. During the next twelve years the number of transatlantic liners equipped with wireless had progressively increased. At the same time all Lloyd's main signal stations were also fitted with wireless. The principal items of the day's news were regularly transmitted from Poldhu and Cape Cod on 2,000 metres. Doctors had prescribed, and games of chess had been played, by means of wireless telegraphy. When the cruiser *Gladiator* and the American liner *St Paul* collided in a blizzard in 1909, the full details of the disaster were known the same night to every ship fitted with long-distance wireless apparatus within 1,500 miles of Poldhu. The death of Edward VII was actually known at sea within two hours of its announcement in London; and next year, while in mid-Atlantic, passengers booked seats by wireless for George V's coronation procession which they had seen advertised in the ship's newspaper. At a lecture delivered in this same summer (1911), Marconi declared: 'Those who make long sea journeys are no longer cut off from the rest of the world; business men continue to correspond at reasonable rates with their offices in America or Europe; ordinary social messages can be exchanged between passengers and their friends on shore; a daily newspaper is published on board most of the principal liners giving the chief news of the day. The chief benefit, however, of radio-telegraphy lies in the facility which it affords to ships in distress of communicating their plight to neighbouring vessels or coast stations.'

In the small hours of Friday, April 12th, Jack Phillips, the senior operator, sat at the table in the wireless cabin with the telephones on his head and the Morse key at his elbow. The *Titanic* was now something like 180 miles west of the Fastnet. Except for the 'black gang' in the stokehold, and a handful of men on duty on the bridge and on various stations elsewhere throughout the ship, nearly everyone was in bed; and the promenade decks and the public rooms were almost wholly deserted.

Phillips was a pale-faced, rather serious young man who stood high in the confidence of his superiors in the Marconi Marine Company. Born at Farncombe in Surrey in 1887, he had spent several years at Godalming Grammar School, worked for some time as a telegraphist in the local post office, and in 1906 joined the Marconi training-school at Liverpool. At his Postmaster-General's Examination Phillips headed the list of successful candidates and in the course of the following years went steadily to the top, serving successively in the *Teutonic*, *Lusitania*, *Mauretania*, *Campania*, and *Oceanic*; he also spent three years at the high-power transmitting station at Clifden in western Ireland. During the last appointment he had struck up a radio friendship with Walter J. Gray, the officer-in-charge at the corresponding station at Glace Bay, Nova Scotia, of whom more will be heard later. Phillips had celebrated his twenty-fifth birthday on the previous day.

Like so many of the young wireless operators of those days, he was utterly and completely absorbed in his work. He was justly proud of his service in the *Oceanic*—one of the smartest mail boats that ever crossed the Atlantic—and exultant on being appointed, in 1912, to the *Titanic*. At the same time it is worth noticing that during his Christmas leave he had confessed to a friend who had been at school with him that he would rather have been in a smaller ship than in the giant liners which were now running. He may, perhaps, have missed the easier, more informal relationship that existed between the deck officers and the wireless men in the smaller ships. On board the *Titanic* it not infrequently happened that the operator on duty did not even know the name of the Officer of the Watch when he had to go up on the bridge with a telegram. During the same conversation Phillips is said to have told this friend that he had a great dread of icebergs.[11]

In the adjoining cabin the junior operator, Harold Bride, lay asleep in his berth. He was a fresh-complexioned, curly-haired youth from Bromley, Kent, who, like Phillips, had originally been a post office telegraphist. At the 'Tin Tabernacle' (as the Marconi training-school at Liverpool was irreverently styled) some eighteen months earlier, he had embarked upon an intensive course embracing elementary electricity and magnetism, the principles of radio propagation, the theoretical and practical knowledge of various types of wireless apparatus, the location and repair of faults and failures, the rules and regulations laid down by the Radiotelegraphy Convention, and general shipboard routine. After completing his training, Bride had gone to sea in the summer of 1911, serving in the *Haverford*, *Lusitania* (as junior operator), *Lanfranc*, and *Anselm*. He was twenty-two years old.[12]

Chapter 5

On Her Course

By daybreak on the 12th the *Titanic* was well out in the Atlantic and running at something like 21 knots. The weather still continued fine, and the sea was calm with a gentle swell that affected none but the worst sailors among the passengers. The early morning sunlight streamed into the white-painted bathrooms, the glass-sheltered promenade decks, and the trim dining saloons where stewards were putting the last touches to their breakfast tables. The breeze that blew down the newly swept corridors and staircases was pure and invigorating as it seldom is on shore. Quite a number of the passengers rose early and tramped for miles along the different decks to work up an ocean appetite. Others resorted to the gymnasium on the boat deck, the squash rackets court, or the swimming bath.

Before them stretched a long carefree day with nothing to do but to enjoy themselves. An army of several hundred stewards and others existed solely to minister to their comfort and pleasure. A large number of the passengers elected to do nothing in particular but to recline in deck-chairs in the sun on one of the sheltered promenade decks, their eyes sometimes straying from book or writing-pad to the wide horizon; or perhaps to take coffee in the verandah café high above the sparkling waves, or to sit lazily listening to another fine concert given by the ship's orchestra. Others settled down to long sessions of auction bridge or poker. The more energetic played for hours at deck quoits and other shipboard games. The squash rackets court and swimming pool, being novelties at sea (a swimming pool in an ocean liner, even the largest, had been unheard of until the first was installed in the *Olympic*) were in continuous demand.

'The weather was fine and the sea calm,' Dr Washington Dodge has observed. 'At all times one might walk the decks, with the same security as if walking down Market Street, so little motion was there to the vessel. It was hard to realize, when dining in the large spacious dining saloon, that one was not in some large and sumptuous hotel.'[1]

'I enjoyed myself as if I were in a summer palace on the seashore, surrounded with every comfort,' declared Gracie, '—there was nothing to indicate or suggest that we were on the stormy Atlantic Ocean. The motion of the ship and the noise of its machinery were scarcely discernible on deck or in the saloons, either day or night.'[2]

As a floating hotel-de-luxe the *Titanic* was certainly unsurpassed by any other ship afloat. The White Star Line offered the most marvellous value for money, in whatever class they travelled. The second class were enjoying a standard of living well above that to which most were accustomed ashore. They did not regard costly luxuries as necessities of life and were more than content with the comfortable and congenial surroundings in which they found themselves. Beesley, who had never before been out of sight of the shores of England, was enjoying every minute of the time. Yesterday he had spent many hours on deck watching the Irish coast slip by as they ran down to the Fastnet. He had gone up on the boat deck again after nightfall, and noticed that the large flock of seagulls which had followed them from the Cove of Cork were still wheeling and circling in their wake. Next morning, he observed, when he went on deck again they were gone. He continued to spend much of his time in the open air, enjoying the prospect of the sea and the sky. For the rest he was content with the pleasures of conversation with a number of interesting people, and with long spells of reading and letter-writing. When he was not on deck, his favourite haunt was the library.

Among the acquaintances that Beesley had made on board during the last few days were the Rev. Ernest Carter and his wife, Lilian, who was the daughter of Thomas Hughes, author of *Tom Brown's Schooldays*, a well-loved nineteenth-century classic. A friendly argument between the two men on the relative merits of their respective universities—Oxford and Cambridge—had led on to talk of 'the lack of sufficiently qualified men to take up the work of the Church of England'.

It was the first of several such conversations. The Carters were childless; but Mrs Carter's intense love of children had led her to spend much of her time with the children of her husband's East End parish. Their visit to America was the first real holiday that the Carters had enjoyed for years.[3]

Beesley and his friends, the Carters, formed part of a fairly numerous British middle-class element in the *Titanic's* passenger list—nearly all of them in the second class. A book which Beesley was to write later in the year, *The Loss of the 'Titanic'* throws a revealing light on the normal British middle-class outlook of his day—staid, sober, industrious, decorous, circumspect and conscientious as it was: though, as was to be expected, it was truer of the professional, than of the business community, of this era.

The steerage accommodation, cheap as it was, represented the height of luxury to most of the youngsters hailing from some remote village where the conditions of life, in 1912, were, to say the least of it, primitive. For the first time in their lives they had nothing to do, for days on end, but to put all cares behind them and to have a good time. In the steerage quarters a boisterous skipping game was a general favourite with both sexes, and in the smoking-room several card schools were usually in progress. At night there was singing and dancing. In the third class common-room on C Deck was installed one of the sixteen pianos carried on board the *Titanic*. It may be mentioned that one small hardship in the case of the single men (whose sleeping quarters were situated forward) lay in the fact that, in order to enjoy a smoke or a game of cards, they were obliged to traverse the whole length of the ship and back, entailing a walk of over one-third of a mile.

The emigrants came from all over Europe and beyond—there were Norwegians, Swedes, Danes, Russians, Finns, Poles, Dutchmen, Spaniards, Italians, Greeks, Roumanians, Arabs, and even—despite the American immigration laws—Chinamen. Some of these people in the steerage had never set eyes on the sea or a ship before. Hardly any of them had ever come into close contact with so many foreigners. There was an astonishing variety of garb and racial features. They eyed one another with frank curiosity. The language problem presented a difficulty.

Those who came from the various Scandinavian countries could understand one another reasonably well—their languages, after all, were similar; Yiddish was the usual medium of communication among the Jews: but, for the majority, the jangle of strange tongues all around sounded like so much gibberish. The services of Herr Müller, the ship's interpreter, were in frequent demand. For the most part the various nationalities kept themselves to themselves; though they were generally ready enough to join in lively party games where a knowledge of foreign languages was unnecessary. The steerage passengers also saw, and heard, a good deal of one of their number who played the bagpipes.

Almost every known variety of craft and calling seemed to be represented among the emigrants, both skilled and unskilled. The range was apparently endless: baker, butler, barman, bricklayer, clerk, compositor, chemist, carpenter, dressmaker, engineer, farrier, farmer, groom, gardener, jeweller, labourer, mason, miner, painter, plumber, servant, shoemaker, tailor, tinsmith, waiter—all these, and many others besides.

From the third class promenade deck in the stern they looked down on the maelstrom of dazzling white foam and swirling blue-green water churned up by the enormous screws and the broad white wake stretching away to the far horizon . . . the track that led back to Europe and home . . . the track that most of them, as they very well knew, would never retrace. . . .

The usual shipboard coteries were now firmly established. Sometimes they were composed of old friends and neighbours; sometimes of people who were attracted to one another by some common interest or occupation; sometimes they were formed purely by chance. Members of these coteries were nearly always to be found together, at certain times and places, throughout the day.

An interesting feature of the *Titanic's* passenger list was the large number of newly wedded couples on board. There were Mr and Mrs Lucien Smith, of Virginia, who were on the last lap of a honeymoon trip round the world; there was the eighteen-year-old Mrs Daniel Marvin who was returning to New York with her husband after a crowded three-weeks honeymoon in England of parties, dances, and sight-seeing;

there was another youthful bride, a Spanish girl of only seventeen, lately married to Senor Victor de Satode Penasco, who was eighteen. In every class, in fact, there were all these young men and girls who were starting on their new life with an Atlantic crossing in the world's largest liner.

One of the chief attractions on board was the ship's orchestra.

It is hard to recapture the spirit of this era, before the onset of two world wars and of cataclysmic change transformed the old order of things out of recognition; but it can still, perhaps, be recalled momentarily for us in some haunting Lehar waltz, in one of the enchanting refrains of Ivan Caryll, Paul Rubens, or Lionel Monckton, or in the rollicking, roistering Alexander's Ragtime Band'. Three elements, in particular, had combined to produce the flood of joyous, light-hearted music that was heard everywhere in 1912: Viennese operetta, English musical comedy, and American ragtime. It was as if a wave of melody had swept the world.

These were the years when Franz Lehar attained the height of his fame. His greatest operetta, *The Merry Widow*—containing one of the most popular waltzes ever written—took London by storm (it ran for nearly eight hundred nights), its success at Daly's far eclipsing its success in Vienna. *The Merry Widow* was followed in turn by *The Count of Luxemburg* and *Gipsy Love*. Another composer in the great Viennese tradition was Oscar Straus, whose two principal works were *The Waltz Dream* and *The Chocolate Soldier*. The characteristically English contribution to the popular music of the period was musical comedy, then at its heyday in this country. From that day to this the melodies from such outstanding successes as *The Arcadians*, *The Country Girl*, *Our Miss Gibbs*, *The Quaker Girl*, *Miss Hook of Holland*, and *San Toy*, with their cherished memories of Daly's and the Gaiety, have never ceased to enchant successive generations of hearers. In 1912 this kind of music was played all over the country by orchestras and military bands. The third element was utterly different. In complete contrast to the graceful, romantic waltz measures of Franz Lehar and Lionel Monckton blared out the strident, compelling, intoxicating rhythm of American ragtime. It was acclaimed as the distinctive rhythm of the new century, with its ever-rising clamour of harsh, mechanical din; and Irving Berlin was its prophet and high priest (his 'Alexander's Ragtime Band' was all the rage in 1912). If the waltzes from Vienna and London were evocative of a bygone era, ragtime was, surely, the sign and portent of things to come. It had captivated the younger generation on both sides of the Atlantic. Such exotic measures as 'The Bunny Hug', 'The Turkey Trot', and their like had become immensely popular.

Wallace Hartley and his orchestra had brought these melodies into the midst of the ocean. Hartley was from one of the northern counties where the love of good music was traditional. In his early years he had played in a number of hotel orchestras, and he had toured with the Carl Rosa and Moody-Manners opera companies. He had been for some time in the *Mauretania*; and then, early in 1912, he had been engaged by the White Star Line for the maiden voyage of the *Titanic*. His young violinist, Jock Hume, was well known throughout the Line; from commander to page-boy, everybody liked Jock. His last ship had been the *Olympic*; and, after the collision last year, his mother had earnestly begged him not to go to sea again. But the pay offered him was good and Jock was soon to be married. Fred Clarke, the bass viol, had signed on for a similar reason. Unlike Jock, he had never been to sea before; but the winter concert season had ended, and he had a widowed mother to support. Both the 'cellist and pianist came from the *Carpathia*. Hartley's orchestra, eight in all, was probably the best afloat. The well-attended concerts that were performed each day in various parts of the vessel contributed in large measure to all the gaiety and high spirts that prevailed on board the *Titanic*.

One of the stewardesses recalls how, just before dinner on the night of Friday, April 12th, while she stood by the companion-way chatting with Thomas Andrews, she saw old Dr O'Loughlin waiting for him on the landing below and calling him by his Christian name, 'Tommy'. She noticed that Andrews seemed harassed and out of sorts, which was probably due to over-work. It was a relief to him after a long and hard day's work to talk of Ardara and home to this friendly Belfast woman; as also to two new friends he had made at the Doctor's table, a young Canadian couple, Mr and Mrs Albert A. Dick, from Calgary, in Alberta.[4]

'The ship is as firm as a rock, and the sea is like a millpond,' Stead had written to his wife a few days earlier. 'If it lasts I shall be able to work better here than at home, for there are no telephones to worry me, and no callers.'[5]

He had brought with him the proofs of his recently completed autobiographical sketch to complete on the voyage. He found his pleasant, airy state-room an admirable study, and Stead was enjoying himself. He had a seat at the Purser's table, where, as was to be expected, he quickly captivated his companions. A New York lawyer, Frederick K. Seward, who sat next to him, related that all at that table were 'almost spell-bound by the humour, and beauty, and breadth of vision of Stead's conversation'. With his richly stored memory, resonant, cheery voice, keen sense of humour, and unfailing flow of good spirits, the old journalist dominated that circle from the first night of the voyage. The talk centred first on Theodore Roosevelt, the stormy petrel of American politics; and later on William Randolph Hearst (whom Stead greatly admired), then at the height of his power and influence. On another occasion Stead spoke at length of the incredibly savage persecution to which Lloyd George and he had been subjected during the late war. Seward was presently taken to task by one of the English passengers for being so much in the company of one who had been an uncompromising opponent of the South African War. 'My dear fellow,' remonstrated the Englishman, 'do you know he was *a pro-Boer*?'[6]

On the evening of Friday, April 12th, Stead was at the top of his form. The eight men at his table sat up until far into the night recounting ghost stories and discoursing on superstitions. The great journalist, who could never resist the chance of a 'scoop', wound up the session in characteristic fashion.

The story he told concerned the finding and translation of an inscription on a mummy case discovered in an Egyptian tomb. The inscription warned the finder that whoever should repeat the story narrated in its mysterious hieroglyphics would, without doubt, meet with a violent death. Stead thereupon proceeded to tell the story. . . .

'To prove that I am not superstitious,' said Stead in conclusion, 'I call your attention to the fact that it was Friday when I began this story and the day of its ending, my watch tells me, will fall upon a thirteenth.'[7]

Gracie relates that after dinner he used to go with his table companions, James Clinch Smith and Edward A. Kent, to take coffee in the palm court, where, strolling round among the tables, he would usually meet some of the people whom he knew, such as Hugh Woolner, son of a famous English sculptor, or H. Björnström Steffanson, the newly appointed Swedish naval attaché in Washington, who had been acquainted with his wife's relatives in Sweden. From the palm court Gracie would proceed to the smoking-room to talk politics with some of the well-known figures he might count on meeting there: George D. Widener, John B. Thayer, Arthur Ryerson, Archie Butt, Frank Millet, or Clarence Moore. For many of the men on board these nightly sessions in the smoking-room were probably the best part of the voyage.

Early that year Major Butt had begun to suffer increasingly from depression and fatigue; his health looked like breaking down, and President Taft had suggested a trip to Europe. The truth was that recent political developments had imposed an almost intolerable strain on Taft's handsome and debonair aide-de-camp. Formerly military aide to Roosevelt, Butt had been invited to continue in that office under his successor; but the situation became a harassing one for him when recriminations presently arose between Taft and Roosevelt, and he found himself torn between two allegiances. In these circumstances he readily fell in with his friend Millet's invitation to accompany him in the *Berlin* to Italy, where they would spend several weeks before returning in mid-April to the United States.

'I am completely tuckered out,' Butt wrote to his sister-in-law before his departure, 'and the doctor advises me to take a rest, and the President is willing that I should go. . . . Don't forget that all my papers are in the storage warehouse, and if the old ship goes down you will find my affairs in shipshape condition. As I always write to you in this way whenever I go anywhere, you will not be bothered with my presentiments now.'[8]

Gracie also saw a good deal of old Isidor Straus and his wife Ida. Mrs Straus's health had benefited greatly from their winter holiday among the pines and olive-groves of Cap Martin; and they were returning home in good spirits. Every day Straus and the Colonel would pace the promenade decks together, deep in conversation.

In the course of these walks the old man spoke much of his youthful days in America. How he had come out in the fall of 1854 with his mother and brothers and sister to join their father, Lazarus Straus, in Georgia, where he had made a home for them all. How as a young man he had returned to Europe in 1863 with a Confederate mission to purchase supplies for the South, and how he had later worked in a Liverpool shipping office. There followed forty years of toil and endeavour and steadily increasing prosperity. In 1888 Isidor and his brother Nathan had become partners in Macy's and in 1896 its sole proprietors; under the new management the various departments of the store were multiplied and it became the largest concern of its kind in the world. The two were in fact complementary to each other. What business qualities one brother lacked in the highest degree the other possessed, and *vice-versa*. While Nathan was jovial and free-spoken, mercurial and impulsive by temperament, and working by fits and starts, though swift to seize an opportunity and given to flashes of brilliant insight, Isidor was reserved and circumspect, industrious, dignified and even-tempered, patiently and systematically following every detail of the business. The two brothers also developed the Brooklyn store of Abraham and Straus. Isidor in his later years became a director of several banks. He had taken an active part in the campaign which secured Cleveland's re-election as President in 1892. He sat in Congress from 1893 to 1895 and had much to do with the working out of the Wilson Tariff.

Isidor and Ida Straus had been married for more than forty years. The old couple were all in all to each other. The evening of their lives was filled with a certain quiet happiness. The long years of struggle lay behind them. Isidor, a man of high integrity and simple tastes, was possessed of much more wealth than he would ever expend on himself. He was interested in many Jewish charities. In recent years the active management of the great store had devolved more and more on Isidor's sons.

For Harry Widener, also, the trip to Europe had been a success. In March he had spent a good many hours with his friend and counsellor, Bernard Quaritch, at Sotheby's. He had been fortunate enough to obtain a number of pamphlets containing caricatures by George Cruikshanks (already he possessed one of the finest collections of Cruikshanks's caricatures in existence), and in addition, at the Huth sale, the very rare second edition of Bacon's *Essaies* (1598), which he had thereupon slipped into his pocket, observing to Quaritch, who stood by, 'I think I'll take that little Bacon with me in my pocket, and if I am shipwrecked it will go down with me'.[9] The remark was not meant to be taken seriously, of course; already Harry Widener could see these newly acquired treasures in their proper place in his private library in Philadelphia: a library which was the envy of book-collectors all over the world.

For John Jacob Astor the return to his native land looked like being a turning-point in his fortunes. He was once more entering the social arena. First the Maiden Voyage, and then the New Start.

If the enviable owner of $150 millions could not live his life in his own way—in fact, get whatever it was he wanted— really, one was tempted to wonder who *could*. Astor's divorce had been arranged for him with the utmost smoothness and discretion. It was with regard to his re-marriage that everything had gone wrong. The fact was, he had wholly miscalculated the strength of the opposition which confronted him. It was impossible to find an Episcopalian rector willing to unite the multi-millionaire to his eighteen-year-old bride, even for a fee of $1,000. Eventually a clergyman did offer his services, not in church, but in the ballroom of Astor's mansion at Newport. After a honeymoon spent in the West Indies, Astor proposed to hold a great ball at 840 Fifth Avenue, his town house. The ball was 'cut' by most of his friends and acquaintances, as was also the Astor box at the Metropolitan Opera on the opening night of the season. With a lordly disregard for all the obstacles in his path, Astor had envisaged a programme of balls, banquets, and other festivities throughout the winter of 1911–12. Once again he was rebuffed. He was pilloried in the national press, and virtually ostracized by the Four Hundred. So the situation had stood when, abandoning the contest for the time being, he had sailed in the *Olympic* with Madeline, in December, for Europe.

The issue of the struggle was still undecided. The future alone would reveal whether, in the end, the Astor millions would work the imperious will of their owner; crowd his great houses with hosts of guests as in former days; and set Madeline securely on the throne occupied for so long by his mother, Caroline.

Far removed from all that world of wealth and luxury was the little coterie of deck officers whose lives at sea revolved around the bridge and the officers' quarters at the forward end of the boat deck. There were seven of them all told, besides the Master—three watch-keepers (the Chief, First, and Second Officers), and four juniors (the Third, Fourth, Fifth and Sixth Officers). Bred to the sea from their boyhood, they had mounted the ladder rung by rung, first in sail and then in steam, and had so far earned the approval of the ruling lights of the Line as now to be singled out for the high honour of serving as officers in the magnificent new liner on her maiden voyage.

Behind them lay the camaraderie of the half-deck with its memories of the seasick misery of their early days at sea; of the unforgettable thrill of going aloft for the first time, and of learning the ropes under the aegis of the Third Mate— traditionally the boys' mentor; of the halcyon experience of the Trades, with the ship snoring along with sails set and yards trimmed for days on end, in radiant 'flying fish weather'; of gathering in the second dog watch for the evening sing-song; of learning to prepare and enjoy those time-honoured confections of the half-deck, crackerjack and dandyfunk; of sweltering days in the Doldrums with the sails slatting idly against the masts and long weary spells of 'pulley-hauley'; of freshening winds and rising seas as they got down into the Forties and the ship laid her lee rail down to the water and the watch tailed on to the main topsail halyards to the chorus of 'Sally Brown'; of pitch-black nights off the Horn with the ship labouring in mountainous seas and men washed about the flooded decks, or clinging to the jackstay lashed by sleet and hail; of the peremptory cry of 'Wear ship!' and of the fearsome ordeal that would follow; of the favouring slant which finally enabled them to make their westing, and then to reach milder latitudes; of the open anchorage at Iquiqui, where the ships lay out in tiers loading nitrates for Europe; and of the ceremony of 'Hoisting the Southern Cross' and cheering the homeward-bounder as each ship in turn completed its lading and sailed for home.

Though textbooks like Lecky's *Wrinkles in Practical Navigation* and Todd and Whall's *Seamanship* would accompany their owner to sea, they usually lay about neglected in the half-deck until the apprentice's final voyage and the approach of the Second Mate's examination. Then would ensue furious spells of 'swatting up' mathematics, nautical astronomy, seamanship, and navigation at some Navigation School ashore. After another year there would be similar preparation for the Mate's examination. And later still they would pass for Master, receiving the coveted slip of blue paper that qualified them to command at sea.[10]

In the nineteen-hundreds an increasing number of young officers were also passing for Extra Master, which was of considerable advantage to those aspiring to an appointment in the Western Ocean mail boats, where it was essential, among other things, to have a thorough mastery of the spherical trigonometry underlying the solution of Great Circle problems.

The prestige and glamour of these great Atlantic liners drew the keenest, smartest men in the British merchant service like a lodestone. The short voyages, the regularity and frequency of shore leave (this was of particular importance to the family man), were powerful arguments in their favour; as were also the admirable living conditions, and the good and abundant food. With the long, gruelling years in sailing ships still fresh in their memory, it was as if they had entered the Elysian fields 'This is the life!' the youthful James Bisset had whispered to himself on his first night on board an Atlantic mail boat; and then, with a contented sigh, turned his face to the bulkhead and fell fast asleep smiling. . . .

The White Star Line demanded and secured some of the ablest officers, the best navigators, the finest seamen afloat. What was required of an applicant for one of these coveted mail boat berths was that he should have been trained in sail, gained all his certificates (including, if possible, the Extra Master's), and belonged to the Royal Naval Reserve. The young men coming on in the Cunard and White Star Lines usually had these qualifications. They found the standard of discipline and navigation obtaining in the fast passenger steamships was something scarcely any of them could have dreamed of before. In effect, what the Masters and Mates of the famous China tea clippers had been in their day, so now, in the early nineteen-hundreds, were these officers of the North Atlantic mail boats—the élite of the British mercantile marine.

'If ever there was a kill or cure,' Lightoller declared, 'it was a Western Ocean mail boat in winter time.' When the paramount consideration was to make a passage, the vessel used to be driven smashing through everything and anything in the way of weather, regardless of the heavy damage done.[11] (There was an unwritten law that except in a grave emergency the Officer of the Watch must not use the telegraph without the authority of the Master.) The demands made upon an officer's stamina and powers of endurance were terrific. Only the fittest and toughest could survive the ordeal.

After long years at sea in square-sail, traversing some of the loneliest regions of the ocean, where possibly one might not sight another vessel for weeks and even months, it was a nerve-racking experience for the young officer when he was first introduced to the harsh realities of the North Atlantic trade. It called for a novel kind of seamanship, apparently. The usual rules seem to have been suspended or turned upside-down. Everything was devoted to making a passage, with the result that year in, year out, the mail boats would run to schedule like express trains. (It is on record that the *Oceanic* had made two consecutive runs of over three thousand miles and not one minute of difference between them; and three consecutive runs and only one minute of difference between the times of leaving Sandy Hook, off New York, and passing the Wolf Rock, off Land's End.[12]) These crack steamships would be driven for all they were worth. The fast liners that were advertised to waft their passengers from New York on Monday, to take dinner in London on Saturday, seldom failed to arrive on time. Rarely would the Master dream of reducing speed—except to a quite insignificant degree—in the worst conditions of weather and visibility. The unwritten rule of the service appeared to be, 'Get on or get out!'

'Great luxury and great speed,' commented the *Nautical Magazine*, 'and "schedule time", are now demanded from the American liners, and this, in the resultant, means that the commanders of these vessels may be required, or may be unduly tempted, to take the most dangerous risks.'[13]

According to a mail boat officer of those days, the Officer of the Watch was normally reluctant to call the commander in hazy weather (which he roughly defined as 'one part clear to two parts thick', as opposed to *fog*), until he had experienced one or two really bad scares. Thus, after his ship had narrowly escaped collision with a huge iceberg, the officer's first concern was to hush the matter up. 'Needless to say, I called the Master after the danger had passed, and kept mum over the affair too.' On his next voyage, under similar conditions, the ship nearly collided with one of the crack German liners, the 23-knot *Deutschland*. 'Again,' the O.O.W. related, 'luck was in my way, for nobody was about except the few sailors washing the decks, the time being the middle watch, midnight to 4 a.m.'[14]

As time went on, however, and nothing untoward occurred—only occasional 'near misses' which stopped short of actual disaster—the young officer would gradually become hardened to these moments of acute tension and anxiety and presently take small acount of them. After a few years on the North Atlantic run experience taught him that risks which at first sight would have appeared unjustifiable could generally be taken with impunity provided that one knew what one was doing, kept a cool head, and was ready to act swiftly and decisively in an emergency. His heart was no longer in his mouth when shearing through a fog off the Newfoundland Banks or running at full speed in thick weather for the entrance of the Channel. Thus at the cost of an unknown number of fishermen's lives fast passages were regularly achieved.[15] The mail boat officer knew very well that he had to accept these risks in order to make a passage; and, moreover, in all circumstances he must keep up an appearance of nonchalance and sangfroid before the passengers. This last was highly important.

What was to be regretted was that the conditions of the mail boat service also bred a false sense of security. Just as at the present time a driver in the warmth and comfort of a modern motor-car often tends to underestimate the hazards of the icy roads and drifting snow-squalls without, so an officer, pacing the bridge of a crack Atlantic liner, was apt to lose his seaman's sense of danger. Wholly exposed to the elements and with his every sense on the alert, the officer on the poop of a sailing ship was in very different case. The mail boat officer could well remember his time as Second Mate and Mate when watching every yard, sail, and rope, his eyes would be constantly on the sea and sky and expectant of every sign and token of a change in the weather. He did not then need to be reminded of what was at stake and of the need for unceasing vigilance. But those days were past and gone. With the enhanced accuracy of modern navigation and the phenomenal advance of modern shipbuilding, their ancient enemy, the 'old grey wolf', the Sea, seemed somehow to have become far less formidable. Some years earlier Captain Smith had publicly stated that he could not conceive of any vital disaster happening to one of these great liners—'I cannot imagine any condition which would cause a ship to founder. I cannot conceive of any vital disaster happening to this vessel. Modern shipbuilding has gone beyond that. . . '16 The *Daily Telegraph* was soon to put the matter in a nutshell—'Under the influence of years of immunity from serious marine disaster, a sense of security in the adequacy of modern passenger ships to triumph over all the chances and hazards of navigation had been engendered.'

Moreover, what many of these mail boat commanders and officers failed to take into account was that the risks were steadily increasing as the ships became faster, larger, and proportionally weaker. They thought that they were running the same risks which had been run with impunity for years; but they were wrong. The risks they were running in 1912 were not the same risks that had been run in 1892; or even in 1902: but greater—very much greater.

The Chief Officer, Henry Tighe Wilde, was a tall, broad-shouldered, powerfully built man of thirty-eight. Formerly Chief Officer of the *Olympic*, he had been appointed to the new liner just for that one voyage. Wilde belonged to the older school of White Star Officers; and, like Murdoch, he possessed only an ordinary certificate. The Line, nevertheless, must have rated Wilde's qualities very highly indeed to have appointed him to such a position in their two finest ships. Alone among the *Titanic's* officers, Wilde was reluctant to accept the new appointment; for some time, in fact, he hesitated; and only when a number of his friends declared that he would be mad to refuse this chance did he finally, and with much misgiving, accept it.[17]

William McMaster Murdoch, formerly Chief Officer of the *Oceanic*, was the First Officer. He was a Scot from Dalbeattie, in Galloway, and came of seafaring stock. After serving his apprenticeship in sail and gaining all his certificates, he had joined the White Star Line, serving first in the *Medic* and *Runic* on the Australian run, after which he had been transferred to their Atlantic steamers, serving successively in the *Arabic*, *Adriatic*, *Oceanic*, *Olympic*, and, finally, *Titanic*. He was hoping in the near future to be offered a command in one of the smaller vessels of the Line. Murdoch was at this time just under forty: an officer of ripe experience, cool and steady judgment, and instant presence of mind. Only a few years earlier, when serving in the *Arabic*, he had displayed all these qualities in consummate degree in coolly, skilfully, and, in the nick of time successfully averting a collision. It happened one night on the outward passage, one day from Nantucket Light, with a fresh north-westerly breeze and a light impalpable mist (known as 'a Scotchman'), which rendered visibility difficult and set up a false horizon. Just after 10 o'clock Murdoch came up on the bridge to relieve Fox, the O.O.W. Before taking over, the former as usual took a few turns while accustoming his eyes to the darkness. There came a sudden warning from the lookout: 'Light on the port side!' Fox, without observing the light himself, promptly shouted, 'Watch your port helm' (i.e. *be ready to alter course to starboard*). He moved over to the side, Murdoch following; then, seeing the light, gave the order to port the helm. At the same instant Murdoch also suddenly saw, almost under the *Arabic*'s bows, a single red light. Realizing there would be no time to alter course, he acted with swift decision: already the quartermaster had begun to port the helm when Murdoch, rushing to the wheel, shoved the man aside, brought the wheel back a few spokes, and held on. They saw a large sailing vessel with all her sails set, with the wind on her port quarter, making good speed. Involuntarily the officers ducked as the ship swept past them—so close, that it seemed as if her yard-arms must sweep the bridge. For a few seconds nobody spoke. Then Murdoch murmured to the junior officer, 'All right, Chang! Go and steady her on.'[18]

Charles Herbert Lightoller, the Second Officer, was what sailors called 'a hard case'. He had once boasted to his sister, who was inclined to worry about him, that he would never be drowned. 'Don't you bother,' he would say reassuringly; 'the sea is not wet enough to drown me. I'll *never* be drowned.' The story of his life was more crowded with drama and danger than any adventure yarn out of the *Boy's Own Paper*. As a boy he had sailed under Old Jock Sutherland, one of the most daring 'crackers-on' out of Liverpool. He had been one of the turbulent half-deck crowd of the *Holt Hill*, who had made a number of ports too hot to hold them. He had experienced a fire at sea, had been cast away on a desert island, had served as Second Mate of a three skysail yarder, and had passed for master at the age of twenty-three. His subsequent exploits had included some lurid passages-at-arms with the notorious Bully Waters out on the West African coast, and he had later taken part in the Yukon gold-rush. Afterwards, having joined the White Star Line, he was appointed to one of their new ships, the *Medic*, on the Australia run. While out in Sydney he had conceived the admirable project of simultaneously firing the cannon and hoisting the Boer flag (it was the middle of the South African War) on Fort Dennison in Sydney Harbour—an exploit which resulted in his first being 'carpeted' by the White Star Marine Superintendent at Liverpool, 'Old Daddy Hewitt', and then being transferred to the New York service. Serving under such outstanding commanders as Captain John Cameron and Captain Edward J. Smith, Lightoller's advancement was rapid. He later became Second Officer of the *Oceanic*, First of the *Majestic*, and then First of the *Oceanic*, before finally being appointed Second of the *Titanic*. He held an Extra Master's certificate.[19]

Herbert John Pitman, the Third Officer, had served for three years as an officer in a sailing ship before going into steam. He had then served twelve months in the Blue Anchor Line, six months in the Shire Line, and five years in the White Star Line. Joseph Grove Boxhall, the Fourth Officer, had also served for five years in the White Star Line. His father and several of his other relatives had been in the North Atlantic trade before him. Boxhall, who had an Extra Master's certificate, seems by all accounts to have been the outstanding navigator among the *Titanic's* officers. Harold Godfrey Lowe, the Fifth Officer, was, like Lightoller, 'a hard case'. He had run away to sea when he was fourteen and served first in schooners. His father wanted to apprentice him in the usual way, but the boy would not have it. 'I said I would not be apprenticed; that I was not going to work for anybody for nothing, without any money, that I wanted to be paid for my labour. . . . He took me to Liverpool to a lot of offices there, and I told him once and for all that I meant what I said. I said, "I am not going to be apprenticed, and that settles it." '[20] Lowe went on from schooners into square-rigged ships, got all his certificates, spent five years on the West African coast, and, early in 1911, joined the White Star Line. This voyage in the *Titanic* was his first experience of the North Atlantic run. James Pell Moody, the Sixth Officer, had gone from the *Conway* to sailing ships, and thence to the *Oceanic*. Like the other officers, he had found the enormous proportions of the *Titanic* somewhat daunting. 'Have been here a week,' he had written home from Belfast, 'chiefly occupied trying to find my way about the big omnibus.'

'I am quite sure,' the First Officer's sister related many years afterwards, 'none of these men even for a moment thought of any accident happening to their ship—all were anxious for the honour of being posted on the world's greatest liner. . . .'[21]

An important part of the day's—or rather, *night's*—work in the *Titanic's* wireless office consisted in taking down the news. Phillips sat at the operating table with pencil and pad. Soon he would be entering on the last three hours of his long spell of duty (8 p.m. to 2 a.m.). A glance at the clock on the bulkhead showed him that it was getting on for the time when Poldhu would begin to transmit its nightly news bulletin. He rapped out a CQ, or general message, informing all ships and shore stations that he would be 'Standing by' for press; and then he adjusted his tuner to MPD's wave-length.

On the stroke of the hour the customary signal was heard in the headphones. The giant spark at Poldhu was calling, '*All ships subscribing to the Marconi news service*'. Poldhu first announced that a number of private messages for certain vessels would be sent immediately after the press; and then began to transmit the news, which consisted of telegrams received from all parts of the world.[22] With the headphones pressed tightly to his ears Phillips, scribbling rapidly, took down on the pad before him paragraph after paragraph of highly compressed information which he would presently send down to the Purser, who in turn would forward it to the ship's printer for reproduction in the *Atlantic Daily Bulletin*.

The signals at this range were loud and clear, and the reception of the news presented no particular difficulty. It was another matter altogether when, far out in the Atlantic, conditions were bad—it might then be necessary to take down part of the transmission from Poldu, part from Cape Cod, and, occasionally, part from neighbouring ships which had picked up words or sentences that the other operator had missed.[23] Any gaps still remaining the latter would have to fill in with the aid of his imagination.

The transmission of the press, at approximately eighteen words a minute, lasted about half an hour. At the end of this period the operator again adjusted his tuner to the shipping wavelength, and both received and transmitted telegrams so long as the *Titanic* continued within range of these other ships.[24]

Four bells . . . 2 o'clock in the morning—half-way through the 'graveyard watch'. The sharp clang of the bell on the bridge was echoed by a distant clang forward. At about the same moment, in accordance with their usual arrangement, Harold Bride came on duty.[25] With a thankful 'good night' Phillips turned the station over to his junior and then withdrew to their little sleeping cabin.

Bride glanced at the Communication Chart to learn what ships were likely to be within range during his spell of duty. Then he ran his hands over the various switches, wound up the clockwork of the magnetic detector, and adjusted the telephone receivers on his head—at once he was in touch with the outside world and listening to the staccato mutter and buzz of Morse. The night was alive with whispers. Both near and far ships were communicating with one another concerning call-signs and positions . . . winds and weather conditions, ice-warnings, and reports of floating derelicts . . . crops and cargoes . . . commerce and finance. From time to time a personal message, too, would be flashed across the ether. There were telegrams of greeting and good wishes, of congratulation and condolence, and of other important family events. As she swept proudly on across the ocean, the *Titanic* was also getting occasional messages of congratulation from other ships on her maiden voyage —though there were by no means as many of these as her sister-ship had received the previous year.

It is, as a wireless operator of those days has related, hard for the layman fully to appreciate the keen interest and fascination of sitting alone in a small cabin at dead of night while gliding across the silent ocean, and 'having under one's hand an invisible cord that links up the world and gives the latest news from lands which sank astern days ago, and from ships and other lands which are yet many leagues ahead'.[26]

In those days wireless operators did not rank as officers. Their position on board great liners like the *Olympic* and *Titanic* was, indeed, an anomalous one. They did not mess with the ship's officers or associate with them. They did not even wear their uniform, but that of the Marconi Marine. They received little pay for long hours of work. Though on some days their duties were not especially onerous, on others, when there was a heavy spate of traffic, they could be very exacting; and in any kind of emergency, as will later be seen, they were expected to work practically all round the clock. But the compelling interest and delight of the work itself more than made up for the hardships of their lot.

They would sit for hours at the operating table, sometimes sending, sometimes receiving, but more often than not just listening to the rapid volleys of Morse from ships within a range of several hundred miles. The operators could often distinguish one another's touch on the key as they could recognize some other ship by the note of its spark.[27] On occasion the other ships were very close and the transmissions almost deafening; at other times they were so far away that the signals were faint whispers that even the keen hearing of the operator could scarcely catch. Sometimes a third party would suddenly 'chip in' during a conversation over the ether. A personal message from some ship or shore station announcing 'a happy event' would be greeted with ribald comments. Most of these young men were well-known to one another, either personally or by reputation, having met in the same training college or fore-gathered in home and foreign ports. Their communications with one another consisted largely of abbreviations: the official 'Q' code being supplemented by unofficial, but universally recognized, other abbreviations. The object always aimed at was to get their message across in the shortest possible number of words. QRA (*what is the name of your station?*), a distant whisper would inquire. QRA MGY (*The name of my station is the* Titanic), would come the response. TU OM GN (*Thank you, old man, good night!*). In the morning they would greet each other with, GM OM (*Good morning, old man!*), and at night they would take leave of each other with, GN OM (*Good night, old man!*). An operator busy with his own traffic would rap out a warning QRT (*Keep quiet, I'm busy*) to some importunate neighbour; or more bluntly, GTH OM QRT (*Get to hell, old man, keep quiet, I'm busy*).

In mid-Atlantic the patient ether resounded with the buzz and splutter of spark. The cacophony was sometimes unbelievable; in this early era it was a radio free for all. The wave emitted, says Baarslag, 'was broad and interfering; so that any ship, while it was transmitting, made it virtually impossible for all others within forty or fifty miles to hear anything else.'[28] There was a fierce competition for paid traffic among the rival systems—Marconi, Telefunken, Lee De Forest, and United Wireless. Except in an emergency, Marconi men were not allowed to communicate with a vessel equipped with another system. Not only was there no co-operation between these warring companies, but actual enmity among them. Operators belonging to rival systems would deliberately jam one another's transmissions.[29]

In addition to such man-made manifestations, there was the interference, sometimes serious, due to atmospherics, or X's; and also fading, or 'freaky' reception, occasioned by the influence of the ionosphere on the propagation of wireless waves. The governing factors with regard to fading were the time of day or night, solar cycles, and the *aurora borealis*; as a rule it was particularly pronounced at twilight.

Bride might well consider himself lucky to have obtained this berth in the *Titanic*. After all, he had only entered the marine service the year before; it was something of a 'plum'. During his first few days in the new liner he had not found his duties particularly exacting; and Phillips and he got on very well. Much the greater part of the responsibility for the operation of MGY of course devolved upon the senior. As has already been said, the Marconi men did not associate with the ship's officers. They were thrown very much on their own resources. With his knowledgeable and experienced senior Bride could argue amicably about some professional wrinkle, browse over the current *Marconigraph*, compare past experiences of faults and repairs, and discuss the vagaries of radio communication generally. Both of the young operators were well aware of their good fortune in serving under such a commander as Captain Smith, who did not share the antipathy of so many of the older school to the new invention of wireless.

Gradually the time passed. The 'graveyard watch' gave place to 'the coffee watch'. The sun came up over the eastern horizon. Hands were busy washing down the decks. The stewards were sweeping the corridors. Soon he would he be relieved. At last the junior operator was glad to see the hands of the clock pointing to 8 o'clock and to hear the cheerful notes of the bugle sounding breakfast.

Chapter 6

Mid-Atlantic

As day followed day, the general admiration for the great liner increased. The comfort and stability which had been remarked upon in the *Olympic* was even more pronounced in the sister-ship. Steaming, as she drove on to the westward, at a speed of 21 knots, the absence of vibration was thought to be extraordinary. At night, the low throb of the engines could scarcely be felt; it was only when standing on the deck of touching the bulkhead that one could feel the vibration. Those who had crossed the Atlantic many times considered the *Titanic* the most comfortable ship in which they had ever sailed, and declared that they much preferred her to the crack Cunarders which held the blue riband of the Atlantic—the *Mauretania* and *Lusitania*. The fine weather still continued; on the bridge they had solar observations every morning and stellar observations every evening. Occasionally, as some other ship was sighted, the signal flags would flutter up the halliards in greeting.

'We were out on a lark and revelry was the keynote. The weather was superb, the comfort and luxury aboard all that had been promised,' related Mrs René Harris many years later. '. . . The days passed too quickly. I felt as if I would like to go on until the end of time. Dinner parties, bridge parties, dancing, auction pools, midnight repasts were indulged in to the *n*th degree.'[1]

'The weather was fine and clear, the ship palatial, the food delicious,' Jack Thayer declared, '. . . and, needless to say, being seventeen years old, I was all over the ship.'[2]

'The boat was so luxurious', said another of the passengers, Mrs Douglas, 'so steady, so immense, and such a marvel of mechanism that one could not believe he was on a boat.'[3]

To the comfortable, cosseted life of the modern transatlantic traveller the new medium devised by the genius of Marconi had added the final touch. For several years past newspapers had been printed daily in the larger liners on the North Atlantic run. The first newspaper of its kind, the *Transatlantic Times*, was published on board the American liner *St Paul*, bound from New York to Southampton, in the autumn of 1899. The construction of high-power transmitting stations at Poldhu and Cape Cod, which supplied a regular service of news from land, made possible a daily issue of the ship's newspaper. In 1904 the *Cunard Daily Bulletin*, published on board the *Campania*, gave its readers throughout the voyage the latest news of the Russo-Japanese War. A total of several thousand copies was now published daily at sea.

Every morning, about the time the bugle-call for breakfast was sounded, the steward would bring his passengers the current copy of the *Atlantic Daily Bulletin*. This was a remarkably well-thought-out and attractive production, comprising about a dozen pages and arranged in the form of a magazine; most of it being printed ashore before sailing, the news being added, day by day, at sea. The centre pages were reserved for the press reports, along with certain Stock Exchange quotations from London, Paris, and New York, the movements of Liverpool cotton, and the racing results. In addition to the news, the *Atlantic Daily Bulletin* contained articles of literary, artistic, and scientific interest, the latest social and theatrical gossip from London and Paris, and a good many advertisements, together with the menu of the day's dinner, and the previous day's run. The *Atlantic Daily Bulletin* was eagerly sought after by the passengers and was considered very good value at several shillings a copy. The news appearing in its columns was discussed at length in the smoking-room and on the promenade decks.[4]

From day to day, therefore, passengers were aware of what was happening in the outside world. How the Irish Home Rule Bill—the third that had been attempted—had been introduced in the House of Commons by the Prime Minister, H. H. Asquith; how serious rioting had broken out among the Lancashire miners; how the great Coal Strike had at long last been settled; how Dr Seddon, sentenced to death for murder at the Old Bailey, had, after the failure of his appeal, petitioned the Home Secretary, Reginald McKenna, without success; how Chinese soldiers stationed at Nanking had mutinied, and how the Queen Victoria Memorial at Nice had been unveiled. With the Democrats ready to take advantage of the estrangement between President Taft and Theodore Roosevelt, there was also plenty to read and talk about in American affairs. Much interest was taken in the respective merits of the four Democratic aspirants for the presidential nomination—Senator Champ Clark, and Oscar Underwood, Governor Woodrow Wilson, and William Jennings Bryan. In the United States, as in our own country, 1912 was a year of social unrest.

For the moneyed class wireless telegraphy had proved a real and necessary business accessory. Even in mid-ocean it was possible to watch the movements of securities in which one was interested. The leading Stock Exchange quotations were always available in the *Atlantic Daily Bulletin*, and any of the others might be swiftly and inexpensively ascertained by a marconigram. The story is told of a passenger who noticed in the ship's newspaper that certain rubber shares which he held were then very high and telegraphed to his secretary in New York to sell. A few hours afterwards he received a reply, whereupon he remarked with satisfaction to the operator that he had just netted $185,000 and intended, as soon as he landed, to 'buy a motor-car and take a drive through Europe'. He could well afford to![5]

The past week had witnessed exceptional activity in the London Stock Exchange. Business was booming. There was unexampled buoyancy not only in one market, but in several. High prices were reached by such different securities as Hudson's Bays, Canadian Pacifics, London Omnibus stock, and Marconis. The American market was less active.

The Captain's table stood in the centre of the huge white dining-room. The stewards would come to attention as he approached, and his 'tiger' would draw back his chair. As he took his place in their midst, a ripple of low-voiced comment would go round the room. The passengers liked to see him sitting among them there, just as they liked to see him pass by on the stairway or promenade deck. The Captain was accustomed to be at his place in the dining-room for most of his meals.[6]

'E.J.' could expect to see gathered round his table some of the most celebrated men and women of his day. In his own lifetime he had become a legend. The veterans of the smoking-room swore by him. He enjoyed the confidence alike of millionaires and bishops. ('He never took a risk,' was the considered opinion of the Bishop of Willesden.) He was a familiar figure to thousands of American and British travellers, not a few of whom had crossed the ocean with him many times. One of the chief pleasures of the crossing for the regular traveller was the opportunity of foregathering with the genial, white-haired commander and hearing again his deep voice and well-remembered chuckle. Children, too, adored him, and were sure of being noticed by him. It was due at any rate in part to 'E.J.'s' great popularity that the Company had been accustomed to appoint him to the command of each of their finest ships as it came into operation. A maiden voyage without Captain Smith in command was almost unthinkable! This was the kind of Master that the White Star Line appreciated. He had done all they wanted of him. Apart from that unfortunate affair with the *Hawke*, he had experienced no sort of accident in all his career. In any case it was far from certain that the collision had really been caused by the *Olympic* (the case, in fact, was still *sub judice*); and to mark their continued confidence in Captain Smith the Company had been pleased to appoint him to his present command. 'E.J.' was drawing a higher salary than any other commander afloat.

A seat at the Purser's table was almost as eagerly sought after as a seat at the Captain's. Hugh McElroy was a tall, well-built man approaching retiring age who seemed to know everybody and everything. He was possessed of a strong sense of humour which, in a Purser, is almost as desirable an attribute as outstanding business ability. He had proved himself able to hold his own with the most difficult and unreasonable type of passenger without giving offence. He was so popular in fact with regular travellers that they would often time their journeys so as to sail in the same ship with him. How many famous people he had known! Only the day before the *Titanic* sailed McElroy and his wife had left at the Southampton theatre a large bouquet of roses in red and white—the Danish colours—for the great ballerina, Mlle Adeline Genée, who was to appear there later in the week. (The colours were still fresh when their donor was no more.)[7] It would not be by any means easy to do justice to the share of prosperity which had accrued to the Company in recent years through the great popularity of the Captain and McElroy. Lately they had attracted many a wealthy and influential passenger to the *Olympic*; it was now confidently anticipated that they would do as well by the *Titanic*.

The Doctor, F. W. N. O'Loughlin, was, like the Purser, Irish and a Catholic. McElroy and he were old shipmates, having been promoted successively from the *Oceanic*, *Baltic*, *Adriatic*, and *Olympic* to the *Titanic*. After a brief spell as dispensary doctor in Ireland, O'Loughlin had entered the White Star Line, with which Company he had served for more than forty years. At the Doctor's table was Thomas Andrews, his companion on many a past voyage. The historic antagonism between north and south in Ireland had not prevented a close and enduring friendship from springing up between the Catholic from County Cork and the Protestant from County Down.

For his part 'E.J.' might well survey that brilliant scene with serene satisfaction. The bridge was one half of his professional life; but this, after all, was the other half. The first class accommodation of one of these large Atlantic liners was the marine equivalent of the Adlon or the Ritz. Around him were the heirs of the Gilded Age; for whose pleasure and gratification this great floating palace had been called into existence. 'It was built,' said the *Nation*, 'for the great men of the earth, for the financial giants of our time, men who could lightly pay for this single voyage the year's keep of ten British families.' There sat the great men of industry, commerce, and finance; a sprinkling from the aristocracies of Europe; leading figures in the theatrical and cinematograph world; a well-known member of Lloyd's, one or two country squires, an important American publisher, the doyen of British journalists, a famous metallurgical engineer, and dozens of other celebrities. All this array of wealth and fashion, all this fine show of new Parisian gowns and shimmering jewels beneath the lovely Jacobean ceiling, was, in fact, the outward and visible sign of that ever-increasing share of the lucrative Atlantic passenger traffic which the Line had gained at the expense of its rivals.

Not all the first class passengers took their meals in the great dining-room. With the rising standards of service at sea, experience had shown that the wealthier class of passengers expected, as a matter of course, not only to get the best of everything, but also to indulge themselves at all sorts of inconvenient hours. To meet this demand, however, meant that the cooks and stewards would often be unable to attend to their regular duties and that the service in the dining-room would suffer in consequence. Again, it sometimes happened that some of the passengers might want to give a dinner-party for a number of their friends. Hence the addition of a restaurant to the other amenities of the first class accommodation.

This represented an important and much appreciated innovation in modern ocean travel. In the restaurant, with its large staff of French waiters and a *maître d'hotel* from Paris, passengers could give their dinner-party as in a first-class hotel ashore. The menu cards were prepared and printed in the ship's printing office and were often preserved by the guests as mementos of a happy evening. The restaurant was open at all times throughout the day. In short, in the restaurant passengers could choose whatever it was they fancied from the menu and take their meals when and with whom they chose. Through the inauguration of this new amenity the more exacting type of passenger was satisfied, the pressure on the staff in the dining-room was materially relieved, and the standard of service much improved.[8]

The spacious reception room with its white Jacobean panelling and splendid tapestry was generally crowded after luncheon and dinner, and at afternoon tea. The lounge, which had plenty of comfortable nooks and corners that were much sought after, was also very popular with the passengers. The reading and writing-room, on the other hand, which had been intended mainly for the ladies, had not been resorted to nearly as much as had been expected. The large, square, mahogany panelled smoking-room, with its friendly leather armchairs and benches, was, as is invariably the case on board these Atlantic liners, the great masculine stronghold. A favourite rendezvous of the younger set in the evening was the verandah café, with its comfortable wicker chairs set out under the trellised vines.[9]

A well-known contemporary writer, Filson Young, has portrayed the general lay-out of the floating palace in a passage which is worth quoting.

If, thinking of the *Titanic* . . . you could imagine her to be split in half from bow to stern so that you could look, as one looks at the section of a hive, upon all her manifold life thus suddenly laid bare, you would find in her a microcosm of civilised society. Upon the top are the rulers, surrounded by the rich and the luxurious, enjoying the best of everything; a little way below them their servants and parasites, ministering not so much to their necessities as to their luxuries; lower down still, at the base and foundation of all, the fierce and terrible labour of the stokeholds, where the black slaves are shovelling as though for dear life, endlessly pouring coal into furnaces that devoured it and yet ever demanded a new supply— horrible labour, joyless life; and yet the labour that gives life and movement to the whole ship. Up above are all the beautiful things, the pleasant things. Up above are the people who rest and enjoy; down below the people who sweat and suffer.[10]

Broadly speaking, the established structure of society was reflected in the division of the *Titanic's* passengers into first, second, and third class. In the first were the 'rulers', represented by the Big Business men and their satellites; in the second, the middle class so faithfully portrayed in Beesley's book; and in the third, the people of the working class, i.e. the manual workers.

A large proportion of the first class passengers, as has already been said, fairly wallowed in ease and luxury, 'enjoying the best of everything'. (A few of them even spent the entire day in bed, emerging only at nightfall from their state-rooms to join the rest at dinner.) But even amongst those fortunate ones situated 'up above', who were said 'to rest and enjoy', there were not a few men who, from time to time, with the assistance of secretaries, stenographers, and the ship's radio station, were hard at work. The President of the Canadian Grand Trunk Railroad, who was engaged in planning and building new hotels along the line of recent extensions to his system, was naturally interested in studying the palatial accommodation provided in the *Titanic*. For the Chairman of the White Star Line (with whom Hays had several interesting conversations) the maiden voyage was no mere pleasure trip.

Perhaps the busiest man in the ship was Thomas Andrews, who was certainly one of those 'up above' (his cabin was on A Deck). Like Martha he was careful and troubled about many things; though some of the things that concerned him do not seem to have been particularly important. From the first day of the voyage the hot press in the restaurant galley had apparently been giving trouble; then there was the number of screws in the state-room hat racks, which he thought excessive, and the colour of the pebble dashing on the private promenade decks, which struck him as rather too dark. Andrews was always at hand to repair a defective electric fan, or to settle a quarrel among the stewardesses. From the early morning, with the eight men from the Island Yard at Belfast, he was continually about the ship; attired in a boilersuit, he would go down into the stokehold; he would be closetted with the Chief Engineer; he would dine with Ismay to discuss alterations; he would sit writing up his reports in his cabin till late into the night—and always the *Titanic* was in his thoughts. 'As Chief Designer and Naval Architect,' says his biographer, Shan Bullock, 'he planned her complete. As Managing Director he saw her grow up, frame by frame, plate by plate, day after day throughout more than two years; watched her grow as a father watches his child grow, assiduously, minutely, and with much the same feelings of parental pride and affection.'[11]

It is worth noting that the staff employed in the running of the floating palace was many times more numerous than those engaged in navigation (including the officers, there were no more than a few dozen seamen in the whole ship). To minister to the wants of the passengers, there was a whole army of stewards and stewardesses. From early morning until late at night the latter were almost continually on their feet. Their one desire was to please their own particular passengers. Their tireless attentions and unfailing cheerfulness were in fact largely responsible for the general feeling of contentment and well-being that pervaded the ship. They had to sweep out and tidy the public rooms before any of the passengers were stirring, and they had to prepare and take round the early morning tea; they had to lay the tables in the dining saloons and have everything ready for breakfast, and then clear away again; they had to set to rights the state-rooms and make the beds; no sooner was this done than they had to lay the tables for luncheon, afterwards clear away again; after a short interval there was afternoon tea to be served, and, while the passengers were dressing for dinner, the stewards were laying the tables in the dining-room; after waiting on the passengers and clearing away again, they had to get the dining-room ready for the morrow and also see to the state-rooms. Whenever there was an entertainment or religious service to be held in any of the public rooms it was the stewards who had to make the necessary preparations. They had to take their meals and their rest when they could. Nevertheless, there is no evidence to suggest that the stewards considered their lot an unhappy one. If they did their best to content their passengers, the latter, for their part, usually expressed their appreciation of these services in lavish tips. Not a few of these men, beginning as bell-boys, had risen steadily in the department. To be a steward in one of the larger liners was accounted a secure and rewarding career.[12]

It is probable that even of the stokehold Filson Young's description conveys a somewhat exaggerated impression. Whether the 'black gang' really appreciated the hardness of their lot to anything like the same degree as a casual visitor to those regions—the 'literary gent' who came, saw, and shuddered!—is more than doubtful. 'A tougher bunch than the firemen on a Western Ocean mail boat,' observed Lightoller, who knew them well, 'it would be impossible to find.' In many thousands of working-class homes in certain sea-ports the men traditionally followed the sea either as firemen or as trimmers. It was the only life they had ever known. They were no keener to change their calling than were the miners. The hardship, to their mind, did not lie in the servitude of the slicer and the shovel, but in the lack of it. After a long spell of unemployment

1   Captain E. J. Smith (*Photo: Popper*)

2 The Boat Train. John Jacob Astor about to board the Boat Train for Southampton on
April 10th, 1912 (*Photo: Popper*)

Sailing day (*Photo: Popper*)

3 The Ocean Dock, Southampton, in 1912 (*Photo: Echo Commercial*)

4   The *Titanic* leaving the Ocean Dock (*Photo: Syren and Shipping*)

Steaming down Southampton Water (*Photo: Radio Times Hulton Picture Library*)

5   The *Titanic* off Cowes (*Photo: Beken & Son*)

6　Dropping the Pilot off the Nab (*Photo: Echo Commercial*)

'Past the headlands of the west.' The *Titanic* running down the south coast of Ireland on April 11th, 1912 (*Photo: Popper*)

7 The dining saloon
(*Photo: Popper*)

The writing and reading room
(*Photo: Illustrated London News*)

8 Harold Bride, the Junior Operator
(*Photo: Marconigraph*)

Harold Bride in the wireless cabin
(*Photo: Popper*)

Jack Phillips, the Senior Operator
(*Photo: Marconigraph*)

due to the recent coal strike most of these men were only too glad to sign on in the new liner. In any case, what Filson Young wrote of their 'fierce and terrible labour' was much truer of an earlier era, when the White Star Line still ran their express service to America from Liverpool, when life in the stokehold consisted of one endless drive and the last ounce of steam had to be kept up at all costs, and when 'Brutal Bootle' was a by-word. In those days it was no uncommon occurrence for several men in a watch to be overcome by the terrific heat, so that they had to be hoisted up the ash-shoot with a bucket chain looped under their arm-pits and left on deck to recover.[13] There was a different breed in the stokehold since the switch to Southampton. The Southampton men were tough enough physically, in all conscience; but they were not the brutes that the inhuman conditions in the stokehold had made of so many of the Liverpool Irish.

Between the Boat Deck and the stokehold there was a diversity of activities in progress—the duty watch washing down decks and cleaning the paintwork, shifting and stacking chairs, and cleaning up generally; T. W. McCawley, the white-flannelled gymnasium instructor, assisting people to ride the mechanical 'horse' and 'camel'; chefs and their underlings endlessly preparing dishes in the various galleys; the restaurant cashier busy with her accounts; the nurse on duty in the sick bay; library stewards filling in or cancelling slips as books were taken out or returned; page-boys hurrying on the track of errant passengers; the Purser's staff keeping the ship's books, receiving the reports of the stewards and cooks, and supervising the issue of the day's stores; lift-boys wafting passengers up and down between the different decks; the ship's printer and his assistant busy among their formes; the post office clerks in the mail-room sorting letters destined for many different lands; Müller, the interpreter, grappling with the Babel of diverse nationalities in the steerage; Fred Wright, the rackets professional, coaching his clients in the squash court; Wallace Hartley and his orchestra preparing for another concert; mechanics cleaning automobiles down in the hold. Elsewhere in the giant liner were to be found clerks, writers, storekeepers, Turkish Bath attendants, barbers, barmen, florists, butchers, bakers, electricians, window-cleaners, scullions, and platewashers, all intent on their various occupations.

The floating palace was still a ship. With the exception of the Master, the deck officers of the *Titanic* rarely came in contact with the passengers; they lived, in fact, in a different world. For most of the passengers this maiden voyage was simply a holiday; for the officers and crew it was their daily work. 'As day followed day,' says Lightoller, 'officers and men settled down into the collar, and duty linked up with duty until the watches went by without pause or hitch'.[14]

The navigating bridge was about 190 feet from the bow. On the after part of the bridge was the wheel-house, containing the wheel and steering-compass, and telephones leading to the crow's nest, engine-room, poop, and foc's'le head. In the wheel-house, too, was the course-board, on which the course would be chalked, illuminated after dark by a small light. The chart-room was immediately abaft the wheel-house. Inside was a long mahogany table with drawers underneath to hold the charts. The chart in use—No. 2058, a large double sheet, the North Atlantic Track Chart—was spread out on the table. The sextants and chronometers were kept in the chart-room, as well as all the navigational instruments—compasses, dividers, parallel rulers, etc.—and the various *Pilots*, or Sailing Directions, and other navigational works. The chart-room also contained the master-clock, which activated electrically, at minute intervals, all the other clocks. On the starboard side of the wheel-house were the Captain's quarters and some of the officers' rooms; the others being on the port side. Abaft the forward funnel casing was the wireless cabin.

In their larger ships the White Star Line were accustomed to carry six look-outs, who did nothing else, night and day, except keep a look-out, two at a time, up in the crow's nest. This was situated high up on the foremast and was reached by a spiral staircase fitted inside the mast itself. The men in the crow's nest would keep a sharp look-out and report to the bridge anything they sighted from their lofty perch, such as a distant light, a trail of smoke on the horizon, a derelict, a piece of wreckage, or an iceberg. From long experience the look-outs had become expert in detecting such objects afar off. Their hours of duty were two hours on and four hours off. In addition to drawing the ordinary monthly pay of an A.B. these men received five shillings per voyage 'look-out money'. The task of the look-outs was at all times onerous, what with the monotony and constant strain; and doubly so when the weather was bad and the visibility poor.

Every two hours the quartermaster stationed on the poop would note the reading on the dial of the patent log fixed to the taffrail, telephone it to the bridge, and enter it in his log-book; it was also his duty to report anything that was amiss—for instance, should a passenger fall or jump overboard he was to drop a lifebelt or lifebuoy, at the same time informing the bridge.

There would be a stand-by quartermaster on the bridge for running messages, looking at the lamps in the standard compass and trimming them, and doing other odd jobs, like reading the thermometer, barometer, the temperature of the water, and the log. Every half-hour the stand-by quartermaster would sound the bell. He would relieve the helmsman after his two hours' trick at the wheel.

The men in the crow's nest would repeat the bells, and during the night they would look at the navigation lights, and call out, 'All's well and lights burning brightly!'

At the end of each watch, as the quartermaster sounded the bell, a new helmsman appeared on the bridge and took the wheel, repeating the course as it was given him; the look-outs were also relieved. At the same time a new Officer of the Watch came on duty, and, after ascertaining the ship's position, course, and speed, examined the chart, checked the course being steered as marked on the course-board in the wheelhouse, and learned from his predecessor all the 'items of interest', as they were called, relating to his watch—the weather conditions, wireless messages, and so on. At night he would sign the night order book in the chart-room, after which the officers would stand together yarning for a few minutes while the new O.O.W. was getting his eyes used to the darkness; as soon as he could see all right he would signify that fact to his predecessor, and officially 'take over'. From time to time the

Officer of the Watch would pace the weather, and his junior the lee, side of the bridge. While on duty the senior officer was normally responsible for everything that occurred during the watch; from time to time messages were brought or telephoned to the bridge from the various departments: only in an emergency was the Captain to be called. The junior officers occupied themselves with various duties; they worked out the sights taken by their senior and checked the deviation of the compass by the bearing of a star or the sun; they attended to the telephone when necessary and kept a watchful eye on the steering. One of the duties of the Fifth and Sixth Officers was to note the temperature of the air and water. All this was done so that the O.O.W. could be in full and absolute charge of the bridge and have nothing to worry his head about.[15] Sometimes the junior officers would see the Captain in his chart-room, in the wheel-house, or on the outer bridge; they would go and report to him the revolutions of the engines, the various calculations they had been working out, and the ship's position by dead reckoning.

Shortly before noon all the officers, armed with their sextants, would assemble on the bridge to take the sun. They would follow the sun as it rose with their sextants and then, when it reached its zenith, where it must remain stationary for a few seconds, they would take its altitude from the horizon. The latitude would be calculated from this meridian altitude. The Master would afterwards retire to his chart-room and the others either to the officers' chart-room or to their own cabins to work out their sights with pad and pencil and tables of logarithms. This, combined with the longitude found by observations during the forenoon, 'longitude by chronometer',[16] and then brought up to noon, would give them their position. When the ship's position had thus been ascertained, it would be marked on the chart; and the next course to be steered would be laid off, to correspond, as closely as possible, with the Great Circle track. The clock on the grand staircase would be put back and the day's run posted up on the various notice-boards.

One way of getting a good fix was by taking altitudes of stars at dawn or twilight, when both horizon and stars could be seen clearly in the sextant. The usual practice was for the O.O.W.

to take a set of stars. In that way one position checked another. He would take two stars for latitude, and two for longitude, one star north and one star south, one star east and one star west. If he found a considerable difference between the two latitude stars, he knew at once there must be mistake somewhere. If there was a difference between the east and west stars, he also knew there must be a mistake. The junior officer would take the time for the observations, and the O.O.W. the stellar observations. The latter would call out 'Stop!' and the former would at that instant take the exact time from the chronometer and write it down.

Between these solar and stellar observations the ship's approximate position would be found by dead reckoning—i.e. by estimating the course steered and distance run, with due allowance for set of currents and leeway from wind and sea. The O.O.W. would take into consideration the reading of the patent log and the revolutions of the engines as reported to the bridge, Dead reckoning would also be resorted to of necessity if, through mist or overcast skies, an observation were impossible; and this, in the North Atlantic trade could happen sometimes for days and even for weeks on end. Even with the greatest possible care, however, D.R. was not to be relied on over an considerable period.[17]

The steering of an accurate Great Circle course demanded, in all circumstances, very careful navigation. As has already been explained, frequent alterations of course were necessary, and these were liable to produce a different degree of deviation; from which it followed that solar and stellar bearings would have to be taken periodically in order to check the compass error. Both the ship's track on the chart and the course steered by the helmsman would have to be carefully watched.

On the western side of the ocean the need for unremitting vigilance and care was greater than ever. Not only was there danger of fog, but also the vertex of the Great Circle track came well within the limits of the region where ice had often been reported during this particular season. The track was, in fact, only entirely safe during the late autumn and winter months. During the time of year when ice would sometimes drift far to the southward passengers were quite unaware of the risks taken to bring them across in good time; and commanders would be congratulated on a smart passage. Due warning of this hazard to traffic on the North Atlantic passage was given in the Sailing Directions published by the Hydrographic Department of the Admiralty; but in practice it was all too frequently ignored.

One of the chief dangers to which vessels are exposed in crossing the Atlantic lies in the probability of encountering masses of ice, both in the form of bergs and of extensive fields of solid compact ice, released at the breaking up of winter in the Arctic regions, and drifted down by the Labrador Current across their direct route. Ice is more likely to be encountered in this route between April and August, both months inclusive, than at other times.

The route chart of the North Atlantic, No. 2058, shows the limits within which both field ice and icebergs may be met with, and where it should be carefully looked out for all times, but especially during the spring and summer seasons. From this chart it would appear that whilst the southern and eastern limits of field ice are about lat. 42° N. and long. 45° W., icebergs may be met with much farther from Newfoundland; in April, May, and June they have been as far South as lat. 39° N., and as far east as long. 38° 30′ W. It is, in fact, impossible to give, within the outer limits named, any distinct idea of where ice may be expected, and no rule can be laid down to ensure safe navigation, as its position and the quantity met with differs so greatly in different seasons. Everything must depend upon the vigilance, caution, and skill with which a vessel is navigated when crossing the dangerous ice-bearing regions of the Atlantic Ocean.[18]

It was because of these dangers and the rapidly increasing number of fast steamships crossing the Atlantic that on November 15th, 1898, agreement had been reached at a conference held in London under the chairmanship of J. Bruce Ismay, attended by the representatives of many of the leading steamship companies of the world, on the fixing of shipping lanes to enable the traffic to keep as clear as practicable of the ice and fog liable to be encountered on more northerly routes. These lanes were to be adapted to the ice conditions which might be expected at different periods of the year.

In their eagerness to make a smart passage, however, some commanders would ignore these arrangements and steer as far to the north as they could. It was possible thereby for vessels steaming on the southern or summer track to shorten the passage to an appreciable degree: since, at the point commonly known as 'the corner', the angle in the rhumb or straight-line course was so acute; and attention had lately been drawn by the mail boat officer quoted above to the significant fact that it was on the southern or summer track, on the westward run, that the smartest passages were made; he added, that all Lines were more or less guilty of the practice.

The *New York Times* recalled that in recent months a certain liner, cutting the corner to save time, ran in so close to the land that her passengers were able to distinguish people strolling on the beach at Cape Race. This revealed the lengths to which some commanders were ready to go to save a few hours' time and coal.[19]

Chapter 7

Revelry by Night

From noon on the 11th to noon on the 12th the *Titanic* had run 386 miles; from the 12th to the 13th, 519 miles; from the 13th to the 14th, 546 miles. It was confidently predicted that the next twenty-four hours would see an even better performance; and Gracie records that Captain Smith had prophesied that, with continued fine weather, they should make an early arrival record for this maiden trip. 'The time the boat was making was considered very good', another passenger, Mrs Douglas, observed; 'and all were interested in getting into New York early.'[1]

Late in the forenoon of Friday, the 12th, a greeting had been telegraphed from the *Empress of Britain*, '*Officers and self send greetings and best of luck to the* Titanic, *her officers and commander.* Murray'; to which the *Titanic* had responded, '*Many thanks for your kind message from all here.* Smith'.[2]

On Sunday morning more boilers were lighted. As on the maiden voyage of the *Olympic*, the year before, the engines were warming up; profiting from the experience gained with the prototype, it might even be possible to improve upon her performance. By Sunday night the *Titanic's* speed had not only increased to 22½ knots, but it was apparently still increasing. . . . A few days before (it was during the call at Queenstown) Ismay had summoned the Chief Engineer to his room, and, after inquiring about the quantity of coal on board, had spoken of driving the ship 'at full speed' on the 15th or the 16th if the weather were entirely suitable. Ismay has said that he told Bell that it was not possible for the *Titanic* to arrive in New York on Tuesday, that there was therefore no object in pushing her, and that they would arrive there at 5 o'clock on Wednesday morning.[3] However that may be, it would seem that they *were* pushing her. In fact, there was every expectation that, if the speed they were making throughout the 14th were maintained, the ship would arrive in New York on Tuesday evening and berth at the White Star pier vacated only two days before by the *Olympic*.

Sunday, the 14th, was an altogether delightful day. The fine weather still continued. The sea was smooth, with a moderate south-westerly wind. Everyone was in good spirits. Little groups of people foregathered in the glass-sheltered promenade decks, in the comfortable smoking-rooms and libraries, in the Café Parisien, and in the spacious writing-room. Some sought out snug and secluded corners to which they would presently retire with a book chosen from the well-stocked ship's library. In the blast of a steady, rushing wind—chill, but invigorating— the hardier spirits among them paced briskly up and down the Boat Deck. Later on in the day a rumour went round that ships to the westward had transmitted reports of icebergs and ice-floes. Some thought that distant icebergs had actually been sighted. People were interested but in no way alarmed by all this talk of ice. The more experienced travellers knew very well that there was always the chance of sighting ice in this region of the ocean, at this particular time of the year. All around the Atlantic stretched away to the far horizon, smooth and sparkling in the sunshine. From the sheltered promenade decks of the *Titanic*, so high above the water, the western swell was barely perceptible.

Breakfast was followed by one of the principal events of Sunday at sea—Captain's inspection. Headed by 'E.J.', an imposing procession, comprising the Captain, the Chief Officer, the Chief Engineer, the Purser, the Chief Steward, and the Senior Surgeon—all the Heads of Departments, in their best uniforms—proceeded with measured tread from stem to stern, and from the topmost to the lowest deck, in and out of the public rooms, visiting every part of the great vessel.

It is worth noting that Sunday, in the White Star Line, was the usual day for boat drill; but on this particular Sunday— probably to the secret relief of the crew—no boat drill was to be held.

At 11 o'clock there was a church service held in the first class dining-room. Instead of an organ there was the ship's orchestra, and instead of the Book of Common Prayer there was the Company's special Prayer Book. The second and third class passengers came in rather shyly and took their places. It was the Master's prerogative to conduct this service in person— though on occasion he might relegate the duty to one of the clergymen on board. (It was the prudent practice of a certain White Star Captain to stipulate, whenever he did so, that the service was not to last more than forty minutes, and nothing must be said which might offend the other passengers—'as, after all,' observed 'Bertie' Hayes, 'we have only contracted to take them as far as London, and are not responsible for where they eventually reach. . . .'[4]) 'E.J.', however, took this service himself. He was a fine figure of a man as he stood before them in his Captain's uniform, with the four gold rings of his rank on either sleeve, gravely reading the prayers, and holding the attention of his congregation with considerably more success than the local clergyman usually did ashore. With his quiet, even voice he led them through the General Confession and the Prayer for Those at Sea, various other prayers and psalms, and ended with Hymn No. 418, 'O God our help in ages past', which was sung with a will.

When service was over the stewards hurried in to get the dining-room ready for luncheon, the congregation dispersed on their various occasions, and Captain Smith went up on the bridge to preside over a different ritual. From the noon observations the ship's position and the day's run would be known.

As usual in these transatlantic liners there were sweepstakes got up for passengers to bet on the day's run; and at noon, after the siren blew, the passengers who had entered for the sweepstake went along to the smoking-room, and on their return announced that the ship had covered 546 miles. Somewhat later there came a rumour from the engine-room that the engines were turning three revolutions faster than at any time on the passage.

The figures for that day's run sent a thrill of satisfaction through the ship. There was much conversation about it at luncheon in the second class saloon. The second day's run of 519 miles, the assistant purser told the others at his table, had been a disappointment; and his belief had been then that they would not dock until Wednesday morning instead of Tuesday night, as had been expected. But following the last day's improved performance, it was thought they might arrive in New York, after all, on Tuesday night.

'They are not pushing her this trip and don't intend to make any fast running,' Mr Barker went on: adding, 'I don't suppose we shall do more than 546 now; it is not a bad day's run for the first trip.'[5]

In the course of the day a good many passengers visited the Purser's office with personal or business messages to be sent by wireless. The Strauses dispatched a greeting to their son and daughter-in-law who were crossing to Europe in the *Amerika*. Two girls sent a telegram to their uncle and aunt who were bound for the Mediterranean in the *Carpathia*, telling them how greatly they were enjoying the voyage. There were also a large number of business messages to be dealt with. Later on the pressure of wireless traffic increased to an almost intolerable degree; though probably no one on board gave a thought to this except the two overworked operators. Since the departure from Southampton they had sent off nearly 250 marconigrams.

Early that afternoon it became intensely cold, and many people forsook the open deck for warmer quarters. The English schoolmaster made for one of his favourite haunts, the library. On the way he paused in the second class foyer to glance for a moment at the notice-board showing the day's run and to observe the ship's position on the chart. One of the acquaintances he had made on board, the Rev. Ernest Carter, was similarly engaged. The two men fell into conversation, in the course of which the parson asked Beesley, who sat at the assistant purser's table, to request the use of the dining saloon for a service of hymns which he wished to hold that evening. Beesley made the request, to which Mr Barker readily agreed.

The library that afternoon was more than usually full of people, owing to the cold. But the sunshine streamed in through the large windows, and the sky was perfectly clear. Everyone expected that, if the fine weather continued, they would land in New York on Tuesday evening. To the end of his life Beesley could vividly recall the scene in the library, on that sunny April afternoon. It was a wide and airy, well-proportioned room with white fluted wooden columns supporting the deck above. Flanking three sides of it were comfortable writing-desks, and along the remaining side were glass-cased bookshelves. In one corner of the room sat a young American cinematograph photographer and his young French wife, playing patience. In the opposite corner were two American ladies, dressed in white, whose conversation was frequently interrupted by a child clasping a large doll. At a table in the middle of the room were two Catholic priests: one of them, who was quietly reading, was a middle-aged Yorkshireman on his way to officiate at his brother's wedding; the other, a dark and bearded Austrian Benedictine, was speaking in German to another man of the same religion. In anticipation of their arrival in New York the library steward was busy serving out declaration forms for the passengers' luggage. In the glass-sheltered corridor outside a number of children were happily playing.[6]

After dinner about a hundred people assembled in the dining-saloon for the hymn-singing. Seated at the piano was a young Scottish engineer, who was going out to join his brother on a fruit-farm in the foot-hills of the Rocky Mountains. The choice of the hymns was left to the congregation. The Vicar introduced each hymn with a few appropriate remarks. It was noticeable that not a few of the hymns that they chose that night dealt with the perils of the sea and included the well-loved 'Eternal Father, strong to save', which a certain Western Ocean skipper had once described as 'the finest prayer from the sailorman to God that was ever offered'.[7] Beesley recalls the hushed and earnest tone with which they all sang:

> Eternal Father, strong to save,
> Whose arm hath bound the restless wave,
> Who bidd'st the mighty ocean deep
> Its own appointed limits keep.
> > O hear us when we cry to Thee
> > For those in peril on the sea.

The hymn-singing continued until well after 10 o'clock, when the Vicar brought the service to a close with some words of thanks to the purser and a warm tribute to the great ship which was bearing them all safely and speedily to their destination.[8]

A Cornish family party, which was not present at the hymn-singing but sat in one of the glass-enclosed promenade decks where the children might play, in after years recalled the intense cold that night. A young woman sat there with her baby clasped to her breast. Near by, her mother was oppressed with a strong foreboding. Soon after nightfall she had heard, or else fancied the had heard, the sound of a cock crowing, which, among the older generation in Cornwall, was regarded as an augury of some great trouble impending.[9]

Auguries were not troubling the steerage that evening. In the third class common-room on C Deck there was music and dancing, which was momentarily interrupted by the incursion of a stray rat. After a spirited chase by some of the young men present, the dancing was resumed. By all accounts it was the liveliest evening of the voyage. . . .[10]

Mrs René Harris had been playing poker with her husband and several others in a comfortable corner near the grand staircase. Hearing the bugle-call for dressing, she was on her way down to her state-room when she missed her footing on the stairs, and took a bad fall. Some men rushed to her side and helped her up. The surgeon presently diagnosed a broken arm. Mrs Harris was in considerable pain; but, with the injured arm set in plaster, she insisted on going into dinner in the restaurant.

Thomas Andrews, who had been worried and out of sorts during the past few days, was now feeling much better. He had successfully resolved all the lesser problems concerning the new liner which were on his mind. 'I believe her to be as nearly perfect as human brains can maker her,' he said to Albert A. Dick, while they were discussing ship design in the smoking-room. When he went into dinner that night, one of the stewardesses declared, 'he looked splendid'.[11] At dinner he talked to the Dicks as usual about his wife and small daughter and their home at Coomber on the banks of Strangford Lough. Afterwards he returned to his cabin where he changed into working clothes and settled down to write.

It was a happy evening for the Strauses, who had just

received a marconigram from their son and daughter-in-law in the *Amerika* in reply to the greeting they had sent them earlier in the day. Isidor Straus had lately finished reading Gracie's book, *The Truth about Chickamauga*, which he had borrowed from the author.

That night the Wideners were giving a dinner party in the restaurant at which Captain Smith, Mr and Mrs Thayer, Mr and Mrs Carter, Major Butt, and their son Harry were guests. The party was going well. It was almost as if they were celebrating the *Titanic's* triumphant début in anticipation of the customary firefloat and siren welcome they might expect to receive in New York Harbour a couple of days later. There was boundless satisfaction at the success of the maiden voyage and the excellent speed they were making. From time to time 'E.J.'s' pleasant, even voice and deep-chested laugh were heard. Seeing Mrs Harris and her injured arm, the Captain came over and congratulated her on her spirit. After dinner 'E.J.' settled down to smoke. He was in no hurry to leave the party. The crystal chandeliers shone down on the beautiful evening gowns, the jewellery, and the bowls of hothouse flowers. It was altogether a great night for these wealthy Americans and their English sailor.

Among the other diners present were the Astors, and Sir Cosmo and Lady Duff-Gordon. In a neighbouring alcove Ismay was dining with old Dr O'Loughlin. The doctor told him, 'We have turned the corner'. . . . This was a great night for Ismay also. The praise of the new liner that was going up on all sides was as music in his ears. He must have known that he was not a popular man; he was too much of an autocrat, and something of a bully; but there could be no doubt whatever that he was a highly successful one. Under Ismay's leadership the White Star Line was entering on a new and brilliant era. The *Olympic* and *Titanic* would skim the cream of the transatlantic traffic. There had never been passenger lists to compare with those of the two giant liners whose construction had been rendered possible by the creation of the Morgan Combine. All around Ismay were the rich and famous: men who might fairly be said to have reached the top of their respective trees. They had attained their life's ambition. They

had got there. They had made their pile. They were in every
way disposed to eat, drink, and make good cheer. . . .

'E. J.' lingered long in these congenial surroundings. Presently, he knew, he would have to go up on the bridge; but
there was no special need for haste. Captain Smith loved a good
cigar; and this night he had two. He sat there in a kind of
smoker's Elysium, and the time slipped by. Everything was
going well—very well indeed. The *Titanic* was really showing a
remarkable turn of speed. If only the fine weather held up, it
looked like being a fast passage. . . . His last command! Well,
he had had a long innings. Soon he would be following old
John Pritchard and the rest into retirement; soon he would
have done with the sea for good and would be joining his wife
and young daughter in their quiet home on the edge of the New
Forest. . . . It was nearly nine o'clock (according to one of the
women sitting nearby it was even later) when he finally excused
himself and quitted the revels.

In the dining saloon, too, there was gaiety and high spirits,
with enthusiastic praise of the *Titanic* and jubilation at the
prospect of a smart passage. The chefs had put on a sumptuous
Sunday dinner. A number of buyers for the great department
stores who had previously been entertained by Emil Brandeis in
his private suite on B Deck were seated at one table. The
Hudson Allisons of Montreal, with their little daughter,
Loraine, and several of their compatriots, were at another.
The Strauses had a small table to themselves. Jack Thayer
was the only member of his family at their table that night;
his parents being at the Wideners' dinner party in the restaurant.
Among other absentees was W. T. Stead, who, owing to a minor
indisposition, was dining in his state-room. Elsewhere in the
great room, Mrs J. J. Brown, James Clinch Smith, Francis
Millet, and Hugh McElroy were as usual entertaining their
respective circles.[12]

After dinner there was a general move towards the Louis
Seize lounge on A Deck. Coffee was served at the numerous
little tables under the palms while the people listened to a concert by the ship's orchestra. The concert ended with a selec-
tion from Offenbach's *Les Contes d'Hoffmann*, with its memories
of lantern-hung Venetian balconies, star-crossed lovers, gliding

gondolas, evil magicians, and students roistering in taverns. The triumphant finale mingled with a loud burst of applause, the conductor smiling and bowing to the audience. With the strains of the lovely barcarolle ringing in their ears, most of the people then wandered off in the direction of their state-rooms. A few, venturing out on the open decks, remarked on the loveliness of the night. As so often happened, the music chosen by Wallace Hartley exactly suited the mood of the moment. Many of the passengers had seen *Les Contes d'Hoffmann* at one of the great opera houses of Europe or America. Few of them could have listened to that music in a more romantic setting. They were in mid-Atlantic, in the largest ship that the world had ever seen, racing through the darkness under a blaze of stars. There were a large number of honeymoon couples on board the *Titanic*. This, surely, was one of those magical nights which all these young people would remember as long as they lived.

> *Belle nuit, ô nuit d'amour,*
> *Souris à nos ivresses!*
> *Nuit plus douce que le jour,*
> *Ô belle nuit d'amour. . . .*

Even the seventeen-year-old Thayer boy was struck by the surpassing beauty of the sea and sky that night as, with a warm coat over his evening clothes, he took a few turns up and down the deserted and lonely Boat Deck, where the wind whistled through the stays and volumes of oily, blackish smoke poured from the funnels. 'It was a brilliant, starry night,' he recalled. 'There was no moon and I have never seen the stars shine brighter; they appeared to stand right out of the sky, sparkling like diamonds. . . . It was the kind of night that made one feel glad to be alive.'[13]

Mrs J. J. Brown had been enjoying herself with the rest of them. She ended the evening with a talk with her much-travelled Philadelphian friend, Mrs Bucknell, who repeated a remark she had previously made while they were waiting to go on board the *Titanic* at Cherbourg. The latter said that she had again experienced a premonition of disaster. However, Maggie only laughed at these misgivings and soon after retired to her state-room.[14]

Somewhat later a few congenial spirits foregathered in the smoking-room. The Swedish naval lieutenant, Björnström Steffanson, with a number of others came up from the verandah café, where it was becoming rather too cold for comfort. Major Peuchen sat chatting with a few of his compatriots for about half an hour, and then said, 'Good night; I am going to turn in'. Charles Williams, the world rackets champion, who was on his way to New York to defend his title, had come up from the squash court. At one table Gracie, Butt, Clarence Moore, Harry Widener, and some of their acquaintances were enjoying a final cigar, while several others were playing auction bridge (the Chief Steward had waived the usual White Star Line rule of no cards on Sunday). Three or four men sat reading in the deep leather armchairs. Most of the women had gone to bed. The conversation turned on Moore's adventures in the Virginian mountains where he had once repaired with a journalist to interview a famous outlaw, Captain Anse Hatfield. Before he went to his room Gracie had a long talk with Charles Hays. One of the last things which the President of the Canadian Grand Trunk Railroad said to Gracie was this: 'The White Star, the Cunard, and the Hamburg-Amerikan lines are now devoting their attention to a struggle for supremacy in obtaining the most luxurious appointments for their ships. But,' said Hays earnestly, 'the time will soon come when the greatest and most appalling of all disasters at sea will be the result.'[15]

Soon after this Gracie went to bed, after instructing his steward to call him early next morning, in time for a game of squash and a swim before breakfast.

High up under the great dome above the main staircase, Honour and Glory crowned yet another hour of Time as people passed, laughing and chatting, on their way to bed. Slowly the public rooms emptied. The Astors and the Wideners sought their 'millionaire suites' on B Deck. Some of the business magnates on board were working late, and Andrews was still poring over his notes and diagrams. Because of the intense cold, people were turning on the electric radiators in their cabins. Gradually the ship became silent, save for the low throbbing of the engines.

After undressing and climbing into his berth, Beesley settled down with a book for half an hour. It was during this period that he became gradually aware of the increased vibration of the engines (his cabin was on D Deck, directly above the engine-room) and rightly concluded that they were steaming faster that night than at any other time since they sailed from Southampton.[16]

When they retired to their cabin at about 10 o'clock, C. E. Henry Stengel, who was familiar enough with machinery in his leather manufacturing business, drew his wife's attention to the fact that the engines were running faster than at any other time. Later on, when the Douglases also retired, they both remarked that the vessel was going faster than she ever had before.[17]

Deep down in the stokehold the 'black gang', stripped to the waist, were ministering to the harsh demands of the furnaces. The firemen ceaselessly shovelled the coal from the piles left handy for them into the hungry fires. The trimmers trundled their barrows along the dark and narrow alleyways that led from the bunkers, and shot their loads against the furnaces. They hurried continually to and fro, filling and tipping, filling and tipping. Close on a hundred tons of coal would be fetched from the bunkers during the watch. From time to time a fireman would be outlined against the glare as he swiftly cleared a furnace with his long slice. There was the incessant clang and scrape of metal as doors slammed-to on furnaces and shovels dug deep into mounds of coal. The atmosphere was thick with coal dust. It was hard to realize, in the terrific heat of the stokehold, that up on deck it was nearly freezing. Hour after hour it would continue, watch after watch, day after day. Such was the merciless, unremitting, back-breaking labour that kept up the pressure of steam and drove the huge propellers.

In the engine-room the officers on duty were hard at work tuning up and adjusting the machinery in readiness for the turn of speed which Ismay and Bell had called for on the morrow. Every engineer seemed to be perpetually watching and listening. The steady throb of the reciprocating machinery mingled with the low hum of the turbine and the whine of the dynamos. Twenty-four out of a total of twenty-nine boilers were lit—more than had ever been in use at any previous stage of the voyage. Originally designed as a 21-knot ship, with the addition of the turbine which drove her centre screw the *Titanic* was capable of speeds far above 21 knots. Knowing what was expected of them, the engineers were on their mettle.

With hillocks of foam flinging wide from her bows, her glistening wake stretching far away into the darkness, her lofty promenade decks and her serried tiers of port-holes ablaze with light, the great ship drove on through the night. . . .

The week-end had not passed so agreeably for the two young men in the Marconi office. Late on Friday night they discovered that something was wrong with the transmitter. Phillips thought at first that the condensers had gone; and they accordingly had these out for examination.[18] It was imperative that the trouble should be put right without delay. For nearly six hours Phillips strove to locate and rectify the fault. In the end Bride and he discovered that the leads of the transformer secondary had burnt through inside the casing and were making contact with the iron bolts securing the frame to the woodwork, with the result that the current was being largely short-circuited to earth. After binding the damaged leads with insulating tape, the pair had the transmitter in good working order again. It was owing to all this trouble that Bride had undertaken to relieve Phillips on Sunday night at midnight, instead of at the usual time, 2 a.m., as he seemed so very tired.

During the past few days news had been coming in from ships in the vicinity of the Grand Banks revealing an unusual number of bergs encountered and the presence of enormous quantities of pack ice which had drifted far to the southward of its usual limits. The relevance and urgency of these reports varied considerably; but there could be no question that the general situation in this particular area of the North Atlantic was more than usually hazardous.

On the first day out a number of ice-reports had been received and posted in the chart-room. On Friday, the 12th, the French liner, *Touraine*, had been in communication with the *Titanic* during the afternoon and evening until 9 p.m. It was in the evening that the former dispatched an ice-warning:[19] '*My position 7 p.m., G.M.T., lat. 49.28, long. 26.28. Dense fog since this night. Crossed thick ice field lat. 44.58, long. 50.40 "Paris" '; saw another ice field and two icebergs lat. 45.20, long. 49.09 "Paris"; saw a derelict lat. 40.56, long. 68.38 "Paris".*[20] *Please give me position. Best regards and* bon voyage. *Caussin.*' Presently a reply arrived from the *Titanic.* '*Thanks for your message and information. My position 7 p.m. G.M.T. Lat. 49.45, long. 23.38 W. Greenwich. Had fine weather. Compliments. Smith.*'

Throughout the 14th the ice-reports became more frequent and more pressing. At 9 a.m. the following telegram was received from the *Caronia*: '*Captain,* Titanic.—*West-bound steamers report bergs, growlers, and field ice in 42° N. from 49° to 50° W*'.[21]

At 11.40 an ice-report was received, via the *Caronia*, from the *Noordam.* '*Congratulations on new command. Had moderate westerly winds, fine weather, no fog, much ice reported in lat. 42° 24' to 42° 45' and long. 49° 45' and long. 49° 50' to 50° 20'.*'[22]

Shortly before one o'clock a message arrived from the *Baltic.* '*Captain,* Titanic.—*Have had moderate, variable winds and clear, fine weather since leaving. Greek steamer* Athenai *reports passing icebergs and large quantities of field ice today in lat. 41° 51' N., long. 49° 52' W. . . . Wish you and* Titanic *all success. Commander*'.[23]

Each of these messages was formally acknowledged by the Master.

Ismay was standing talking to some passengers on A Deck when Captain Smith approached and handed him, without comment, the marconigram which had just come in. Ismay took the paper and put it casually into his pocket, while the Captain continued on his way. Next moment the bugle sounded luncheon, and there was a general move towards the companion way.

The message from the *Baltic* reposed in Ismay's pocket for six hours or more; the officers on duty, in fact, had no knowledge of it; and it was not until shortly before dinner that evening that Captain Smith, seeing Ismay sitting in the smoking-room and suddenly remembering the ice-report, said, 'By the way, sir, have you got that telegram which I gave you this afternoon?' 'Yes', replied Ismay, searching for it in his pocket and returning it to the Captain—'here it is.' The

Captain explained that he wanted to put it up in the officers' chart-room.[24]

Shortly after the arrival of this telegram, a message from the *Amerika* to the Hydrographic Office in Washington was intercepted by the *Titanic*. '*Amerika passed two large icebergs in 41° 27' N., 50° 8' W., on April 14th*'.[25] At 7.30 another telegram, this time from the *Californian* to the *Antillian*, was picked up by the *Titanic* and delivered to the bridge. '*To Captain*, Antillian. *6.30 p.m. apparent ship's time; lat. 42° 3' N., long 49° 9' W. Three large bergs five miles to the southward of us.*'[26]

During the afternoon of Sunday, April 14th, the *Titanic* would reach the vicinity of the 'corner', or turning-point, in 42° N., 47° W., where vessels were accustomed to alter course for Sandy Hook. It was with some surprise, therefore, that when the Fourth Officer came on duty in the first dog watch (4–6 p.m.) he noticed that the night order book was written out and that there was an order for course to be altered at 5.50. He remarked on this to Wilde, the O.O.W., observing that if it were intended as usual to alter course at 'the corner', course should surely have been altered considerably earlier.[27] Actually it would appear that the commander, in thus continuing on the south-westerly course which had been followed since leaving the Fastnet, was endeavouring to steer clear of some of the ice which had been reported.'[28]

In the crow's nest Jewell and Symons came on duty at 6, relieving Hogg and Evans.

'Nothing doing,' reported Hogg; 'keep a look-out for small ice. . . .'

It would appear that this was some kind of joke or catch-phrase in use among the men in the crow's nest on the North Atlantic run.

Seven ice-reports at least reached the *Titanic* that Sunday. Early in the afternoon Lightoller, as usual, relieved Murdoch while the latter was having his luncheon. During this time Captain Smith came up on the bridge and showed him the message from the *Caronia*. Lightoller later informed Murdoch, who merely replied, 'All right'. The Second Officer then went below and turned in.

When Lowe, the Fifth Officer, came on duty in the second dog watch (6–8 p.m.) he noticed a chit lying on the chart-room table with the word 'ice' pencilled upon it and a position written underneath. He roughly worked out the position in his head and concluded that the ship would not have reached the ice region before the end of his watch.[29]

Wilde was relieved by the Second Officer at 6 p.m. The latter, as soon as he arrived on the bridge, asked the junior officer for the computations on which he had been engaged, and they were given him about half an hour later. Shortly afterwards there was some talk about the ice in the officers' quarters. The general opinion was that they would be 'up with the ice' somewhere between 10 p.m. and midnight.

The watchkeepers who were on duty from 6 o'clock onwards were certainly on the look-out for it. Various precautions were taken. At 7.15 Samuel Hemming, a lamp-trimmer, came up on the bridge and reported to the O.O.W. that all the lights had been placed. The man was about to leave the bridge when Murdoch called him back, saying: 'Hemming, when you go forward get the fore scuttle hatch closed. There is a glow left from that, and as we are in the vicinity of ice I want everything dark before the bridge.' Hemming went and closed the hatch himself.[30]

As on the previous evenings, the O.O.W. took a set of stars as it was coming on dusk—three stars for latitude, and three for longitude; while the Third Officer stood by the chronometer, and noted the exact time as his senior gave the call; after which he retired to the chart-room to work out the O.O.W.'s observations.

The Fifth Officer was engaged in working out the slip table, which was a table based upon so many revolutions of the engines and so much per cent. slip,[31] so as to calculate the miles per hour; and also in working out a dead reckoning position of the ship at 8 p.m. for the Captain. He left the completed slip report on the chart-room table, so that the ship's position might be filled in in the night order book. Just as Boxhall had done, Lowe glanced at the course laid off in on the chart at noon and surmised that, judging from the distance run, they had held on their course for something like three-quarters of an hour after reaching 'the corner'. He thought that course ought to have been altered at about 5 o'clock.

The Third Officer was busy in the chart-room. He could see from the marconigrams stuck up on the frame that there was no ice reported anywhere near the track. Nothing to worry about, apparently. As usual, he took a stellar bearing to check the compass error. Towards the end of his watch, at about twenty minutes to eight, he had started working on the meridian altitude of the star for latitude when his relief appeared on the bridge. He handed over the task thankfully to Boxhall, saying:

'Here is a bunch of sights for you, old man. Go ahead!'[32]

Boxhall and Moody came on duty. Pitman and Lowe went below. The quartermasters and look-outs were also relieved. Robert Hitchens, a Cornishman, who had the first two hours of the watch as stand-by, was presently told to give the Second Officer's compliments to the carpenter and to advise him to look to his fresh water, as it was about to freeze. He did so; and soon after the carpenter appeared on the bridge and reported the duty carried out. About the same time Lightoller sent word to the engine-room to take the necessary precautions for the winches. Later on Hitchens was told to go and find the deck engineer and bring him up with a key to open up the heaters in the corridor of the officers' quarters, also in the wheel-house and chart-room, on account of the intense cold.[33]

In the Marconi cabin the senior operator was, as usual at that time of night, on duty; while Bride had turned in. Phillips, tired out as he was after the long struggle with the defective transformer, still had to face long hours of work. Message after message had shot down the pneumatic tube which led from the Purser's office into the wire receptacle at his side. His most pressing anxiety had been to re-establish communication with Cape Race at the earliest possible moment (they had already been in touch with the station at about 4 a.m.—but communication over such distances during the hours of daylight was impossible); there was in consequence a large accumulation of telegrams awaiting dispatch. At last the first faint signals from this station, MCE, were heard; and work began. By one of the two clocks in the wireless office, which kept ship's time, it was now 9.40; by the other, which kept New York time, it was 7.50. Just then there came an interruption.

Some two hundred miles to the eastward, S. H. Adams, the radio operator of the *S.S. Mesaba*, of the Atlantic Transport Company, had begun to transmit.

'*From* Mesaba *to* Titanic . . . *Ice-report in lat. 42° N. to 41° 25' N., long. 49° to 50° 30' W. Saw much heavy pack ice and a great number large icebergs. Also field ice. Weather good, clear.*'

After a brief interval the answer came back: '*Received; thanks*'. Then silence. The *Mesaba's* operator stood by for a while, fully expecting to hear that Captain Smith would presently acknowledge the message. Such a message, he knew, should have been delivered to the Master at once; and it was customary for the Master to reply. But Adams waited in vain; apart from the bare acknowledgment already mentioned (*R. Tks.*), no response was forthcoming from MGY, which he could again hear calling Cape Race.[34]

In point of fact, the message was never delivered to the bridge at all. What with all the hours of work devoted to repairing the damaged transformer the previous night, and all the heavy backlog of private traffic which had to be worked off the following day, Phillips was fagged out. It seemed as if his work would never end. The senior operator was nearly at the end of his tether. Naturally pale-faced, he now looked wan and exhausted. It was for this reason that Bride had undertaken to relieve him at midnight, instead of at 2 a.m., the usual time. Conditions were fairly good that night; though not a few operators in this region of the ocean had occasion to complain of 'freaky' reception, static, and serious jamming.[35]

Phillips toiled on while the *Mesaba's* message lay, forgotten, under a paper-weight on the operating table.[36] The telegrams from Cape Race piled up at his elbow as he took them down. Then he in turn began to transmit, dispatching messages from the *Titanic* to the shore station,[37] whence they would be transmitted by wire or cable to New York or London. The need to clear the passengers' telegrams and complete his accounts was uppermost in his mind. The regulation about always giving priority to messages affecting the navigation of the vessel was disregarded.[38] . . . Several hundred miles away at Cape Race Gray had taken over the key earlier in the evening; and the two friends had a brief chat. Phillips was full of the wonders of the magnificent new vessel on her maiden voyage, and spoke of her remarkable passenger list. Finally Gray bade him goodnight and left the key.[39] The work continued. Phillips appears to have cleared all the Cape Race traffic by seven bells, 11.30 p.m.

He was still busy at the operating table when there arrived yet another warning out of the night. About half an hour earlier a Leyland liner, the S.S. *Californian*, brought to a halt and apparently encompassed by ice, dispatched the last of the ice-reports received by the *Titanic* that day; it came over with a roar, completely blotting out the signals from MCE, and Phillips told her operator curtly to shut up—'*Shut up. Shut up. I am busy; I am working Cape Race*'. To MCE he signalled, '*Sorry; please repeat; jammed*'.[40]

Such were the circumstances in which the second of the urgent ice-reports wirelessed to MGY was ignored and no intimation of these warnings ever reached the bridge. The *Californian's* operator made no further attempt to communicate with MGY. Phillips cleared the last of his telegrams while Bride slumbered fitfully in the adjoining cabin. The *Titanic* was now running at over $22\frac{1}{2}$ knots—the highest speed she had ever achieved.

Chapter 8

The Collision

The Officer of the Watch stood on the bridge looking out on a sea which just then seemed almost motionless; though appearances could be deceptive, as he and every other experienced mail boat officer well knew, since from the height of a ship's bridge it was often impossible to detect a slight swell.

It was a beautiful night, and there was not a cloud in the sky. Since about 6.30 p.m. the temperature had been steadily falling; in fact, when he had relieved the Chief Officer after dinner Murdoch had remarked that the temperature had dropped four degrees (from 43° to 39° Fahr.) in the last half-hour. Later that evening the quartermaster had from time to time reported the continued fall in the temperature. When it had dropped to 33°—only one degree above freezing—the Second Officer, as we have seen, had sent to warn the carpenter and the engine-room. Despite the peace and serenity of the night, the weather conditions were not altogether to Lightoller's liking. What somewhat disturbed him was the absence of wind and the smoothness of the sea.

According to his reckoning they had almost reached the region—long. 49° W.—where ice had been reported. They might perhaps sight an iceberg or a growler (a berg which is very nearly submerged) or perhaps they might not. One of the surest indications of a mass of ice at night was the white foam fretting round its base. Experience had shown that under the usual conditions ice could be sighted in time, and avoided. But in an oily sea like the present the margin of safety would be greatly reduced. It therefore behoved the O.O.W. to keep a sharp look-out.

Lightoller was not unduly apprehensive of sudden emergencies. If such occurred, he was well prepared to deal with them, as he often had in the past. That was what was expected of him. It was because of his standing and experience that he was now a watch-keeper on board 'the Biggest Ship in the World'.

Just before 9 o'clock 'E.J.' came up on the bridge. He remarked that it was cold.

'Yes, it is very cold, sir,' agreed Lightoller. 'In fact, it is only one degree above freezing. I have sent word down to the carpenter and rung up the engine-room and told them that it is freezing or will be during the night.'

'There is not much wind,' said Captain Smith presently.

'No, it is a flat calm, as a matter of fact.'

'A flat calm.'

'Yes,' said Lightoller, 'quite flat, there is no wind.' He added that it was rather a pity the breeze had not kept up whilst they were going through the ice region. (What he meant by this, as has already been explained, was that because of the oily calm they could not expect to receive warning of the ice through the ripples breaking on the base of the berg.) Something was then said to the effect that, even if the blue side of the berg might be towards them, in all probability the white outline would still give them sufficient warning, and they should be able to see it at a good distance.

By this time 'E.J.' was getting his eyesight after the brightly lighted restaurant and the cheery party which he had lately left, and he murmured:

'It seems quite clear.'

'Yes, it is perfectly clear,' agreed Lightoller.

Captain Smith in conclusion observed that if it became in the slightest degree hazy they would have to slow down; then he went to his room, saying, 'If it becomes at all doubtful let me know at once; I will be just inside'.[1]

On his way he visited the chart-room, where at about 10 o'clock he put down on the chart the ship's position as calculated by the Fourth Officer at 7.30. He also discussed some stellar bearings that Boxhall had taken.[2]

As soon as the Captain had left the bridge, Lightoller told the Sixth Officer to warn the two men in the crow's nest to keep a sharp look-out for ice, particularly small ice and growlers, until daylight. Moody at once telephoned the look-outs and the

O.O.W. heard him saying, 'Keep a sharp look-out for ice, particularly small ice and growlers, until daylight'.[3]

If it was cold on the bridge, it was colder still in the crow's nest. Jewell and Symons were 'on' from 8 to 10. Symons, who had travelled this route many times in the past few years, glowered at the slight surface haze which lay along the western horizon. It was apparently more or less the same, neither thickening nor dispersing, throughout the whole of the two hours' watch. Once or twice Symons, as he stared ahead, sniffed the keen air knowingly.

Presently Jewell turned to his mate and murmured:

'It is very cold here.'

'Yes,' replied the other; 'by the smell of it there is ice about.'

Jewell then asked him what he meant by this, and Symons replied:

'As a rule you can smell the ice before you get to it.'[4]

Slowly the time passed.

Somewhere in the waste of dark waters beyond, more than nine centuries earlier, a shipload of Norse mariners under one Bjarni Herjólfsson had sighted, for the first time in history, the American mainland. The ship in which they sailed was an undecked sailing craft of some 30 tons. The vessel in which certain of their compatriots were now voyaging to the New World, at a speed and in conditions of comfort beyond the Vikings' wildest imagination, was more than 1,500 times as large. In the time of Bjarni Herjólfsson the mariner's compass was still unknown, so that when they were driven southward by north winds into a haze which lasted for days they lost their reckoning and all sense of direction; and this went on until finally they saw the sun and were able to get their bearings. On these ventures the Norsemen would resort to such adventitious aids to navigation even as 'birds from Ireland' and 'birds and whales from Iceland'[5]. . . . Nautical science had come a long way since the time of the Vikings. Nowadays, with the aid of the navigational instruments carried in the *Titanic*, the Officer of the Watch could be certain of his position, within reasonable limits, at every stage of the voyage.

The two men keeping their lonely vigil in the bitter cold of the crow's nest, high above the welter of foam and broken water streaming back from the liner's thrusting stem, were hardly any better off, so far as creature comforts were concerned, than the sturdy Norsemen who had sailed with Bjarni Herjólfsson; but at least they had the consolation of knowing that, at the end of their spell of duty, they would have four hours' rest in warmth and comfort below.

During the rest of his watch Lightoller took up a stationary position on the bridge, where, clear of back-stays, stays, and so on, he had an unobstructed view right ahead, and perhaps a couple of points on either bow. Mindful of 'E.J.'s' parting injunction, he was closely watching the weather, and keeping a sharp look-out for ice as well.[6] Knowing that if there was ice about there might well be a certain amount of surface haze, he often used his glasses. From time to time he would raise them to his eyes, gazing ahead to see if he could see anything, relying on both glasses and eyes.[7]

At a quarter to ten the stand-by quartermaster went to call the First Officer, to let him know that it was one bell. He also took the thermometer, barometer, temperature of the water, and the log.

Four bells . . . Fleet and Lee ascended the foremast by the spiral stairway and entered the crow's nest to relieve the two look-outs.

'Keep a sharp look-out for icebergs and growlers until daylight!'

The two men who had just come on duty repeated the order; and shortly after Jewell and Symons left the crow's nest and clattered off down the stairway.

Shadowy figures had appeared on the bridge. The helmsman's relief entered the wheel-house; and presently Robert Hitchens, the Cornishman, took the wheel.

'N. 71 W.,' murmured Oliver.

'N. 71 W.,' Hitchens duly repeated.[8] Firmly he grasped spokes, staring into the softly glowing binnacle.

At the same time Murdoch had arrived on the bridge to relieve Lightoller. He was wearing his overcoat, and he murmured, 'It is pretty cold'. 'Yes,' replied Lightoller; 'it is freezing.' The latter proceeded to pass on the items of interest— the ship's position, her course and speed, weather conditions, ice reports, etc. Before leaving the chart-room, Murdoch had also to inspect the night order book, which that night contained a footnote regarding ice. The Second Officer remained on the bridge for a few moments while his relief was getting his eyes used to the darkness. As they stood there, side by side, gazing ahead, they both remarked on the ship's steadiness and the absence of vibration. Once again the conversation turned on the ice reports that had been coming in. Lightoller passed the remark that they might be 'up around the ice about now'. About this time mention was made of the lack of definition between the horizon and the sky—which would make an iceberg all the more difficult to see at a distance—particularly if it had a black side, and that should be, by bad luck, turned their way.

Lightoller also reported the commander's visit to the bridge, and he told Murdoch about the order that he had had telephoned to the crow's nest, and the warning that he had sent to the carpenter and the engine-room as to the temperature.[9]

What neither of these officers was to know was that about half an hour earlier the message from the *Mesaba* had been received, warning the *Titanic* of an immense mass of ice lying dead in her track. But the message had never reached the bridge. It was still lying on the table in the Marconi office, impatiently shoved aside under a paper-weight.[10]

The position now was as follows: the various masses of ice which had been the subject of successive warnings from neighbouring ships—the *Caronia* ice, the *Baltic* ice, the *Amerika* ice, the *Antillian* ice, and the *Mesaba* ice—would, if they had all been plotted on the chart, have formed a rough oblong, or parallelogram, into the midst of which the *Titanic* was driving at full speed.[11] It was not in the event of crucial importance whether or not the *Mesaba's* message was actually delivered to the bridge; since, as will presently be seen, the O.O.W. did, shortly after, receive warning of the ice in his track.

The Second Officer set out on his rounds, moving swiftly from deck to deck. A good many of the passengers had by this time turned in or at least had gone to their cabins. The concert in the palm court was drawing to a close. Soon the public rooms would be emptying. In a ship of the *Titanic's* size, 'doing the rounds' meant traversing a mile or more of decks, as well as several hundred feet of ladders and staircases. It was intensely cold, and Lightoller thought longingly of his warm bunk. After covering several decks, he went down through the working alley-way known as 'Park Lane' ('Scotland Road' to the crew), and came out by a short cut on the after deck and the freezing cold. Here he had to look round and see that the quartermaster and the others were on their stations.

Before Lightoller had completed these duties and retired to his cabin, another warning had reached the *Titanic*. All this time the great vessel ran on, at 22½ knots, into the ice region. No extra look-outs were put on. No other precautions were taken, indeed, than those already mentioned. These were deemed to be fully sufficient to meet the needs of the situation. In accordance with the customary practice of the Western Ocean express service, the First Officer had confidently accepted the risk of encountering ice as, an hour or so earlier, 'E.J.' and Lightoller had accepted it. Presently Murdoch accepted an even greater risk. At about five bells—10.30 p.m.— a steamer was sighted on the opposite course to the *Titanic's*. It was a Furness Withy vessel, the *Rappahannock*, eastward bound from Halifax. Her acting Master, Albert E. Smith, had just taken over from her former commander, incapacitated by illness. The *Rappahannock* had lately emerged from a great icefield where, steaming cautiously among the heavy pack-ice and occasional ice-bergs, she had sustained severe damage to her rudder. Out of the darkness a signal-lamp began to wink.

After ascertaining the name of the westward-bound vessel the acting Master of the *Rappahannock* signalled, '*Have just passed through heavy field ice and several ice-bergs.*' The *Titanic* replied briefly in acknowledgment, '*Message received. Thanks. Good night*'.[12]

Soon the Furness Withy vessel had been left several miles astern . . . while the *Titanic* drove on to the westward, towards the imminent danger, now less than 25 miles ahead of her. Still confident, however, that even if they did encounter ice, he would be able to manœuvre safely around it, Murdoch held on the course laid down by the commander, and at the

same high speed. Another half-hour went by. At six bells—
11 p.m.—yet another ice-report reached the *Titanic*, from the
Leyland liner *Californian*, which was then lying with her
engines stopped on the fringe of the same icefield through
which the *Rappahannock* had lately passed. Like the message
from the *Mesaba*, this warning never reached the *Titanic's*
bridge, though it was apparently known to both her wireless
operators.[14]

The crucial factor at this stage was the visibility. It will be
remembered that Captain Smith had expressly warned the
Officer of the Watch that if it became in the slightest degree
hazy they would have to slow down. The danger was not only
the likelihood of encountering mist while in the ice region, but
also the difficulty, under certain conditions, of detecting mist
when it was there. In other words, a dangerous situation might
suddenly arise before they were aware of it. Haze is a deceptive
subject at all times, but particularly at night. It can sometimes
be seen from above, e.g. from the crow's nest, when it is quite
invisible lower down, e.g. on the foc's'le head.

Up in their lonely perch the two look-outs, Fleet and Lee,
gazed intently at the uncertain horizon. The mist was apparently thickening. It was much more noticeable now than it had
been earlier in the evening. Fleet is said to have remarked that
if they could see through that haze they would be lucky.[14]
Slowly the moments passed. It was getting on for 11.40—two
hours after the *Mesaba's* message had been received, an hour
after the ice-report from the *Rappahannock* had been acknowledged. The watch was nearly over. Twenty minutes more and
it would be eight bells, and they would be thawing out with
cocoa in the warmth and light of the mess-room.

It was then that Fleet suddenly fixed his eyes on something
half seen in the hazy darkness ahead. Whatever it was, was
barely visible, it was only the top of the object he could see
at first. Next moment he struck three bells, and then went to
the telephone, informing the bridge, '*Iceberg right ahead!*' after
which he returned to this own place on the port side of the
crow's nest.

Moody, at the telephone, quickly repeated the warning to
the Officer of the Watch, who immediately gave the order,

'Hard-a-starboard!' and telegraphed to the engine-room, 'Stop. Full speed astern.' At the same moment he pulled over the switch which closed the water-tight doors in the engine and boiler rooms. The quartermaster put the helm hard over, and presently the ship's head veered slowly two points to port.

It was too late. No sooner was the helm hard over than they all felt a sudden jar, followed by an ominous grinding noise far below along the ship's side. The Captain came rushing out of his room.

'Mr Murdoch, what was that?'

'An iceberg, sir. I hard-a-starboarded and reversed the engines, and I was going to hard-a-port round it but she was too close. I could not do any more. I have closed the water-tight doors.'[15]

Chapter 9

The Eight Rockets

The Captain, with Murdoch and the Fourth Officer, who had just returned to the bridge, rushed out on to the port wing, where, gazing astern, they saw the iceberg, 'a small black mass not rising very high out of the water', a little on the starboard quarter. Murdoch stood with outstretched hand pointing to the berg, while Boxhall hurriedly left the bridge to try and find out what damage had been done. The great vessel gradually lost her headway, and at last lay motionless in the dark, still water under the glittering stars.

As Boxhall made his way forward the alarm bells were ringing for the closing of the watertight doors; and he went down into the steerage quarters beneath the foc's'le head to try and discover the extent of the damage. Pushing through the crowd of third class passengers swarming up the stairway, he descended to the lowest steerage, and then inspected all the decks as he came up again; but nowhere could he see any sign of water entering the ship. Back on the bridge he reported to the Captain and First Officer that he could discover no damage whatever.[1]

'Go down and find the carpenter,' was the next order he received, 'and get him to sound the ship.'

Boxhall met the carpenter coming up to the bridge to report. The carpenter said, 'The ship is making water'. Next he met a mail clerk who wanted to know where the Captain was.

'He is on the bridge,' the officer replied.

'The mail hold is filling rapidly.'

'Well, you go and report it to the Captain and I will go down and see.'

Boxhall went down to the mail hold where the bags of mail were floating about and the clerks were hurriedly removing letters from the racks. For the first time the gravity of the situation was borne in upon the officer. He returned to the bridge and made his report.

The Chief Officer then hurried to the bridge and asked the Captain whether he thought the damage was serious. 'Certainly,' was the reply. 'I'm afraid it's more than serious.'

During this time Captain Smith had been to the wheel-house to look at the commutator, which was a small instrument mounted in front of the compass for indicating how the ship was listing. He observed to his consternation that it already showed a list of five degrees to starboard. 'Oh, my God!' he muttered in his beard.

Lightoller had been just on the point of falling asleep when he felt a sudden vibrating jar run through the ship. Next moment he was out of his bunk and running across the deck in his pyjamas. First he looked over the port side, and then seeing nothing there, raced over to the starboard side; but saw nothing there either and returned to his bunk. He was waiting there when, shortly afterwards, the Fourth Officer came into the room and said, 'We've hit an iceberg'.

'I know you've hit something,' said Lightoller.

'The water is up to F Deck in the Mail Room,' said Boxhall quietly; and without another word exchanged he went out, closing the door behind him, while Lightoller hurriedly dressed. [2]

Lying half waking, half sleeping, in his bunk, the Third Officer had heard a sound like 'the chain running out over the windlass', accompanied by a slight vibration. It was not enough to rouse him to full wakefulness. After a few minutes he got up and looked out of the door; but neither seeing nor hearing anything unusual he returned to his room and lit his pipe.

However, as it was near his watch, he started to dress and was already half-dressed when Boxhall came in and told him that the water was flooding into the mail room. Pitman drew on his coat and went on deck, where he saw the seamen uncovering the boats and clearing them away. Presently he met Moody, who told him that there was ice on the forward well deck. He went first to look at the ice and then to the foc's'le head, where he could find no damage. On his return he saw a crowd of firemen coming up with their bags. The officer asked,

'What is the matter?' 'The water is coming in our place', they told him. 'That is funny,' said Pitman. He looked down No. 1 hatch and saw the water flowing over the hatch.

Meanwhile Ismay had arrived hurriedly on the bridge, where he asked the Captain whether he considered the damage was serious; and Smith replied that he thought it was. Then he went below, and, meeting the Chief Engineer at the head of the staircase, asked him, too, whether he thought the ship was seriously damaged. Bell's reply was that he thought she was, but he hoped the pumps would be able to control the water.

This hope proved in vain. In rather less than ten seconds a submerged spur of the iceberg had torn a 300-foot gash along the ship's side and the water burst in like a cataract. Presently Smith, in company with Andrews, who had been hurriedly summoned to the bridge, went below to investigate. They strode past the mail room and the squash rackets court, both of them flooded. They found that the sea was pouring into the six forward compartments and gaining on the pumps which had been started soon after the collision. Nor could the collision be confined to the six compartments which had been damaged; since, though there were sixteen watertight compartments in the ship, the transverse bulkheads had not been carried up to the deck-heads, and, as each compartment flooded, the water poured over into the next. It was apparent that the *Titanic* was doomed.[3] Andrews, in fact, gave her only an hour or perhaps an hour and a half to live. Returning to the bridge, the two men hurried through the A Deck foyer, now filled with anxious passengers. Shortly after midnight, Captain Smith told the Chief Officer to get the lifeboats uncovered.

Under the bridge the Bo'sun had piped, 'all hands up and get the lifeboats ready!' The men came swarming up ladders and scudding along alleyways. Since the stoppage of the engines the steam had been roaring off at all the eight exhausts, Lightoller relates, 'kicking up a row that would have dwarfed the row of a thousand railway engines thundering through a culvert'. In the face of this terrific din speech was impossible; but a tap on the shoulder and a wave of the hand was enough to set the Port Watch hurriedly stripping the covers and hauling tight the boats' falls and coiling them on deck. On the starboard side the work of clearing away the boats went forward under the supervision of the First Officer.[4]

The work did not proceed quickly at first. It was some time in fact before most of the hands arrived on the boat deck; and a great deal of confusion ensued owing to the fact that the men did not know their respective boats—as has been said, there had been no proper boat drill, not even a boat muster. Charles Hays, Major Peuchen, and a number of other first class passengers hurried forward to assist them. One of these volunteers was the excitable and over-impatient J. Bruce Ismay, who was presently urged by Lowe (who had no idea of his identity) 'to get to hell out of it!'

For some minutes the Fourth Officer went round the decks helping to strip the covers off the lifeboats. The Captain then told him that the position that had been sent out in the general distress call was the 8 p.m. dead reckoning one and enquired how it compared with the 7.30 p.m. stellar position. Boxhall went at once to the chart-room and worked it out [5]

The present position, calculated from the stellar observation at dusk, was found to be lat. 41° 46′ N., long. 50° 14′ W., which showed the ship to be about 20 miles ahead of the D.R. position. The Captain ordered him to take it to the wireless office. Boxhall obeyed. Owing to the ear-splitting din of the escaping steam, he simply scribbled the position on a slip of paper and left it beside Phillips on the operating table, afterwards returning to the boats.

Meanwhile down in the engine-room and stokehold there was furious activity. When the alarm was sounded all the engineers off duty rushed to their emergency stations. They were presently assisted by the men from Harland and Wolff's. The necessary orders were given: with the water very soon rising above their knees and waists, the engineers hurriedly directed the drawing of the fires; others dragged forward the great heavy suction hoses as far as they possibly could in order to keep the inrush of water under control; the largest pumps in the ship were set going, and thousands of tons of water sent thundering down into the sea. The Chief Engineer and his assistants switched on the emergency dynamos situated well above the waterline so as to keep the pumps, lights, and wireless apparatus working. By midnight most of the fires in the forward boiler-rooms had been drawn. Though the flood continued to gain on the pumps, the rise of the water was at any rate retarded. For well over $2\frac{1}{2}$ hours after the collision the lighting and wireless apparatus were still working. Nearly all the ventilators had been switched off in order to save current. At last, at about 1.40 a.m., the firemen were ordered up on deck; but the engineers remained. It was almost entirely due to the heroism and devotion of these officers that the ship remained afloat as long as she did. They did their duty to the end.[6]

Shortly after midnight Bride had climbed out of his bunk and joined his senior in the wireless cabin. He had been fast asleep and knew nothing of what had happened. On the operating table lay a large batch of telegrams from Cape Race that Phillips had been engaged in taking down. Bride presently donned the headphones, and Phillips got ready to turn in, casually observing as he did so that they must have hit something, as the ship had stopped. He said he thought they would have to return to Belfast, and went on with his undressing. It was then that the Captain suddenly appeared in the doorway.[7]

'We've struck an iceberg,' he said; 'and I'm having an inspection made to tell what it has done to us. You had better get ready to send out a call for assistance. But don't send it until I tell you.'

The Captain hurried back to the bridge. After his departure, the two operators turned to each other in amazement. Why, everyone knew that the *Titanic* was unsinkable! A few hours earlier Phillips had been telling his colleague at Cape Race all about the wonderful new liner, and what a marvellous experience it had been. The idea that there could be any possible danger seemed to them absurd. For a while they laughed and joked, and 'said all sorts of funny things to each other'.

All this time they could hear a confused murmur of voices, and much coming and going on the deck outside; but nothing at all to indicate that there was any real cause for alarm. They were quite ready to obey the Captain's orders. Thanks to all the work they had put in the previous night, the ship's wireless was once again functioning perfectly. In ten minutes or so the Captain reappeared.

'Send the call for assistance!' he said abruptly, barely putting his head inside the door.

'What call should I send?' the senior asked, as he resumed the headphones.

'The regular international call for assistance. Just that!'

A turn of the hand started up his transmitter, and Phillips bent over the table and sent out the general distress call, CQD, six times, followed by the *Titanic's* call sign, MGY, and the vessel's approximate position. '*Have struck an iceberg. We are badly damaged.* Titanic. *Postition 41° 44′ N., 50° 24′ W.* The call was received by several ships and by Cape Race.

The Captain returned after an interval and asked:

'What are you sending?'

'CQD', replied Phillips.

'Send SOS,' Bride suggested. 'It's the new call, and,' he jested mildly, 'it may be your last chance to send it!' At that they all laughed. When the Captain had gone away again the two operators went on saying 'lots of funny things' to each other, while Phillips sent out the SOS.

The first response came from the German *Frankfurt*, whose operator went off to inform the Master. On his return he was informed that the *Titanic* was sinking by the head. Then a Cunard liner, the *Carpathia*, replied. As has already been said, by this time Boxhall had worked out the correct position of the ship, based on the star position at 7.30 p.m.; and another message was promptly sent.

'CQD CQD SOS SOS CQD SOS *Come at once. We have struck a berg.* CQD OM [*It's a CQD, old man.*] *Position 41° 46′ N., 50° 14′ W.* CQD SOS.'

Soon after the staccato mutter of Morse began anew. The following message was picked up by a Japanese ship, the *Ypiranga*, which heard the *Titanic* give her position fifteen to twenty times.

'MGY CQD *Position 41° 46′ N., 50° W. Require immediate assistance. We have collided with iceberg. Sinking. Can hear nothing for noise of steam.*'

It is to be remembered that all this time the appalling din from the exhausts continued unabated; but at last, in response to an appeal from Phillips, Captain Smith got the noise reduced. Meanwhile the *Carpathia's* operator had hurried off to his Captain. Presently a message came that the Cunarder—then 58 miles to the south-eastward—was turning about and steering for the *Titanic*; and Phillips sent Bride to inform Captain Smith. The young operator made his way with difficulty along the Boat Deck through a surging mob of passengers to the Master's quarters. He said afterwards that he had seen no fighting, but he had heard talk of it.

On his return to the wireless cabin Bride heard his senior giving the *Carpathia* fuller directions. Then Phillips told him to go and get dressed (in the excitement Bride had forgotten that he was still in pyjamas). The latter went into their sleeping cabin and hurriedly dressed, and returned with an overcoat which he slipped round Phillips while he worked. Periodically Phillips would send his junior to the bridge with further messages concerning the *Carpathia's* probable arrival and her speed. On his return from one of these missions Bride noticed that they were putting women and children into the boats, and that the ship's forward list was ominously increasing.

During the first half-hour or so following the collision there was curiosity rather than anxiety or alarm among such of the passengers who happened to be on deck or about the corridors and staircases at the sudden stoppage of the ship. Nobody was thrown out of his or her berth; nobody was jolted against a bulkhead; nobody, in fact, was inconvenienced in the slightest degree; and most of the passengers who had already gone to sleep went on sleeping. Here and there a door opened and a head looked out inquiringly. Here and there a passenger in dressing-gown and slippers sauntered down the corridor and ascended the staircase to find out what was happening. There was silence apart from the subdued murmur of conversation in one or two of the cabins and the occasional sound of footsteps in an alley-way. Nothing was apparently more peaceful and secure that Sunday night than the corridors and public rooms of the great vessel which had already received her death-wound.

As the tremor ran through the hull, small groups of people in lounges or smoking-rooms had looked at each other in surprise and inquired, 'What was that?' Some explanation was proffered or received; and the incident was almost forgotten. In the first class smoking-room they felt what was afterwards described as 'a rip that gave a sort of slight twist to the whole room'. At any rate the shock of the impact was sufficient to bring everyone to their feet, and several of the men ran out through the revolving doors on the port side and stared over the rail. In the second class smoking-room one of the card players caught a fleeting glimpse of a shadowy iceberg through the windows, but nobody, it would appear, had the curiosity to go out on deck for a better view. One of the officers is supposed to have said reassuringly, 'Don't be afraid, we have only been cutting a whale in two'; and there were those who would have considered bumping into an iceberg hardly more serious. Jack Thayer called out to his father and mother in the adjoining state-room that he 'was going up on deck to see the fun'; and the elder Thayer said he would follow him there. Clinch Smith gravely displayed to Gracie a disc of ice, about the size of a watch, which he suggested he should take home as a souvenir. A cotton-broker from Philadelphia was busy dictating in his state-room when the *Titanic* struck the berg. He continued to dictate, wholly unperturbed, during the long period of peaceful silence which followed. Other people went on drinking, or chatting, or reading, or undressing, or whatever else they might have been doing.

Among the very few people who were on deck at the time of the collision were W. T. Stead and the Rev. Thomas Byles. Stead was taking a final stroll before turning in; Father Byles, breviary in hand, was reading his office—it was the one for Low Sunday—in the quiet and solitude of the Boat Deck. Neither of them thought that the accident was at all serious.

A certain number of passengers, more curious than the rest, went up on the Boat Deck to have a look round. They could see nothing; for the iceberg was now far astern. They stood in groups about the deck, and some would stroll from group to group, in search of information. They speculated and asked questions, but were little the wiser. After some time the word went round that it was nothing serious and they had better go back to bed. According to one of the stewards, the ship would be delayed for about two hours, after which she would go on to New York. Many of them returned to their rooms, though a few dozen still remained on the Boat Deck.

It was very different in the foc's'le and steerage quarters. Within ten minutes of the collision the water was swirling round at the foot of the cast-iron spiral staircase leading down from the firemen's quarters to the stokehold. The grinding crash had alarmed or wakened a good many men—both members of the crew and passengers in the accommodation forward. The sudden harsh clang of the engine-room telegraph bell was followed by the simultaneous ringing of the bells that gave warning of the closing of the watertight doors. The engines stopped for a moment; and then began again, with a different rhythm, as they were hurriedly sent astern. Soon after the Bo'sun came to the door of the firemen's quarters and said urgently, 'Get your lifebelts and go to your boats!' Thereupon some of them started 'shaking up' their still sleeping watch-mates. The Bo'sun ran aft through the ship, shouting, 'Close the watertight bulkhead doors!' One of the firemen said after-wards that he thought he was asleep and dreaming of being in a train that had run off the rails. He climbed out of his bunk and went on deck, up on the foc's'le head, which he saw was inches deep with small broken ice. 'Oh, we have struck an iceberg,' he said casually, 'that's nothing.' He thereupon returned to his bunk and went to sleep again. A number of steerage passengers, aroused by the disturbance, were amusing themselves by walk-ing over the ice and kicking it around the deck. And even the firemen far below, who actually witnessed the effects of the col-lision, had no idea that there was any danger.

'We were working away and thinking our watch was nearly up when all of a sudden the starboard side of the ship came in on us. It burst in like a big gun going off, and the water came pouring in. It swilled our legs, and we made a dash into the next section and slammed-to the watertight door quick. There was no time to waste. My section was about one-third of the ship's length from the bows, and we found that the whole of the starboard side was smashed in as far as our section. Well, we got into the next section aft and there we stayed, for, being on watch, it was our business to stay. I did not think, and nobody thought at the time, that the *Titanic* could sink'.[8]

Meanwhile some of the third class passengers, on looking out of their bunks, had seen with astonishment an inch or two of water swirling about the deck. Some were roused by the Master-at-Arms. The men hurriedly dressed and then went off to rouse their sisters and friends in the steerage accommodation aft. Down the broad working alleyway on E Deck they fell in with a good many of the crew making for the boat stations.

As the alarm spread, a crowd of first class passengers gathered at the foot of the grand staircase on D Deck. In the minds of most of them, according to the Canadian, Albert A. Dick, there was 'the feeling that something was going to happen'. At that moment Andrews hurried by on his way up the stairs. To their agitated enquiries he made no reply. But the look on his face was enough. Soon after the report went round that the water was above E Deck (which lay immediately below the deck on which they were standing), and that the baggage hold and the squash racket court were flooded. As he crossed A Deck foyer, Andrews endeavoured to reassure the people assembled there. 'There is no cause for any excitement,' he told them. 'All of you get what you can in the way of clothes and come on deck as soon as you can. She is torn to bits below, but she will not sink if her after bulkheads hold.'[9]

The post office clerks—three American and two British— were hurriedly shouldering all the sacks of registered mail from the flooded mail room up to one of the higher decks. With the assistance of a few stewards they had pressed into service, they carried up 200 heavy sacks of mail.

About this time the Purser was doing his best to allay the anxieties of a number of ladies gathered outside his office. He urged them to return to their rooms and not to alarm themselves; but, purely as a precautionary measure, he advised them to put on their lifebelts.

'That,' Andrews told McElroy, 'is exactly what I have been trying to get them to do. . . .'

To one of the stewardesses Andrews gave urgent instructions:

'Tell them to put on warm clothing, see that everyone has a

lifebelt and get them all up to the Boat Deck.' Presently he added, 'Open all the spare rooms. Take out all lifebelts and spare blankets and distribute them.'

Returning for more lifebelts, the stewardess again met Andrews, who inquired whether all the ladies had left their rooms. She replied, Yes, but she would make sure.

'Go round again,' he urged her; then he added, 'Did I not tell you to put on your lifebelt? Surely you have one?'

'Yes,' was her rather reluctant answer, 'but I thought it mean to wear it.'

'Never mind that,' he said. 'Now, if you value your life, put on your coat and belt, then walk round the deck and let the passengers see you.'[10]

In the midst of all the excitement Mrs J. J. Brown, who was wearing a long black velvet coat over a black velvet dress trimmed with white satin, hurriedly hauled out her lifebelt, enveloped herself in a warm sable stole, and then joined the throng ascending the staircase to A Deck, where her friend Mrs Bucknell whispered dramatically in her ear, 'Didn't I tell you something was going to happen?'

Mrs Lucien Smith came on deck wearing two coats over her woollen dress and knitted hood. Madame de Villiers appeared in a night-dress covered by a long woollen motor-coat, wearing evening slippers without any stockings. Mrs Astor came up smartly turned out as for the Easter Parade. The Thayer boy wore a green tweed suit and vest with another mohair vest underneath his overcoat. Benjamin Guggenheim, too, had been induced by his steward to change into warmer clothing. An English squire wore a large fur coat over his lifebelt. Mons. Gatti, the *maître* of the restaurant, stood by himself in overcoat and top-hat, with a travelling rug neatly folded over his arm. Some of the people were still in evening dress, others in bath-robes and kimonos. Some brought jewels with them, others took books; a few secreted small pet dogs about their persons; one man treasured a lucky charm, and one of the women had a toy pig which would play the 'Maxixe' whenever its tail was revolved.

Three decks below the Purser's office was besieged by an anxious and impatient crowd clamorously demanding their valuables, which McElroy was taking from the safe and handing out to them as quickly as possible.

Crowds collected in the lounge, in the various foyers, and on the Boat Deck. Some people were indignant at this sudden disturbance in the night; others were merely curious to know what had happened. Very few were really alarmed. In certain quarters there was a tendency to treat the whole affair as a joke. Some people put on lifebelts and others laughed at them. Lumps of ice were being handed round, and there was talk of a snowballing match in the morning. Then came a long wait. No officer was anywhere to be seen to warn the passengers or reassure them. They were simply left to themselves.

Even now, however, there were quite a number who, unconvinced that there was any real cause for alarm, much preferred to remain in their rooms. Mrs Henry Sleeper Harper, more concerned about her ailing husband than the possible danger to the ship, went along to enlist the aid of old Dr O'Loughlin.

'I wish you'd speak to my husband,' she said to him. 'He insists upon going on deck and he won't mind me.'

The doctor returned with her to the Harper's state-room and ordered the sick man to undress and get back into bed. He said that he was sure nothing serious had happened.

'Damn it, man,' protested Harper, 'this ship has hit an iceberg! How can you say there's nothing serious?'

After some further argument, Dr O'Loughlin advised him to stay where he was for the present while he went to investigate. It was not more than a few moments before he was back again; and then he merely put his head in at the door.

'They tell me the trunks are floating around in the hold,' he announced gruffly. 'You may as well go on deck.'[11]

By this time the alarm was general. At 12.30 a.m. all the state-room stewards had come on duty again; they hurried up and down the corridors, knocking on the door of every cabin and rousing the passengers. The latter struggled into their clothes, or in their haste simply slipped on dressing-gowns and wraps over their night-clothes, and then joined the throng making for the deck. They came pouring up the grand staircase, past stewards standing quietly on either side with the strange white life-preservers strapped about them, under the great clock, and out on to the Boat Deck. Some of them crowded round the lifeboats, tripping over the falls, badgering the seamen, and getting in the way generally; until the hands, who in any case were far too few for the work, began to get flustered and to lose their heads. Meanwhile the Captain was hurrying round from place to place doing his utmost to stem the rising tide of fear. He was ably supported by the Purser, who went about helping some of the passengers to fasten their lifebelts more securely and persuading others to put on warmer clothing; later McElroy conducted the women and children to the boats.

About this time, too, the ship's orchestra began to play in a corner of the first class lounge, where many of the passengers were assembled. Together with the bright lights all around, the gay and familiar music—it was chiefly ragtime which they played, such as 'Great Big Beautiful Doll' and 'Alexander's Ragtime Band'—was of incalculable help in restoring and maintaining morale.

'Many brave things were done that night,' wrote Beesley, 'but none more brave than by those few men playing minute after minute as the ship settled quietly lower and lower in the sea and the sea rose higher and higher to where they stood; the music they played serving alike as their own immortal requiem and their right to be recorded on the rolls of undying fame.'[12]

While he was preparing the lifeboats for lowering, Boxhall heard the clang of the look-out bell once again. Returning to the bridge, he saw through his telescope that it was another steamship, bearing about half a point on the port bow, and he told the Captain. On asking if he could send up some rockets, he was instructed to go ahead.

The rockets were fired from a socket beside the rail on the starboard side of the boat deck. They soared high into the air and then exploded, throwing out a quantity of white stars. They were regulation distress signals. In all, Boxhall fired eight rockets.[13]

The vessel at which they were looking appeared to be close enough to read a Morse signal, and presently the Captain said, 'Tell him to come at once, we are sinking'. Boxhall thereupon returned to the bridge and started the signal-lamp. He got no answer, but persevered. He would work away with the signal-lamp, and then go ahead and send off a rocket, and then go back and have a look at the other ship, and start signalling again.[14]

As soon as he had got his boats swung out, Lightoller found the Captain, and, drawing him aside into a corner and making a funnel of his hands, bawled into his ear, 'Hadn't we better get the women and children into the boats, sir?' 'E.J.' nodded and Lightoller passed on the order to the Bo'sun. The procedure was to lower a boat until the gunwale was level with the boat deck, and afterwards the women and youngsters were handed across the gap. It was at about this time that the appalling din of escaping steam was suddenly shut off, to be followed by an unearthly, deathlike silence.

Lightoller got nearly forty people into No. 4 boat and then gave the order to lower away, directing the crew to pull round to the gangway door for the purpose of filling the boat to its full capacity; at the same time he told the Bo'sun to take half a dozen hands and open the port lower-deck gangway door abreast of No. 2 hatch. The Bo'sun said, 'Aye, aye, sir,' and hurried away; and that was the last that anyone ever saw of 'Big Neck' Nichols and his men—in all likelihood they were trapped below by a sudden rush of water, for by this time the foc's'le head was within ten feet of the surface.[15]

Even so, Lightoller still hoped that the ship could be saved. He was inclined to believe that the collision had opened up one or perhaps two of the forward compartments, which were swiftly filling and putting her down by the head; but the bulkheads were all new and sound, he knew, and should be able to carry the pressure; the ship would probably trim down by the bow until she balanced her buoyancy; and in that position she would remain.

The loss of the Bo'sun and six of the watch was a heavy blow to the Second Officer. The work in fact became increasingly arduous and difficult as he was obliged to detail two of his remaining hands to go away with each boat as it was lowered. It was now out of the question to fill up the boats at the lower deck doors: they were actually under water. The Second

Officer, therefore, began to load the boats as they hung in the davits with as many souls as he dared.

'Between one boat being lowered away and the next being prepared I usually nipped along to have a look down the very long emergency staircase leading direct from the Boat Deck down to C Deck. Actually, built as a short cut for the crew, it served my purpose now to gauge the speed with which the water was rising, and how high it had got. By now the fore deck was below the surface. That cold, green water, crawling its ghostly way up that staircase, was a sight that stamped itself on my memory. Step by step, it made its way up, covering the electric lights, one after the other, which, for a time, shone under the surface with a horribly weird effect.'[16]

Towards 1 a.m., when one of the smaller boats had been loaded under the direction of the Chief Officer and was about to be lowered into the water, the Master ordered Boxhall to get into the boat and to take charge. After his departure Captain Smith instructed one of the quartermasters, Alfred Rowe, who had been assisting Boxhall with the rockets, to continue signalling; but Rowe's efforts proved no more successful than Boxhall's.

Meanwhile Pitman had been superintending the loading of No. 5 boat. A man in dressing-gown and slippers said to him in a low voice, 'There is no time to waste'. Presently Pitman went along to the bridge and spoke to the Captain. He told him that a man whom he thought was Mr Ismay wanted to get the boat away with women and children in it. 'Go ahead,' replied Captain Smith; 'carry on!' Returning to the boat, Pitman stood inside it and called: 'Come along, ladies!' There was a big crowd, and soon the boat was nearly full. Again he shouted: 'Any more ladies?' None were to be seen; and he allowed a few men to get into it. Then he jumped back on board the ship again, whereupon the First Officer said, 'You go away in this boat, old man, and hang around the after gangway'. The two shook hands and Murdoch said, 'Goodbye; good luck'; and Pitman said, 'Lower away'.[17]

Chapter 10

'Every Man For Himself'

The successive gradations of anxiety and alarm are traced with remarkable lucidity in Beesley's book, to which reference has already been made, *The Loss of the 'Titanic'*, which was published soon after the event. He tells of 'the quietness of the night broken only by the muffled sound that came to me through the ventilators of stewards talking and moving along the corridors, when nearly all the passengers were in their cabins, some asleep in bed, others undressing, and others only just down from the smoking-room and still discussing many things'; and he tells, too, how all this continued both before and after the collision. He went up on the deserted deck and found nothing whatever to alarm him. After a while he returned to his cabin and started to read a book. There was the sound of people moving about the corridors, and, looking out of his door, he saw several ladies in dressing-gowns questioning a steward. He put on warmer clothing, and again he went on deck. This time he found a number of people walking about and looking over the side and asking one another why the ship had stopped. Again he returned to his room. On the way he saw some stewards 'standing unconcernedly against the walls of the saloon'. He resumed his book. Suddenly there came a shout from above: 'All passengers on deck with lifebelts on!'[1]

Again he ascended the staircase from D Deck. By this time there were a good many people assembled in the second class area of the Boat Deck. Some of them were fully dressed and wearing coats and scarves; others were in every kind of *déshabille* and in no condition to face the bitter cold. Despite their growing awareness of the danger, there was not the slightest sign of alarm or hysteria exhibited by anyone in that orderly, decorous, middle-class crowd, who stood quietly together in their own part of the deck, or paced slowly up and down, watching the seamen as they cleared and swung out the lifeboats, preparatory to lowering them into the water. Presently an officer with a white muffler twisted round his neck came hurrying by, and shouted above the roar of the exhausts: 'All women and children get down to the deck below and all men stand back from the boats!'

The men at once drew back from the boats, and the women went down to A Deck. Only in one or two instances was there any difficulty with women who refused to leave their husbands and had to be gently forced away from them. The sense of peril was steadily mounting; but the demeanour of the crowd was unchanged. It was still calm, patient, and obedient. 'They could not have stood quieter,' declared Lightoller, 'if they had been in church.' In this part of the ship, at least, there was no scrambling or confusion. The women and children were assisted into the boats while the men stood quietly looking on. And all the time the great vessel lay, motionless, to all appearances solid and secure, in that calm sea, under the blaze of stars.[2] Within half an hour of the collision the *Titanic* was perceptibly down by the head; though probably few were aware of the slight but ominous forward list occasioned by the flooding of her forward compartments.

But if there were anyone who had not by now realized that the ship was in danger, all doubt on this point was to be set at rest in a dramatic manner. Suddenly a rush of light from the forward deck, a hissing roar that made us all turn from watching the boats, and a rocket leapt upwards to where the stars blinked and twinkled above us. Up it went, higher and higher, with a sea of faces upturned to watch it, and then an explosion that seemed to split the silent night in two, and a shower of sparks sank slowly down and went out one by one. And with a gasping sigh one word escaped the lips of the crowd: 'Rockets!' Anybody knows what rockets at sea mean. And presently another, and then a third. It is no use denying the dramatic intensity of the scene; separate it if you can from all the terrible events that followed, and picture the calmness of the night, the sudden light on the decks crowded with people in different stages of dress and undress, the background of huge funnels and tapering masts revealed by the soaring rocket, whose flash illumined at the same time the faces and minds of the obedient crowd, the one with mere physical light, the other with a sudden revelation of what its message was. Everyone knew without being told that we were calling for help from anyone who was near enough to see.[3]

Down in the broad thoroughfare on E Deck, known as 'Scotland Road', a long procession of men from the steerage accommodation forward was struggling aft with their luggage. In the midst of a large crowd of foreigners was Müller, the interpreter. This hegira was apparently accomplished in the most orderly way. 'You would think they were landing on the tender taking their baggage to New York.' These men joined the growing crowd of married couples and women which jostled around the foot of the main steerage companion. At 12.30 a.m. the order arrived to send the women and children up to the Boat Deck. The usual difficulty was then experienced in separating the women from their men-folk. A good many families were resolved at all costs to remain together. One of the stewards conducted small parties of steerage passengers up the staircase to the third class lounge on C Deck, across the well deck, and then, by a maze of passages through the second and first class accommodation, to the grand staircase leading to the Boat Deck. There were others as well from the steerage who, either singly or in groups, found or forced their way up to the Boat Deck, and the prospect of safety. But the great majority of the third class passengers had for one reason or another to remain in their own quarters while the boats were being loaded. Some, when they attempted to leave the steerage, were peremptorily turned back. One of the junior officers was posted at the head of the companionway leading up from the third class quarters to prevent the steerage passengers from swarming up on to the higher decks. Presently, seeing the boat to which he had been assigned was about to be lowered, he said: 'There goes my boat! But I can't be in two places at the same time, and I have to keep this crowd back.'[4]

It was not in fact until a good while after the collision that a gate which denied access to the higher decks was at last broken down and a large crowd of steerage passengers surged through. Some Irish country girls happened to find their way to the first class restaurant and a spontaneous gasp of wonder and admiration escaped from them as their eyes fell on the array of tables already laid for the following day. For several seconds they forgot the slanting decks and the terror that clutched at their hearts as their gaze took in the rose-coloured carpet, the little table lamps with their pink silk shades, the snow-white napery, the shining crystal and silver, and the flowers. Then they ran on again and finally gained the Boat Deck.

Informed that the ship was sinking, they fell on their knees and began to pray.

There had been no great urgency in loading the first boats; several of them were lowered into the sea only about half-full. For long after the collision many people, including some of the officers, did not really believe that the *Titanic* would founder. Again and again this belief found expression among the waiting crowds. 'This ship cannot sink,' it was said; 'it is only a question of waiting until another ship comes up and takes us off.'[5] A rumour went round that before long the *Titanic* would be ringed by rescue ships. Thus the seamen who were sent away in the boats were not permitted to fetch any of their things; it being confidently expected that they would be back on board again in the morning. It was with difficulty that the women could be persuaded to leave the light and warmth of the great liner for the hazardous descent to the dark and lonely sea. They continued to hang back while the officers and others attempted in vain to induce them to enter the boats. On several occasions the hands, having helped some woman into a boat, were obliged to get her out again because she refused to go without her husband. Thus precious time was wasted. There was ample room, indeed, for all first and second class women and children who were willing to go—while during this period the great majority of the steerage passengers were effectively prevented from reaching the Boat Deck at all. A number of the crew, under the superintendence of the Sixth Officer, formed a ring round the boats as they were being loaded, through which the women and children were passed. On the starboard side some of the men were allowed to enter besides the women and children, if there were still room; but on the port side the rule of 'women and children only' was rigidly enforced.

The band, now wearing their life-jackets, had moved up on

to the Boat Deck, beside the entrance to the grand staircase. All around was a great crowd watching the boats being loaded and lowered, with smaller groups either standing apart or strolling about. The rollicking ragtime tunes, mingling with the low murmur of conversation, did much to keep up people's spirits. The state-rooms on the decks below were silent and empty. The long white corridors which only a few hours earlier had echoed with the shouts and laughter of children at play were traversed only by an occasional hurrying figure. Most of the passengers were either on the Boat Deck or on the deck immediately below it. A few found it warmer and more agreeable to sit in the comfortable wicker chairs of the gymnasium or in the lounge.

The proceedings, at any rate in the first class, were invested with ceremonial politeness and gaiety even. Miss Marie Young, formerly music governess to Theodore Roosevelt's children, was escorted to her boat by Major Butt who 'wrapped blankets about me and tucked me in as carefully as if we were starting on a motor ride'. Young Victor de Satode Penasco led his still more youthful bride to the boats and gave her into the charge of the Countess of Rothes. 'It's all right, little girl,' the nineteen-year old Daniel Mervin told his young wife. 'You go. I will stay.' The testimony of several of these women—Mrs J. J. Brown, Mrs Carter, and Mrs Lucien Smith—is worth quoting.

'The whole thing was so formal that it was difficult for anyone to realize that it was a tragedy. Men and women stood in little groups and talked. Some laughed as the first boats went over the side. All the time the band was playing . . . I can still see the men up on the deck tucking in the women and smiling. It was a strange sight. It all seemed like a play, like a drama that was being enacted for entertainment. It did not seem real. Men would say, "After you," as they made some woman comfortable and stepped back. I afterwards heard someone say that the men went downstairs into the restaurant. Many of them smoked. Many of them walked up and down. . . .'[6]

'We were ordered down to A Deck, which was partly enclosed. We saw people getting into boats, but waited our turn. There was a rough sort of steps constructed to get up to the windows. My boy, Jack, was with me. An officer at the window said, "That boy can't go". My husband stepped forward and said, "Of course, that boy goes with his mother; he is only thirteen". So they let him pass.

They also said, "No more boys". I turned and kissed my husband, and as we left he and the other men I knew—Mr Thayer, Mr Widener, and others—were all standing there together very quietly. The decks were lighted, and as you went through the window it was as if you stepped out into the dark. . . .[7]

'My husband insisted that I get in, my friend having gotten in. I refused unless he would go with me. In the meantime Captain Smith was standing with a megaphone on deck. I approached him and told him I was alone, and asked if my husband be allowed to go in the boat with me. He ignored me personally, but shouted again through his megaphone, "Women and children first". My husband said, "Never mind, Captain, about that; I will see that she gets in the boat". He then said, "I never expected to ask you to obey, but this is one time you must; it is only a matter of form, to have women and children first. The boat is thoroughly equipped, and everyone on her will be saved." He kissed me good-bye and placed me in the lifeboat with the assistance of an officer. As the boat was being lowered he yelled from the deck, "Keep your hands in your pockets; it is very cold weather. . . ." '[8]

Over the final act of the tragedy there hangs a nightmare aura of unreality; the great ship lying motionless on a sea as still as a millpond under the glittering canopy of stars; the rockets soaring aloft into the darkness from the bridge; the lively ragtime airs played by the ship's orchestra assembled near the head of the grand staircase; the passengers standing about in groups, or pacing slowly up and down in the bitter cold; the cheerful, matter-of-fact conversation and occasional jests as one by one the boats were lowered; the extraordinary variety of attire worn by men, women, and children; the strange feeling that not a few of them had of being spectators of a drama rather than actors in it; and all the time the black water rising higher and higher towards the slanting decks. . . .

About this time James Clinch Smith, true to form, delivered himself of a final crack. He drily remarked that he supposed they ought to put a life-jacket on the little dog one of the passengers was carrying.

As the ship sank lower and lower in the water the tempo quickened. 'The splendid monstrous floating Babylon,' as W. T. Stead had called her only a few short days before, was at her last gasp. It was now apparent that the boats offered the only possible chance of safety. At No. 10 boat the First Officer was making the women jump across the gap, nearly two and a half feet wide, between the boat and the ship's side, and then catching the children by their clothes and throwing them in on top of the women.

'Ladies, you must get in at once,' Andrews said urgently. 'There is not a minute to lose. You cannot pick and choose your boat. Don't hesitate. Get in, get *in!*'

A couple of seamen dragged Mrs Collyer from her husband, who begged her to go with them. 'Go, Lottie!' he told her. 'For God's sake, be brave and go! I'll get a seat in another boat!'

'For God's sake, go!' urged Jack Futrelle, as he attempted to force his wife towards the boats. 'It's your last chance—go!' In the end one of the officers hustled her unceremoniously into a boat.

Two men who had followed Mrs J. J. Brown up on to the boat deck presently brought her down again to A Deck and practically threw her into a boat with the words, 'You are going, too!'

The most strenuous efforts of the officers and others had failed to separate Mrs Straus from her husband. They had almost got her into one of the boats, when, at the last moment, she threw her arms round her husband, saying, 'We are old people, Isidor, and we will die together'.

Mrs Hudson J. Allison, of Montreal, also refused to leave her husband, while their small daughter, Loraine, clung to her skirts. Separated from the rest of the family in the confusion, the Allison's Nanny, with their baby son, Travers, held tight in her arms, had found a place in one of the boats.

The children gave far less trouble than the women. The younger ones, naturally, had very little idea of what was happening. Thus abruptly aroused from their slumbers, they might even have imagined that they were still dreaming. The five-year-old son of Dr and Mrs Washington Dodge, who had been rather scared at the roar of the steam blowing off, was delighted at the rockets. This was something like a fireworks display!

That there was a certain tendency among both officers and men to lose their heads is scarcely to be wondered at. One of the former, as has been seen, was actually trying to stop children from entering the boats, if they happened to be of the male sex. (In this connection there is a tradition that John Jacob Astor, cramming a girl's hat on a small boy's head, exclaimed: 'There! now you're a *girl* and can go!')

A few of the boats were lowered so clumsily that they hung at all angles during the descent, to the manifest peril of their occupants. There was no time now to argue with reluctant passengers. As No. 13 boat was being loaded a large woman protested in alarm, 'Don't put me in the boat; I don't want to go in the boat; I have never been in an open boat in my life'. One of the stewards said shortly, 'You have got to go, and you may as well keep quiet'. She was hustled in, and a small child, rolled up in a blanket, was thrown in also, to be neatly caught by the steward.⁹

As the last boats were leaving the spirit of *sauve qui peut* increasingly prevailed. When a Cornishwoman, Mrs Davies, entered her boat she discovered a lot of men lying down in the bottom, several of them stretched out under the thwarts; and before this boat left the ship some more men slid down the falls from the davit heads. More than half the occupants of this particular boat, in fact, were men, for the most part stewards and firemen.¹⁰ In No. 13 boat scarcely half the total number were women. In No. 9 boat also most of the occupants were men, chiefly members of the crew. It would appear that the notorious reluctance of the 'black gang' to participate in boat drill did not extend to taking to the boats in an emergency.

In the meantime Beesley had remained quietly on the starboard side of the Boat Deck waiting upon events. He had watched the boats forward being lowered one by one, stealing slowly away from the ship's side, and then disappearing into the darkness as the men bent to the oars. The First Officer came striding aft along the deck and shouted to the boats being lowered: 'Lower away, and when afloat, row around to the gangway and wait for orders.' 'Aye, aye, sir!' was the reply. The officer hurried by and crossed the deck to the port side. It was soon after this that Beesley's chance came.

'Presently word went round among us that men were to be put in boats on the port side. I was on the starboard side. Most of the men walked across the deck to see if this was true. I remained where I was, and shortly afterwards I heard the call, "Any more ladies?" Looking over the side of the ship I saw boat No 13 swinging level with A Deck. It was half full of women. Again the call was repeated, "Any more ladies?" I saw none coming. Then one of the crew looked up and said, "Any ladies on your deck, sir?" "No," I replied. "Then you'd better jump," said he. I dropped and fell into the bottom of the boat as they cried, "Lower away". As the boat began to descend two ladies were hurriedly pushed through the crowd on A Deck and a baby ten months old was passed down after them.'[11]

In the event No. 13 boat had a narrow escape from final disaster. It descended, slowly and cautiously, past tier after tier of lighted portholes, until at last it dropped into the water. There it was immediately caught in the wash of the condenser exhaust which carried it aft directly under the place where No. 15 boat would shortly be lowered into the sea. Looking up, the occupants of No. 13 saw this other boat already dropping down on them from A Deck and shouted an urgent warning, 'Stop lowering 15!' The passengers and crew in No. 15 repeated the warning to the seamen attending to the falls. But the latter apparently did not hear; for, foot by foot, the other boat continued to descend; and it was only at the last moment that a stoker sprang, knife in hand, into the stern of No. 13 and quickly cut through the falls that held her. She floated clear, only just in time, as No. 15 dropped into the water in the space she had lately filled.[12]

To and fro among the crowds on the Boat Deck above; supervising, ordering, aiding, and encouraging by turns; sweating 'like a stoker' from his exertions, went the *Titanic's* Chief Officer—'one of the bravest men who ever stepped a deck', was the tribute of one of the quartermasters that stood by. A big, brawny, strongly built man, Wilde was possessed of immense reserves of strength and endurance on which he drew to the limit during the ship's last agony; and never did muscular power stand a man in better stead.

Wilde's efforts to avert panic, maintain order and discipline, and get the last of the boats loaded and lowered to the water were valiantly supported by the youngest of the officers, James Moody. Long before this, the latter should by rights have gone away in one of the boats along with the other junior officers. But the seamen left on board were all too few as it was for the work that had to be done. Moody therefore stayed with the ship to the end and was the means of saving many a life that would otherwise have been lost.

All this time, according to a passenger in one of the boats that was standing near by, the *Titanic*, brilliantly illuminated from stem to stern, lay motionless on the dark waters 'like some fantastic piece of stage scenery'. She still appeared remarkably solid and secure.[13]

At about 1.30 a.m. the Captain returned to the wireless cabin and told them that the engine-rooms were flooding and that the dynamos might not last much longer. Phillips quickly passed the news on to the *Carpathia*. Then he went outside for a few moments to see what was happening. During his absence Bride informed the *Baltic* that the *Titanic* had been in collision and was sinking fast; and on his return to the wireless cabin Phillips told his junior that the forward well deck was awash.

Bride went to get their lifebelts and thought how cold the water was. He put on his boots, also an extra jacket. Phillips had just picked up the *Olympic's* signals and sent out another urgent appeal. '*We are in collision with berg. Sinking. Head down. 41° 46′ N., 50° 14′ W. Come as soon as possible.*' As Phillips was tapping out the message, Bride strapped his lifebelt to his back. '*Captain says get your boats ready. What is your position?* The *Olympic* replied: '*40° 52′ N., 61° 18′ W. Are you steering southerly to meet us?*'

Captain Smith must have digested this last message with a sinking heart. Clearly the *Olympic's* commander had no notion how desperate was their plight; in any case, their sister-ship was too far off to have any chance of reaching them in time.

Phillips put the headphones on again, and, after listening for a few moments, jumped up and shouted angrily, 'The ———— fool! He says, "What's up, old man?"' A call had just come through from the German steamship *Frankfurt* which had already been in communication with them. It was all too apparent that her operator had either taken no notice of, or else misunderstood, their original distress call. Phillips and

Bride informed the Captain, who muttered in his beard, 'That fellow is a fool'; an opinion which Phillips evidently shared, for he promptly sat down at the table and rapped out, '*You fool, stand by and keep out*'.

When the Captain left them Phillips suggested to Bride that he should go and find out what the situation was outside and see if all the lifeboats had gone. Bride went out on the Boat Deck and saw some officers and men trying to get an Engelhardt collapsible boat, which had been lashed on the top of the officers' quarters, into the sea. Phillips remained at his post. The ship might be sinking beneath them, but his duty was clear. Still, coolly and imperturbably, he continued sending and sending. His transmission, at a steady fifteen words a minute, was completely unaffected by the ordeal through which he was passing. . . . '*Come quick. Our engine-room flooded up to the boilers.*' Bride returned with the news that the forward end of the Boat Deck was already awash.

It was about this time that Captain Smith again appeared in the wireless cabin. He said in his deep voice: 'Men, you have done your full duty. You can do no more. Abandon your cabin. Now it's every man for himself. You look out for yourselves. I release you. That's the way of it at this kind of a time. Every man for himself!'

After this the Captain returned to the Boat Deck remarking to a man here and there as he passed, 'It's every man for himself!' Then he went back on the bridge.

The two operators had prepared candles for lighting and were ready to change over to the emergency transmitter; but as it happened this was unnecessary, as the power from the engine-room did not completely fail until within a few minutes of the end. Leaving his senior still at the key, Bride went into their sleeping cabin and got all their money together; returning, as he relates, 'to find a fireman or coal trimmer gently relieving Mr Phillips of his lifebelt'. There was a short but savage scuffle; in which, it seems, Bride held the thief while Phillips laid him out. 'We left him on the cabin floor of the wireless room,' the former testified grimly, a few days later, 'and he wasn't moving.'

Amid all the tumult and confusion of 'that last awful fifteen minutes', as Bride declares, his senior went on sending messages; though his signals became weaker and weaker, and at last they ended abruptly. Phillips was aware of this, as he could not get any replies. All this time the two had contrived to keep their *procès verbal*, or wireless log-book, duly written up: their intention being to tear out the pages, and each to take a copy. But in the event there was no time: they could hear the water washing over the boat deck, and Phillips exclaimed, 'Come, let's clear out'.

The end was very near. From aft came the cheerful strains of some ragtime melody; for the band still went on playing, with the water surging towards them across the Boat Deck; only, shortly before the end, the music changed, and they began to play a hymn tune, 'Autumn'. Phillips and Bride glanced for the last time round the familiar surroundings of the wireless cabin where their late adversary lay prostrate on the deck. The water was pouring in through the doorway. Phillips started to run aft, and that was the last Bride ever saw of him alive. For his part Bride scrambled over the top of the wireless cabin and then over the officer's quarters to the place where he had seen the collapsible boat; to his surprise he saw it was still there, with the men struggling to get it launched. One last desperate heave, and it had toppled over into the sea, upside-down, with Bride hanging on underneath. He struggled to free himself and at last got clear, swimming for his life. As he swam, he saw the serried tiers of lighted port-holes and heard the band still playing 'Autumn'.

Such was the shortage of hands that Lightoller had been reduced to the necessity of sending only one seaman away in a boat. On one occasion he found he had only one man left to attend the boat falls for lowering away. 'Someone for that after fall!' he called out; whereupon the seaman he had ordered away to take charge—an old shipmate named Hemming—responded, 'Aye, aye, sir!' and promptly stepped back on board to help lower away.

The boat was already half-way down to the water when someone hailed the officer with the warning, 'We've no seaman in the boat'; and Lightoller called to the crowd of onlookers,

'Any seaman there?' At first there was silence, and then a Canadian soldier, Major Peuchen, came forward. 'I'm not a seaman,' he said, 'but I'm a yachtsman, if I can be of any use to you.' Lightoller looked towards the boat's falls hanging from the davit head, nine or ten feet from the ship's side. 'If you're seaman enough to get out on those falls, and get down into the boat, you may go ahead.' Peuchen swung himself out on to the davit head, and, with some inward trepidation, slid down the falls; he arrived safely and tumbled into the boat.

Soon after this the Chief Officer came over from the starboard side and asked Lightoller if he knew where the firearms were. He explained that Murdoch could not find them.

'Yes, I know where they are,' replied Lightoller. 'Come along and I'll get them for you.'

Accompanied by the Captain, Wilde, and Murdoch, he entered the First Officer's cabin, which had been his own until the re-shuffle of senior officers at Southampton. He went straight to a locker and hauled out the firearms. As he was leaving, Wilde thrust one of the revolvers into his hands, together with a few rounds of ammunition, saying, 'Here you are, you may need it'. Lightoller pushed the revolver and cartridges into a pocket and returned to the boats.[14]

On his way he passed the Strauses leaning up against the deck-house, chatting and apparently quite cheerful. 'Can I take you along to the boats?' he asked Mrs Straus. 'I think I'll stay here for the present,' was her response. 'Why won't you go along with him, dear?' her husband urged her. 'No, not yet,' she said, smiling; and she would not be persuaded. Further on, Lightoller came on a young American couple sitting on a fan casing. 'Won't you let me put you in one of the boats?' he asked the girl. 'Not on your life!' was the frank reply, delivered with a strong Western accent. 'We started together, and if need be, we'll finish together.'

Occasionally he gazed with impotent fury at the lights of the distant steamship. All the time she lay there immobile. She appeared to be deaf and blind alike to the wireless call, the signal-lamp, and the rockets. Lightoller said he longed for 'a 6-inch gun and a couple of shells to wake them up'. Over and over again he had assured the anxious passengers, 'She cannot help but see these signals, and must soon steam over and pick everyone up'.[15]

Long afterwards, he recalled the anguish of that moment. Clearly the *Titanic* could not last much longer. The nearest ship of all, whose lights they could see across the water—their one hope of safety—had failed them. By the time that the other ships arrived to the rescue it would be too late.

From time to time a distant sound of alarmed and angry shouting from the steerage quarters below reached the ears of those on the Boat Deck. Many of the people were now frankly terrified, and there were ugly scenes at some of the boats. At No. 14 a party of foreigners made a rush. They could not understand the order which he gave them, said the Bo'sun's Mate; and he had to use 'a bit of persuasion'—'The only thing I could use was the boat's tiller.' Shortly after he told Lowe that he had had 'a bit of trouble'; and that officer said, 'All right!'. Next moment Lowe had whipped out his revolver and fired two shots between the ship and the boat's side, and at the same time shouted a warning to the men crowding around him that if there was any more rushing he would use it.[16]

The First Officer barely stopped a rush at No. 15. He yelled at the full pitch of his lungs, 'Stand back! Stand back! It's women first!' At one of the collapsible boats forward, a large mob pushed and shoved, trying frantically to climb in. The Purser fired twice into the air, and Murdoch shouted at the crowd, 'Get out of this! *Clear out of this!*'

Lightoller also had trouble with one of the boats on the port side. Despite his rigid rule—women and children *only*—some men, whom he subsequently described as 'Dagoes', had crept in under cover of the darkness. Flourishing his revolver (which in point of fact was not loaded), he quickly evicted them and filled the boat with women and children.

About two hours after the collision, another of the Engelhardts was hurriedly loaded with women and children. Three firemen, a steward, and a barber also took their places in it, with a quartermaster, Alfred Rowe, in charge. At the last moment an American first class passenger, E. C. Carter, and J. Bruce Ismay scrambled into the boat just as it was being lowered to the sea.[17]

Already the water was pouring through the large square ports on C Deck and swirling round the deserted *suites de luxe*. Most of the *Titanic's* state-rooms were now flooded. The lights had dulled and were burning with a reddish tinge. There was a general tendency among the hundreds of people left on the slanting decks to draw back from the rail, as if to avert their gaze from the black water which was steadily rising towards them. About this time, too, some of the crew began to jump overboard; a few of these were picked up by the boats which lay around.

One of the Norwegian emigrants from the steerage remarked to his brother-in-law, a former fisherman, 'We had better jump off or the suction will take us down!' The latter demurred. 'No. We won't jump yet,' he replied. 'We ain't got much chance anyhow, so we might as well stay as long as we can.' The two accordingly waited till the water was only five feet below them, and then they jumped.

Captain Smith was on the bridge with his steward close by him. If during this last terrible hour 'E.J.' had time for reflection, his thoughts must have been bitter indeed. If he chanced to recall them, his own words must have mocked him. '*I cannot imagine any condition which would cause a ship to founder. I cannot conceive of any disaster happening to this vessel. Modern shipbuilding has gone beyond that. . . .*' The words of warning in the sailing directions, explicit as they were, had been treated almost as a dead letter. For twenty years at least it had been the custom to accept these risks—apparently with impunity. Now, at last, the forfeit had been claimed. . . . What would be said and thought of him in the aftermath of this unparalleled catastrophe? On the verge of his retirement from the sea, after a long and signally successful career, the commander of the largest ship which the world had ever seen had worked her up to the highest speed of her maiden voyage just as she entered the danger zone; and then, despite repeated warnings, had driven her full tilt in the darkness into an iceberg which had torn the side out of her while the Master lay slumbering in his berth after a dinner-party!

Thomas Andrews was standing alone in the smoking-room, his arms folded over his breast and his eyes fixed on a painting,

'The Approach of the New World'. His lifebelt was lying on a table near by. A steward said to him, 'Aren't you going to have a try for it, Mr Andrews?' The latter never answered or moved, but 'just stood like one stunned'.[18]

Meanwhile the little group of millionaires stood quietly apart from the rest on the Boat Deck; there were J. J. Astor, George B. Widener, John B. Thayer, and a few others. Astor had $4,250 in his pocket, which was about as much use to him in the present exigency as were the $150 millions he possessed ashore. Guggenheim and his secretary had changed back into evening dress. 'We've dressed up in our best,' the former declared, 'and are prepared to go down like gentlemen.' He gave his steward a message for his wife. Some time earlier Widener's son Harry had taken leave of his mother with the words: 'Mother, I have placed the volume in my pocket—the little "Bacon" goes with me!' Surely the devotion of a bibliophile could go no further.[19]

After the last lifeboat had left the ship, Messrs Millet, Moore, Butt, and Ryerson had returned to the smoking-room. Here, where they had passed so many pleasant hours, the four settled down to cards, apparently indifferent to all that was happening outside. From time to time someone would peer in at the windows; but the players took no notice and continued with their game.[20]

The poor Irish boys and girls from the steerage were more profitably occupied. They were down on their knees, and praying. Only at the last had they been able to gain access to the Boat Deck, when, a gate having been broken down, a huge crowd of steerage passengers came surging up from below. On deck they found the English priest, Father Byles, moving to and fro among the passengers, hearing confessions and giving them absolution. With him was the only other father on board, the Austrian Benedictine. Every moment the black water was drawing nearer and nearer. Gravely the priest urged them all to prepare to meet God. Something like a hundred persons gathered round him on the after part of the Boat Deck, Protestants as well as Catholics. They knelt as he led them in the recital of the rosary, and the people murmured the responses. Many of the Irish there must have remembered how, from their earliest years, they had been accustomed to kneel beside their parents on the cottage floor to repeat the evening rosary. Now, for the last time, they were reciting the old familiar prayers. '*Our Father who art in heaven hallowed be Thy Name . . . Thy Kingdom come . . . Thy will be done on earth as it is in heaven . . . Holy Mary, Mother of God, pray for us sinners . . . now and at the hour of our death. Amen.*' They were still engaged in this ancient devotion of Christendom when presently the water came washing over the deck. . . .[21]

Before loading and lowering the last two lifeboats, Lightoller had paid a final visit to the stairway. So rapidly was the water rising now that he knew the vessel had not many minutes to live. At all costs the two boats still hanging in the davits must be got away. On his return journey he met the Purser, McElroy, with his assistants, Barker and Denison, standing guard over the ship's bags and papers. With them were the two surgeons, Drs O'Loughlin and Simpson. Lightoller was wearing only a sweater and trousers over his pyjamas in the almost Arctic cold; nevertheless, he was sweating freely. Even in the face of death the younger of the surgeons was, as usual, joking. 'Hello, Lights,' he greeted him, 'are you warm?' Little was said, but the officers all shook hands and said good-bye. Lightoller then hurried back to his post on the port side and saw the last remaining lifeboats loaded and lowered safely into the water.

It was about this time that all the engineers came trooping up from below. By their valiant toil at the pumps they had kept the ship afloat, and now there was nothing left for them to do. They came on deck only to see the empty falls hanging from every davit head, and the lifeboats all gone. In the event they were lost to a man; there was not one single survivor out of the whole thirty-five of them.[22]

According to Lightoller, there now remained only two Engelhardt collapsible boats. One was lashed down on deck by the davits of one of the boats which had long since gone; the Engelhardt was hurriedly hooked on to the falls and swung out ready for lowering; in order to give the women a hand over the high rail, Lightoller stood partly inside the boat. When it was loaded and about to be lowered, the Chief Officer came over to the port side, and, seeing no seaman available, said, 'You go with her, Lightoller'.

'Not damn likely!' said the other shortly, and jumped back on board.

The other Englehardt was lashed down on top of the officers' quarters. With one other seaman Lightoller began to cut away the lashings. They prepared to lift up the gunwale and shove her down to the Boat Deck. The other man shouted:

'All ready, sir!'

'Hello, is that you, Hemming?' said Lightoller, recognizing the man's voice.

'Yes, sir.'

'Why haven't you gone?'

'Oh, plenty of time yet, sir!' was the cheerful rejoinder.[23]

The two went over to the starboard side. But the boats were all gone, and there was nothing for them to do. Now the water was right up to the bridge. The throng retreated before the oncoming waves, pushing desperately towards the stern, 'a mass of hopeless, dazed humanity', recalls Jack Thayer, 'attempting, as the Almighty and Nature made us, to keep our final breath until the last possible moment.'[24] Suddenly the ship took an ominous plunge, and a wave came rolling up the crowded deck, washing the people back in a struggling, helpless mass. A few more moments would see the end. Lightoller left the ship with very little to spare before the ship left him. He dived into the sea from the fore part of the bridge. At the same time Hemming slid down one of the falls and, after swimming for a while, was picked up.

Chapter 11

Adrift

Lightoller's survival during the next few minutes was in the nature of a miracle. First, he was all but sucked down the forward funnel by the fierce rush of water; then, quite suddenly, a blast of hot air from the bowels of the vessel blew him clear. He eventually came to the surface alongside the last Engelhardt they had launched. He grabbed hold of a length of rope and held on desperately. Just then the forward funnel crashed down on the sea in the midst of a struggling mass of people with the result that the Engelhardt, with Lightoller still clinging to the rope, was washed fifty yards clear of the wreck. He scrambled up on the upturned boat beside several other men.[1]

Clinging to the flat slippery bottom of the Engelhardt, he was just in time to see the end.

Lights on board the *Titanic* were still burning brightly through the slanting tiers of portholes and on her promenade decks. With her bow now rapidly going down and her stern rising higher and higher out of the water, her enormous bulk stood out black and massive against the starlit sky.

Suddenly all the lights went out. Next moment her huge boilers burst from their beds and hurtled down through the bulkheads with a deep, thunderous roar that travelled far across the water. The giant liner reared herself momentarily on end, bringing her rudder and propellers clean out of the water, until finally she assumed an absolutely perpendicular position, in which she remained for, perhaps, half a minute.[2] Then, slowly at first, but presently with ever-increasing momentum, the fabulous, magnificent *Titanic*, the ship acclaimed as the final and triumphant proof of man's conquest of the ocean, the ship which 'God Himself could not sink', plunged for ever to the depths of the ocean. . . .

The starlight revealed a scene of indescribable horror. The sea all around was covered with a mass of tangled wreckage and the struggling forms of many hundreds of people—men, women, and children—slowly, inexorably freezing to death in the ice-cold water. A sheet of thin grey vapour hung like a pall a few feet above the surface. It reminded Gracie of the unearthly waters of Lethe in the *Aeneid*.

'Add to this,' said the Colonel, 'within the area described, which was as far as my eyes could reach, there arose to the sky the most horrible sounds ever heard by mortal man except by those of us who survived this terrible tragedy. The agonizing cries of death from over a thousand throats, the wails and groans of the suffering, the shrieks of the terror-stricken and the awful gaspings for breath of those in the last throes of drowning, none of us will ever forget to our dying day.'[3]

'The cries,' said Beesley, 'which were loud and numerous at first, died away gradually one by one, but the night was clear, frosty, and still, the water smooth, and the sounds must have carried on its level surface free from any obstruction for miles, certainly much farther from the ship than we were situated. I think the last of them must have been heard nearly forty minutes after the *Titanic* sank.'[4]

The memory of those agonized, unavailing appeals for help made such an impression, indeed, on many of those who heard them that in certain cases it gravely affected their health and even cut short their lives. Long afterwards, Lightoller confessed that he had never allowed his thoughts to dwell on those terrible cries and declared that there were some who would have been alive and well to the present day had they but determined to erase from their minds all memory of those ghastly moments; or at least until time had somewhat dimmed the memory of that awful tragedy.[5]

While the boats were being lowered and were leaving the side of the ship, Captain Smith had on several occasions hailed them through his megaphone, instructing them to return and come alongside. These orders had not been obeyed.

A number of the boats had been so heavily loaded that there could no no question of their going back to pick up survivors.

No. 13 could hold no more, and, in any case, her crew were incapable of such an effort: there was not a seaman among the lot of them; they were for the most part cooks and stewards, with a fireman acting as cox'n. Almost as soon as they were afloat there was shouting and confusion, with the oars continually crossing and clashing. For such a craft to have ventured anywhere near all those hundreds of poor wretches struggling desperately in the icy water would have been courting certain disaster. Nos. 11 and 15 were still more heavily loaded, with seventy souls in each. 'We were loaded down to the gunwales,' declared a steward in the latter boat; 'and we could pull just about half a stroke.'

For fear of the suction which was generally expected to follow on the submergence of so large a vessel, No. 2 boat pulled away, as the *Titanic* sank, to a distance of half a mile or more. In No. 3 a number of firemen in the bow strongly urged the cox'n to get away from the doomed ship. 'She's gone, lads,' cried one of them later; 'row like hell or we'll get the devil of a swell.' In No. 4 somebody in the boat shouted, 'Pull for your lives or you will be sucked under!' One of the passengers in No. 5 related that the officer in charge was urged to steer a little further off. 'We were pulled quite a distance away and then rested, watching the rockets in terrible anxiety and realizing that the vessel was rapidly sinking.' In the event there was little suction even quite close to the wreck, but there can be no doubt there was a general fear of it.

Even when the *Titanic* had gone down there was scarcely any attempt made by those boats which were only half filled to save life. The officer who was in charge of No. 2 appears to have been dissuaded from going back by the protestations of the women in his boat. Similarly in No. 5, when the officer turned the boat round to go to the help of those miserably drowning or freezing to death, there was a terrified protest from the women. 'Appeal to the officer not to go back,' cried one of these women to a man who was pulling. 'Why should we lose all of our lives in a useless attempt to save others from the ship?' The attempt was abandoned. In No. 6 there was a strong feeling that they ought to go back to the sinking liner; but the quartermaster at the tiller, Robert Hitchens, like so many of the crew, was in mortal fear of suction and refused point-blank to make the attempt. 'No, we are not going back to the boat,' he said gruffly; 'it's our lives now, not theirs.' In No. 9 the Bo'sun's Mate, Albert Haines, called the seamen aft to consider the matter. 'There is people in the water,' he said, 'Do you think it advisable? . . . We can't do nothing with this crowd we have in the boat.' Haines later testified they had no room to row, let alone do anything else; and it was no use their going back. He thought it would be very unsafe to make the attempt, having so many in the boat.[6] Then came the terrible endless wails and calls for help. Some of the women whose husbands had been left behind in the sinking ship begged the quartermaster to return. Hitchens flatly refused. He insisted that it was no use going back there—there were only 'a lot of stiffs'. No. 12, which Lightoller had ordered to lay off and stand by close to the ship, made no attempt to return and save life. The excuse was that they had not enough sailors, and neither light nor compass, in the boat.

No. 1 boat, with similar instructions to stand by, was lying about two hundred yards off when the *Titanic* went down. People were screaming and struggling in the water within a short distance of this boat, which still had room for well over two dozen more occupants (there were actually only eleven persons in No. 1—five passengers and six of the crew). A fireman presently suggested that they ought to go back to the wreck, but one of the first class ladies, who was at once supported by her husband, protested that it would be too dangerous. 'We shall be swamped if we go back . . . it would be dangerous to go', etc. There was no further conversation in No. 1 about going back; but later (the exact time has never been settled) the lady who had first spoken observed to her companion, 'There is your beautiful nightdress gone'. The tasteless frivolity of such a remark at such a time brought down an immediate rebuke; not, indeed, from her husband, but from one of the firemen. 'Never mind about your nightdress, madam,' said the man curtly, 'so long as you have got your life.' He added, that he and the others had lost their kits and that their pay was stopped from the moment the *Titanic* went down. On hearing this, the lady's husband at once offered to present each member of the crew

with £5 towards the purchase of a new kit. In the circumstances it was a promise that was liable to be misunderstood and
that he was later to regret.

It appears that the only organized attempt to save life was
that made by Lowe, the Fifth Officer, in No. 14 boat. When the
Titanic went down Lowe proceeded to distribute all his passengers among several of the other boats; and then, hoisting a
sail, he went back to the wreckage, where he and his crew
hauled four men out of the water. 'We turned over several to
see if they were alive,' said a seaman; adding, 'It looked as if
none of them were drowned. They looked as if frozen.' Another
of Lowe's men related that one could hardly count the number
of dead bodies in the water. So many corpses were floating
around, in fact, that they were unable to row. They stopped in
the wreckage, searching for survivors, until daybreak.

Lowe was no lady's man, but a 'hard case' like Lightoller.
'I think the best thing for you women to do is to take a nap,' he
had advised his charges earlier that night; and about this time
he suggested that a good song to sing would be, 'Throw Out
the Life Line'. 'Jump! God damn you, *jump*,' he had adjured
one first class lady, as he was hurriedly transhipping his passengers before returning to the wreck. The lady afterwards
declared indignantly that, in view of his 'blasphemous
language', she believed Lowe must have been drunk. But
another of the women passengers was of a different opinion.
'Mr Lowe's manly bearing gave us all confidence,' she testified.
'As I look back now he seems to me to personify the best
traditions of the British sailor.'[7]

The Marconi station on the bleak headland of Cape Race
stood high on the black, rugged slate cliffs hard by the lighthouse
and the light-keepers' quarters. The ocean swell fretted and
foamed on the rocky ledges below, around which the seabirds
hovered and circled. The whole coast at this south-east ex-
tremity of Newfoundland was bleak and barren in the extreme,
where scarcely a goat could find sustenance. It was a cold, clear,
starlit night.

In the small hours of Monday, the 15th, the officer-in-charge
at MCE was overhauling his transmitter. Some time before,

after receiving the last batch of messages from the *Titanic*, he had taken them off as usual to the local telegraph office, which was then situated in the house of one of the lighthouse men, and had handed them over to the lightkeeper's elder daughter, who acted as telegraphist. He was engaged in inspecting the generator (an 8 H.P. gasoline engine coupled to a belt-driven dynamo) when the operator on watch suddenly left the table and hurried to his side crying, 'My God! Mr Gray, the *Titanic* has struck a berg!'

Gray thereupon rushed to the key and asked what he could do to assist. Phillips in reply requested him to stand-by. It was some little time before the men at Cape Race realized the magnitude of the disaster; that the mammoth liner, with her sixteen watertight compartments and double bottom, could really be in serious danger was to them incomprehensible and unbelievable; the situation, as outlined by the signals received at Cape Race, appeared at first obscure; it was not, in fact, until news came that they were putting off the passengers in the boats and that the liner was sinking by the head did it gradually dawn on Gray that the *Titanic* was doomed. Thereafter came the disturbing reflection that, so far as he was aware, the only vessel that was actually going to the *Titanic's* assistance was the *Olympic*, which was hundreds of miles away from the wreck. (The *Carpathia's* transmitter was unfortunately too weak to be heard at such a distance by MCE's modest receiver, with its single Fleming diode valve detector.) Moreover, about three-quarters of an hour before the *Titanic* went to the bottom, her signals, owing to failing power, could no longer be heard at Cape Race. It was for this reason that Gray strove desperately to discover some nearer vessel to go to her aid.[8]

Some 120 miles to the westward the alarm sent out from MCE was picked up by Charley Ellsworth at Cape Ray (MCR), and thence dispatched by wire to Montreal. From Montreal it was swiftly transmitted to the White Star offices in New York.

Over an ever-widening area of the North Atlantic the dread news spread from ship to ship. Aerials hissed and crackled in the frosty darkness, and operators sat hunched and tense in their little cabins as they listened to the staccato murmur of spark.

They asked one another questions, passed on information, sent assurances of assistance to MGY, and flashed the alarm farther and farther afield. Masters were anxiously poring over charts and conferring with chief engineers. Ships were being hurriedly turned round and racing towards 41° 46′ N., 50° 14′ W. The *Mount Temple, Birma, Virginian, Baltic, Prinz Friedrich Wilhelm, Frankfurt, Amerika, Provence, Parisian, Olympic*, and even *Celtic—* 798 miles to the eastward at the time—were among those that heard and answered the call.[9]

In one case at least the news was received with sheer incredulity. At about about 12.40 a.m. the *Virginian* received a message from Cape Race: 'Titanic *struck iceberg, wants immediate assistance, her position 41° 46′ N., and 50° 14′ W.*' When the operator reported this message to the bridge the Officer of the Watch not unnaturally assumed that 'Sparks' was trying to make a fool of him; and, taking the youngster by the shoulder, was about to run him off the bridge, when the latter, in passing, aimed a terrific kick at the chart-room door. That was sufficient! At once the officer realized that this was no hoax; for no one would have dared rouse the Master in so unceremonious a manner had the message not been genuine.[10]

Both the operators on board the *Virginian* stood by throughout the rest of the night and exchanged positions and news about the *Titanic* with a number of other vessels hurrying towards the scene of the wreck.[11]

At 12.30 the *Titanic* had informed the *Frankfurt* of her position and called, '*Tell your Captain to come to our help. We are on the ice,*' to which the *Frankfurt* responded, '*O.K. Will tell*'. At the same time the *Mount Temple* told the *Titanic* that she was about fifty miles distant and was coming to her assistance. At 12.50 the *Celtic* received the *Titanic's* CQD; and about twenty minutes later the *Caronia* informed the *Baltic* that MGY required immediate assistance and gave her position. Towards one o'clock the *Olympic* (MKC) was receiving messages from Cape Cod when her operator suddenly heard 'MGY signalling to some other ship, and saying something about striking iceberg . . . not sure if it is MGY who has struck an iceberg,' he recorded in his log-book; and he added, '. . . I am interfered [with] by X's and many stations working'. Soon after he received the *Titanic's* CQD and hastened to reply, upon which the latter signalled that she had been in collision with an iceberg and was sinking by the head; giving her position and asking for immediate assistance. At 1.27 MGY informed MKC that her engine-room was flooded, and twelve minutes later, that the passengers were taking to the boats. At 1.50 the *Olympic* signalled, '*Am lighting up all possible boilers as fast as can*'.[12]

At the same time Cape Race sent a message to the *Virginian*. '*Please tell your Captain this: The* Olympic *is making all speed for* Titanic, *but his* [Olympic's] *position is 40° 32' N., 61° 18' W. You are much nearer to* Titanic. *The* Titanic *is already putting women off in the boats, and he says the weather there is calm and clear.*' At 1.45 the *Carpathia* heard the *Titanic* signal, '*Engine-room full up to boilers*'. Two minutes later she picked up MGY again but the signals were unreadable. At 1.55 Cape Race informed the *Virginian*, '*We have not heard the* Titanic *for about half an hour. His power may be gone*'.[13] MGY's power was, in truth, much reduced; at two o'clock the *Virginian* could still hear the *Titanic* calling, but only very faintly. The end was very near.

On board the *Carpathia*, now steaming at $17\frac{1}{2}$ knots, Cottam recorded in his log, '*Titanic calling CQD. His power appears to be greatly reduced*'. A quarter of an hour afterwards he added, '*Calling* Titanic. No response'; and a few minutes later, '*Titanic calls CQD. His signals blurred and end abruptly*'.

The *Virginian* had likewise received the *Titanic's* final CQD. The spark was blurred and rather ragged; the message could not be read; then suddenly all signals ceased, and the faltering spark of MGY was silenced for ever. . . .

'Calling *Titanic* at frequent intervals,' recorded Cottam, 'keeping close watch for him, but nothing further heard.'[14]

Nearly an hour after the *Titanic* had foundered Cottam sent out another message—'*If you are there we are firing rockets*'. Half an hour later the *Birma* signalled, '*Steering full speed for you. Shall arrive you 6 in morning. Hope you are safe. We are only 50 miles now.*' But at 4.18 the *Birma* told the *Celtic*, '*Nobody has heard the* Titanic *for about two hours*'. Shortly after 9 o'clock the *Baltic* turned round for Liverpool, having steamed 134 miles westward in the direction of the *Titanic*; and some time later the *Mount Temple* also continued her voyage.

The little fleet of boats got through the hours of darkness variously. Some of the boats kept more or less together during the remnant of the night, while others pursued their separate ways. 'The brilliancy of the sky,' related one who was in No. 3, 'only intensified the blackness of the water, our utter loneliness on the sea. The other boats had drifted away from us; we must wait now for dawn and what the day was to bring us we dare not even hope.' 'We all prayed for dawn,' said a passenger in No. 4, 'and there was no conversation, everyone being so awed by the disaster and bitterly cold.' In No. 5 the men lay on their oars until daylight. With the first light of dawn the wind increased and the sea became choppy, and they saw icebergs in every direction.

Mrs J. J. Brown in No. 6 boat was in her element. As a girl living beside the Mississippi, she had had experience of boats. Seizing an oar, she began to row; several other women following her example. At times the night was filled with the lamentations of their quartermaster, to the effect that they had neither food, nor water, nor compass, nor charts; he recalled the ill omen at the start of the voyage, and he declared that they did not even know in what direction they were heading—upon which one of the women kindly showed him the North Star, in its usual place. Hitchens simply wanted to let the boat drift. Mrs Brown, however, urged them all to row for the sake of warmth. Hitchens thereupon made a move as if to prevent her; and Maggie told him that, if he came any closer, she would chuck him overboard. . . . After this the quartermaster subsided into sullen silence, and No. 6 boat rowed on with Mrs Brown virtually in charge.[5]

No. 8 boat attempted without success to reach the distant steamer whose lights had been seen by several of the officers and others on board the sinking liner. 'The Countess Rothes was at the tiller all night,' said a steward. 'There were two lights not further than ten miles—stationary masthead lights. Everybody saw them—all the ladies in the boat. They asked if we were drawing nearer to the steamer, but we could not seem to make any headway, and near daybreak we saw another steamer coming up, which proved to be the *Carpathia*, and then we turned around and came back.'

The occupants of No. 13 boat resolved to keep with the other boats as far as possible until they were picked up by the ships which they had been assured were hurrying to their rescue. 'The sea will be covered with ships to-morrow afternoon,' said one of the firemen confidently during the night: 'they will race up from all over the sea to find us.' From time to time the boats would hail one another in the darkness. Occasionally one could be seen gradually drawing near and then pulling away again. There was a boat ahead of them which was certainly two-thirds empty, for they could see she was high out of the water; while No. 13, according to a leading fireman, was loaded 'nearly to the water's edge'. They hailed this other boat (it must surely have been No. 1 Emergency Boat), but without the slightest effect—'They never stopped or answered us.' The sea was like glass, and the reflections of the blazing stars were clearly visible in its mirror-like surface. A fireman remarked that he had been at sea for twenty-six years and had never seen the water so smooth. Another said, 'It reminds me of a bloomin' picnic!' So the time passed. Once a seabird rose from the water nearby with a startled cry, and one of the men exclaimed, 'I like a bird that sings in the morning!' A laugh went round the crowded boat. It was the only laugh they had. There was little conversation. It was scarcely more than an hour after the *Titanic* had foundered when they heard the report of a rocket; and presently, just as the stars were paling, first one, then a second, light rose above the southern horizon. They were the masthead lights of the rescuing steamer, the *Carpathia*.

No. 11 boat was so crowded that some of the people were unable to sit down. It is said that the men remained silent and embarrassed while the women started to quarrel. The latter were also incensed with certain members of the crew for smoking. In No. 11 boat, it is worth noticing, was the Allisons' baby, Travers, who, snug in his nurse's arms, slept peacefully throughout the entire affair. In this boat, also, was the toy pig with the musical box in its interior, which its owner would wind up and play to amuse the children. In No. 3 boat, as the light grew, Mrs Frederick O. Spedden's small son suddenly saw the icebergs. 'Oh, Mummie!' he exclaimed. 'Look at the beautiful North Pole with no Santa Claus on it!'

It was some time before dawn that Lightoller heard from Phillips, who was standing near him on the slippery planks of the upturned Engelhardt, of the vital ice report from the *Mesaba* that had never reached the bridge. At the same time he learned of the different vessels that had answered their call and were hurrying to their aid. According to his calculation, the *Carpathia* would arrive in an hour or so. It was this comforting thought which possibly sustained them during the last part of their vigil, as they stood motionless in their wet clothes on the upturned boat, with the temperature below zero and the sea beginning to get up. The slippery planks were by now well under water, and Lightoller had to correct the boat's roll by ordering them all to 'Lean to the right', 'Stand upright', or 'Lean to the left', as the case might be. Even so, it was a miracle that they managed to keep afloat.[16]

A few had slumped down, slid overboard, and so perished; but the majority were still there when daylight came and they could see a string of boats pulling towards the *Carpathia*. In answer to Lightoller's whistle, two of the boats quickly cast off from the others and pulled towards them. After what seemed to them an interminable wait (for the Engelhardt was leaking and sinking beneath them, so that the water was already up to their knees) they were at last taken safely off, with the exception of poor Phillips, who, shortly before their deliverance, had collapsed and died.

At daybreak Lowe sighted another of the Engelhardts lying at some distance from No. 14. As he thought the boat looked 'rather sorry', he sailed towards her and took her in tow. Later he saw yet another of the Engelhardts, which appeared to be badly damaged; he took off about twenty men and one woman, leaving behind three dead bodies in the abandoned craft—all men. 'I am not here to worry about bodies,' was his inward reflection; 'I am here to save life and not bother about bodies.' With the other boat in tow, he presently made sail towards the *Carpathia*.

As soon as the steamer's lights were sighted, No. 13 boat had swung round and her crew began their long pull. The fireman at the tiller called for a song, and broke into 'Pull for the shore, boys'. The crew took up the hymn quaveringly, and the passengers joined in. They sang one verse, and then gave a cheer. On every side boats could be seen pulling towards the *Carpathia* with shouts and cheers. One of the men in No. 13 said thankfully, 'Well, I shall never say again that thirteen is an unlucky number. Boat 13 is the best friend we ever had.'[17]

Chapter 12

The Middle Watch

Meanwhile, though on the night of the 14th dozens of spark transmissions in diverse keys had filled the ether, from the ship's station which lay nearest of them all to the stricken liner there came not a whisper. This was MWL, the 6,000-ton Leyland liner *Californian*, whose name, together with that of the *Carpathia*, will always be linked with the *Titanic* disaster.

Earlier that night the *Californian*, bound from London to Boston, on a course S. 89 W. true, had run into an immense mass of field ice which stretched as far as could then be seen to north and to south. At 10.20 p.m. she reversed her engines and stopped, and there remained until 6 o'clock on the following morning. At about 11 o'clock a steamer's light was seen approaching from the eastward. The O.O.W., Charles Victor Groves, the Third Officer, went to the chart-room and told the Master, Captain Stanley Lord, that a passenger steamer was approaching.

'Call her up on the Morse lamp,' said the Master, 'and see if you can get any answer.'

Returning to the bridge, Groves pushed in the electric plug and worked away with the signal-lamp; but without success.

The Master went along to the wireless cabin and asked the operator, Cyril Evans, a young man fresh from the training school, whether he had had any ships. Evans said he had had the *Titanic*. He judged by the strength of the signals she was within one hundred miles of the *Californian* in the afternoon. He could hear the other ship working a long time before he actually got into communication with MGY. The Master said, 'Better advise him we are surrounded by ice and stopped'. The operator switched on his transmitter and called up MGY. '*Say, old man,*' he began conversationally, '*we are surrounded by ice and stopped.*' MGY's reply thereupon 'came in with a bang'. '*Shut up, shut up, I am busy; I am working Cape Race, you are jamming me.*'[1]

This was the first of a series of fatal blunders perpetrated that night by someone or other on board the *Californian*. What Evans in the circumstances ought to have done was to ask the Master for an official message (i.e. an 'MSG', Master's Service Message); alternatively, he might have taken the responsibility of writing out the 'MSG' himself, and perhaps getting the Master to initial it then or later. He should then have intimated to the operator in the *Titanic* that he had an 'MSG' for him: but he should not have sent it until he got the K ('*Go ahead*') from MGY. What Evans apparently did was contrary to all the rules and current practices; without a preliminary call, and without listening to find out whether he would be interfering, he sent the ice-warning 'into the air' quite unofficially. In the same way it never seems to have occurred to the Master that it would be prudent, to say the least of it, to insist on getting a reply from the *Titanic*, which—as he obviously realized—might be standing into danger.[2]

Half an hour afterwards Evans still had the telephones on his head and heard MGY still working MCE; this time the former was transmitting passengers' telegrams. At 11.35 p.m. Evans decided to turn in. He put down the headphones, took off his clothes, and climbed into his bunk.

It is necessary at this stage to emphasize the fact that, despite all that was afterwards said to the contrary by Captain Lord, Evans should have remained on watch. The custom of the Marconi Marine service required an operator to remain at his post when anything like emergency conditions prevailed—as they assuredly did on the night of the 14th—for fear of missing an important message. The ice-report which the Master of the *Californian* had just sent to the *Titanic* proves the point. The huge ice-field which had stopped their own ship was a manifest danger to navigation. Ice or fog—the two bugbears of the North Atlantic run—presented just the situation in which collisions were liable to occur and in which recourse to wireless communication might be urgently necessary.[3]

It has also been suggested that, since his engines were stopped, the Master should have shown 'two red lights vertical and no side lights' (for a steamship not under command), which might conceivably have put other ships in the vicinity on the alert.[4]

At about this time the Third Officer, watching the steamer in the distance, saw her lights apparently go out. He remembered that it was then 11.40 because 'one bell was struck to call the middle watch'. When the Master later joined him on the bridge, the other vessel had stopped. Groves believed that 'she had starboarded to avoid some ice'.

'That does not look like a passenger steamer,' observed Captain Lord.

'It is, sir. When she stopped her lights seemed to go out, and I suppose they have been put out for the night.'

After he had been relieved Groves, at about 12.15 a.m., left the bridge. On his way to bed he went into the Marconi cabin and switched on the electric light. Evans and he were on friendly terms, and he would very often drop in for a chat. Wireless interested him, and he had learnt to read slow Morse. Groves now asked Evans what ships he had had, and if there were any news. The latter, still half asleep, told him drowsily that he had had the *Titanic*—'You know, the new boat on its maiden voyage. I got it this afternoon.' Groves picked up the telephones and put them on his head, as he had often done before. He heard nothing at all, for the receiver was 'dead'. The clockwork which activated the magnetic detector had first to be wound up; Groves did not know about this and Evans was too sleepy to tell him. The result was, Groves presently put down the headphones, switched off the light, and left the room, while Evans fell asleep again.

Herbert Stone, the Second Officer, had relieved Groves at midnight. On his way up to the bridge he saw the Master, who told him that the ship was stopped and surrounded by ice; and he pointed to a steamer in the distance, showing one masthead light and a red side-light. Lord asked him to let him know if the bearing of the steamer altered or if she came any closer to them; adding, that the Third Officer had called her up on the Morse lamp and received no reply.

On the bridge that watch with the Second Officer was a young apprentice called Gibson. The latter, looking at the other steamer through his glasses, could make out a mast-head light, her red light, and a 'glare of white lights on her after deck'. He tried, but to no effect, to get into communication with the other ship with the Morse lamp. Later in the watch he had to leave the bridge for about half an hour to do something to the patent log.

While he was gone Stone, pacing up and down the bridge, thought he saw a white flash in the sky immediately above the distant steamer. Lifting the glasses to his eyes, he saw four more white flashes, which 'had the appearance of white rockets bursting in the sky', as they flung out a cascade of white stars. The rockets went up at intervals of three or four minutes. At about 1.15 a.m. Stone reported by voice pipe to the Master that he had just seen five white rockets from the direction of the steamer. Lord asked him if they were 'Company's signals'. Stone replied that he did not know, but they appeared to him to be white rockets; and he added that he had called up the other ship on the Morse lamp. The Master thereupon told him to 'go on Morseing', and when he had any information to send the apprentice down to him with it. On Gibson's return to the bridge Stone told him what had been going on and asked him to call up the other ship on the Morse lamp. Gibson accordingly sent the calling-up signal, but again without success. He called her up for about three minutes, and had just got the glasses on her when he saw her fire three more rockets. His companion saw these rockets with his naked eye. At about 1.20 a.m. Stone remarked that she was steaming away towards the south-west. Slowly the minutes passed. The Second Officer and young Gibson continued to watch the distant steamer, looking at her from time to time with their glasses. 'Look at her now,' Stone said to the apprentice, 'she looks very queer out of the water, her lights look queer.' Gibson gazed through the glasses. He, too, thought there was something wrong about the position of her lights. What it was he could not exactly say, but it appeared to him as if she had a heavy list to starboard. 'She looks rather to have a big side out of the water' (i.e. her port light seemed to be higher out of the water than before); and the officer agreed. Stone went on to observe significantly that, 'a ship is not going to fire rockets at sea for nothing'.[5]

At 2 a.m., about twenty minutes after the eighth and last rocket had been fired, Stone told Gibson to go down to the Master, 'and be sure and wake him up', and tell him that altogether they had seen eight of these white lights like rockets in the direction of this other steamer; that this steamer was disappearing in the south-west, that they had called her up repeatedly on the Morse lamp, and that they had received no answer. Gibson went below and knocked on the chart-room door, then went inside and delivered the message. The Master, referring to the 'white lights like rockets', asked him if he were sure there were no colours in them, red or green. Were they all white? Gibson assured him that they were all white. Captain Lord then asked him the time. The youngster replied that it was five past two by the wheel-house clock. As he closed the door, Gibson heard the Master say something he did not quite catch. He returned to the bridge and reported to the O.O.W.[6]

The officer and the apprentice continued to keep the ship under observation until she disappeared. How it appeared to them, Stone later declared, was 'a gradual disappearing of all her lights, which would be perfectly natural with a ship steaming away from us'. At about 2.40 a.m. the O.O.W. again called up the Master by voice pipe and told him that the ship from the direction of which they had seen the rockets coming had disappeared, bearing S.W. $\frac{1}{2}$ W. The Master again asked him if he were certain there was no colour in the lights; and Stone again assured him they were all white, 'just white'.[7]

When the Chief Officer relieved the Second at 4 a.m., the latter told him about the strange steamer which had puzzled them so sorely in the middle watch, how at one o'clock he had seen some white rockets, and 'the moment the ship started firing them she started to steam away'. The Chief Officer presently called the Master and informed him that Stone had told him he had seen rockets in the middle watch. 'Yes, I know,' said the Master, 'he has been telling me.'

The Chief Officer hurried along to the wireless cabin and roused the sleeping operator. As Evans awoke with a start, Stewart began, 'Wireless, there is a ship that has been firing rockets in the night. Will you come in and see if you can find out what is wrong—what is the matter?' Evans pulled on his trousers and took up the headphones. There was no one working, so he switched on his transmitter and sent out the general call. The *Mount Temple* quickly answered him. '*Do you know the* Titanic *has struck an iceberg, and she is sinking.*'[8]

Chapter 13

'North 52 West'

On the same day that the *Titanic* had left Queenstown the 13,600-ton Cunard liner *Carpathia*, commanded by Captain Arthur H. Rostron, sailed from New York, eastward bound for Gibraltar and the Mediterranean. She carried 120 first class and 50 second class passengers, chiefly American tourists, as well as 565 third class passengers, immigrants to the United States, who were returning to their native lands on a visit. Her extensive passenger accommodation—providentially, as it turned out—was nearly half-empty.

It was some time after three bells in the first watch on Sunday, the 14th, that Captain Rostron came up on the bridge and heard from his Second Officer, James Bisset, the O.O.W., of the latest ice-reports, including the message from the *Mesaba*. He was plainly impressed by these warnings. Summoning the radio operator, H. T. Cottam, he asked him what ships were within his range. Cottam mentioned the White Star Line's new vessel.

'I suppose the *Titanic* will have to slow down,' said Rostron, 'or steer a more southerly course than her usual track. She'll be late in New York. It's hard luck on her maiden voyage. Any other ships near?'

Cottam replied that in addition to the *Mesaba*, *Baltic*, and *Caronia* which he had heard earlier in the day, he had identified five others, the *Frankfurt*, *Mount Temple*, *Virginian*, *Birma*, and— very faint and far away—*Olympic*.

'Thank you,' said Rostron. 'I suppose you'll be turning in presently for the night?'

'Yes, sir,' replied Cottam. 'I may listen to Cape Cod for a while, in case there is any news of the coal strike in England.'[1]

About three hours later Cottam was preparing to turn in. During his watch he had overheard Phillips's snub to Evans in the *Californian*; after which, tiring of the long list of Stock Exchange quotations and private messages, he had changed over from the shipping wave-length, and listened to the news from Cape Cod.[2]

He began slowly to undress and knelt down to unlace his boots. It was now past midnight. For a while he had slipped off the headphones, thereby missing the *Titanic*'s original CQD. Then he put them on again. It occurred to him to call up MGY. He switched on his transmitter and tapped out the message, receiving in reply a curt K ('Go ahead').

'GM OM [*Good morning, old man!*],' began Cottam. '*Do you know there are messages for you at Cape Cod?*'

At the swift response to his enquiry, Cottam's heart nearly missed a beat. For out of the night came the dread CQD, the international distress call.

'CQD CQD SOS SOS CQD SOS *Come at once. We have struck a berg.* CQD OM [It's a CQD, old man]. *Position 41° 46′ N., 50° 14′ W.* CQD SOS.'[3]

In trousers and shirt Cottam raced up on the bridge and breathlessly informed the Officer of the Watch, who in turn awakened the Captain.

On hearing the almost incredible news, the first thing Rostron did was to give orders to turn the ship round. Then he sent for Cottam and questioned him closely.

'Are you sure it is the *Titanic* that requires immediate assistance?'

'Yes, sir,' said Cottam.

'You are absolutely certain?'

'Quite certain,' was the reply.

'All right,' said Rostron. 'Tell him we are coming along as fast as we can.'[4]

Next moment his voice could be heard shouting his orders up to the bridge; whereupon young James Bisset, the Second Officer, roused from his sleep, sprang out of his bunk, hurriedly pulling on his clothes, and dashed up the bridge ladder, to be informed by the First: 'The *Titanic* has struck a berg and has sent out the distress signal!'[5]

Having ascertained the *Titanic*'s position from Cottam,

Rostron hurried off to the chart-room. He glanced down the meridians and picked off the degrees and minutes and then measured off the latitude. He calculated his present position and worked out the course. Returning to the bridge, he addressed the helmsman:

'North 52 West!'

'Aye, aye, sir. North 52 West!'[6]

By this time the other officers, including the Chief Engineer, had assembled on the bridge. Beckoning them all into the chart-room, the Captain quickly outlined the situation. He told them that the *Titanic* was in distress fifty-eight miles away on the bearing N. 52 W. He ordered an extra watch to be called out in the engine-room and every possible ounce of steam to be raised. All seamen were to be on deck to keep a sharp look-out and to swing out the boats: electric clusters to be rigged at each gangway and over the side: all stewards on duty to prepare blankets and refreshments: the doctors to stand by in the dining-rooms. All gangway doors were to be opened, bo'sun's chairs slung out at each gangway, and pilot ladders dropped over-side. Oil was to be got ready to quiet the sea if necessary. He warned them that they might have to pick up more than two thousand people.[7]

Presently the decks began to throb as the revolutions of the engines steadily increased; and, within a few minutes of receiving the call for assistance, the *Carpathia*, a 14-knot ship, was shearing through the water at over 17 knots—a speed which she kept up for well over three hours. Rostron called the Second Officer over to the starboard wing of the bridge, saying:

'Station yourself here, Mister, and keep a special lookout for lights or flares—*and for ice!* I will remain on the bridge. In this smooth sea it's no use looking for white surf around the base of the bergs, but you will look for the reflection of starshine in the ice pinnacles. We'll be into the icefield at 3 a.m. or perhaps earlier. Extra lookouts will be posted on the bows and in the crow's nest, and on the port wing of the bridge, but I count on you, with your good eyesight, and with God's help, to sight anything in time for us to clear it. Give that all your attention!'[8]

'Aye, aye, sir!'

Soon after Cottam came up on the bridge with the news that he had just picked up a message from the *Titanic* to the *Olympic*, asking her to have all her boats ready; also another to the *Carpathia*, asking how long she would be in arriving.

'Say in about four hours,' the Captain told Cottam (actually they did it in three and a half hours), 'and tell her we shall have all our boats in readiness and all other preparations necessary to receive the rescued.'

'*We are coming as quickly as possible,*' Cottam telegraphed to MGY, '*and expect to be there within four hours.*'

'TU OM [*Thank you, old man*]'[9]

After that Cottam switched off his transmitter. He was careful not to do anything which might interfere with the *Titanic's* signals. Presently, however, he overheard her exchanges with the *Frankfurt*, *Mount Temple*, and other ships—though all this time, as has been said, the *Californian*, which lay no more than nine or ten miles distant from the sinking liner, remained silent.

At about 2.45 a.m., when, according to Rostron's reckoning, they must be approaching the ice-region, a green flare was seen in the distance, about one point on the port bow. For a while Rostron had hopes that the liner was still afloat. At about the same time young Bisset, out on the starboard wing, sighted an iceberg glimmering in the starlight three-quarters of a mile ahead on the port bow. He sang out to the Captain, who was standing beside the helmsman. Rostron immediately altered course to starboard and reduced to half speed. He went out on the port wing, and then, seeing that they had easily cleared the iceberg and no more ice was in sight, brought the *Carpathia* back on her former course and moved the handle of the engine-room telegraph once more to Full Speed Ahead.[10]

A few minutes later they sighted another berg, and then another; and then, at intervals, a whole succession of bergs. In his old age Bisset could vividly recall how, with all his senses strung up to the highest pitch of intensity, he kept watch that night on the starboard wing. He had been especially told off for the purpose because he had exceptionally keen eyesight. But there were at least a dozen other men stationed in various parts of the ship to keep a sharp look-out—on the port wing of the bridge, in the bows, and up in the crow's nest. Though the night was clear, there were patches of surface haze. But always the iceberg was seen in time, and avoided. Berg after berg loomed up in the starlight, then fell astern. For half an hour more the *Carpathia*, steaming at forced full speed, zigzagged among the islands of ice, avoiding each in turn with sufficient clearance. None knew better than the Master of the *Carpathia* that the lives of his seven hundred passengers and crew, as well as those of the survivors of the *Titanic*, depended upon the keen eyesight, vigilance, and seamanship of those on the bridge and on look-out. He was taking, as Bisset has related, 'a calculated risk'.[11]

They were now very near the position given in the distress call, lat. 41° 46′ N., long. 50° 14′ W. Shortly before 4 a.m. speed was reduced to half, and then to slow, as Rostron steered the *Carpathia* with the utmost caution towards a green flare on the surface of the water. Bisset discovered to his intense relief that he could distinguish the holes in the gratings: already the first light of day was stealing across the sea. Eight bells was sounded: Hankinson, the Chief Officer, took over from Dean, and the helmsman was relieved. As it slowly lightened, a life-boat was sighted about a quarter of a mile away; she was rising and falling in the long ocean swell, and hardly moving, as if those at the oars were exhausted. There were about two dozen women and ten children in the boat, which was steered by a young officer. Owing to an iceberg which lay directly ahead it was impossible for Rostron to manœuvre his ship so as to give them a lee; and he said urgently to Bisset:

'Go overside with two quartermasters, and board her as she comes alongside. Fend her off so that she doesn't bump, and be careful that she doesn't capsize.'

Bisset hurried off to the fore-deck with the two quarter-masters, and then, as the boat came alongside, clambered swiftly down the rope-ladders and dropped on to her thwarts. After steadying the boat, and fending her off, they dropped astern to an open side door on C Deck, and made her fast. One after another the *Titanic's* survivors were carefully assisted on board, while Bisset conducted her Fourth Officer to the bridge. Long afterwards he thus described the scene:

Without preliminaries, Rostron burst out, excitedly,
'Where is the *Titanic?*'

'Gone!' said Boxhall. 'She sank at 2.20 a.m.'

In the moment of stunned silence that followed, every man on the bridge of the *Carpathia* envisaged the appalling reality, but not yet to its fullest extent. It was now 4.20 a.m. . . .

'Were many people left on board when she sank?'

'Hundreds and hundreds! Perhaps a thousand! Perhaps more!' Boxhall's voice broke with emotion. 'My God, sir, they've gone down with her. They couldn't live in this cold water. We had room for a dozen more people in my boat, but it was dark after the ship took the plunge. We didn't pick up any swimmers. I fired flares. . . . I think that the people were drawn down deep by the suction. The other boats are somewhere near.'[12]

As the pale glow on the eastern horizon brightened and spread, the stars slowly dimmed and died. Low down near the horizon was a pale sickle moon. As it came on full daylight, it was possible to see the vast extent of the icefield which had been the subject of so many warnings.

As far as the eye could reach, from the north-west to the south-east there lay an unbroken expanse of field ice—an awe-inspiring spectacle, with great icebergs from one hundred to two hundred feet high towering above the general mass and glistening in the first rays of the rising sun. Rostron sent a junior officer to the top of the wheel-house and told him to count the largest icebergs. He reported that there were no less than twenty-five between 150 and 200 feet high and that the smaller ones were too numerous to count. Later in the day it took the *Carpathia* nearly four hours to steam round this great mass of ice.[13]

Meanwhile at 6 a.m. the *Californian* had got under way, steering for the position where, as she was presently informed, the *Titanic* had sent out her distress call. An hour or so earlier she had been seen by several of the *Carpathia's* officers and two passengers on the edge of the pack-ice, about ten miles to the northward. Shortly after eight o'clock, steaming cautiously through the ice, she was near enough to the *Carpathia*, whose house-flag now flew at half-mast, for semaphore signalling. On her inquiring what was the matter, the reply came that the *Titanic* had foundered. Later she received a wireless message from Captain Rostron: '*I am taking the survivors to New York. Please stay in the vicinity and pick up any bodies*'.[14]

According to the Master of the *Californian*, no bodies could be found and after an hour or so he resumed his voyage. It is to be observed that he could not have searched very effectively; for there were in fact hundreds of corpses, drifting to and fro on the face of the waters. A cable-laying ship, the *Mackay-Bennett*, was later sent out from Halifax and picked up about two hundred of them. The rest were abandoned. 'Unweighted,' says Bisset, 'and in most cases buoyed by lifejackets, the bodies of the *Titanic*'s dead—the celebrities, the lesser-known, and the humble unknown to fame—were flotsam in the wide Atlantic for weeks, and some, it was believed, for months after the disaster.... The mail steamers for many months gave the region of the floating dead a wide berth; the Atlantic tracks were haunted, and, even to this day shipmasters steer clear of the place where the *Titanic* sank.'[15]

Chapter 14

The Rescue

In the early hours of the 15th the news had reached New York that the *Titanic* had collided with an iceberg and was in urgent need of assistance. Soon after another message arrived to the effect that the liner was sinking by the head and that the passengers were taking to the boats. Other messages followed, but these were so vague that nothing certain could be learned from them. However, the public alarm was partially allayed by reports picked up by the *Olympic* and other vessels that the *Virginian* had taken the *Titanic* in tow. The origin of these mysterious reports was never satisfactorily resolved; but in all probability they were due to the irresponsible activities of a number of American amateur radio operators. As the day advanced, it was assumed that all the passengers had been safely transferred to the various vessels which had responded to the *Titanic's* call for help. That night the *Evening Star's* banner headline announced, 'All saved from *Titanic* after collision'.

A reassuring statement was issued in the morning by P. A. S. Franklin, Vice-President of the International Mercantile Marine Company, to the effect that they were perfectly satisfied that the *Titanic* was unsinkable. The fact that the wireless signals had suddenly ceased meant nothing. It might be due to atmospheric conditions, the arrival of the rescue ships, or something of that sort. They were not worried over the possible loss of the ship, as she would not go down, but they were sorry for the inconvenience caused to the travelling public. They were absolutely certain that the *Titanic* was able to withstand any damage. She might be down by the head, but would float indefinitely in that condition.

Far away in England a wave of consternation had swept across the country at the news of the collision. In the City the newsboys that morning were crying out that the *Titanic* had struck an iceberg; and the early editions of the evening papers carried the headlines, 'The *Titanic* sinking'. 'Women taken off in lifeboats', 'Liners to the rescue'. At Southampton, where most of the crew lived, the first half-pay notes given to the wives and other dependents of the men had just become payable; after receiving their money the women gathered in little groups at the dock gates and anxiously discussed the news. Those who enquired at the White Star offices were assured that the provision of watertight bulkheads was so ample that there was not the least likelihood of the ship sinking. As the after noon wore on, the latest news became more reassuring, and most of the women returned home. After nightfall a silent and anxious crowd, composed almost entirely of men, gathered outside the White Star offices in Canute Street, which remained open throughout the night.[1]

At Oceanic House in Cockspur Street, the London head-quarters of the White Star Line, there had been all that day a steady stream of callers and hundreds of telephone calls. The officials there were unable to satisfy the demand for information, since no further news had come to hand. The newspaper posters displayed at so many street corners bore such announcements as, '*Titanic* disaster', 'Collision with an iceberg', 'All passengers rescued this morning', 'Wireless call for aid'. But at Lloyd's there was consternation. However reassuring the earlier messages might seem to be in respect of the safety of passengers and crew, the gloomiest apprehensions began to be entertained concerning the *Titanic* herself. Should the great ship go down in deep water with mails and cargo on board, the loss to the underwriters would be immense. It would be by far the heaviest blow that had fallen on the insurance market. The moment that the first telegrams from across the Atlantic reached Lloyd's the casualty board was besieged by an anxious crowd of underwriters, brokers, and their clerks: as fast as those in front finished reading and commenting on the news, and moved away, their places were quickly taken by another row: and so it went on. The tension continued unabated throughout the afternoon. However, at 4 p.m., a telegram arrived stating that the *Titanic* was being towed towards Halifax; as a result of which the insurance rate on the liner, which had risen as high as sixty guineas per cent, fell to twenty-five. Throughout this day the Stock Exchange also was unsettled and depressed. [2]

The following day brought the appalling news that the *Titanic* had gone down with two-thirds of her passengers and crew. After well over half a century a good many men and women can vividly recall the stunning effect of those tidings. In countless numbers of homes throughout the country there was a stricken silence as if there had been a death in the family. People on their way to town that morning caught sight of the inscriptions on the newspaper placards and heard the newsboys crying, '*Titanic* sunk' . . . 'Terrible loss of life' . . . 'A national calamity' . . . 'Pa-aper!' They discussed the full implication of the news in train, omnibus, and tram. Later editions of the national dailies came on the streets, and people hastened to buy them. Women were sobbing as they read. The shadow of an unexampled tragedy hung over the land. There had been nothing like this since the terrible 'Black Week' of the South African War.

That afternoon in the House of Commons, as the Prime Minister advanced to the dispatch box in response to an enquiry from Lord Charles Beresford concerning the loss of the *Titanic*, members in all parts of the House removed their hats. Deeply moved, Asquith proceeded to read the brief message received by the Board of Trade from the White Star Line to the effect that the *Titanic* had foundered, and then continued:

'I am afraid we must brace ourselves to confront one of those terrible events in the order of Providence which baffle foresight, which appal the imagination, and which make us feel the inadequacy of words to do justice to what we feel. I cannot say more at this moment than to give a necessarily imperfect expression to our sense of admiration that the best traditions of the sea seemed to have been observed in the willing sacrifices which were offered to give the first chance of safety to those who were least able to help themselves, and to the warm and heart-felt sympathy of the whole nation to those who find themselves bereaved of their nearest and dearest in their desolated homes'. [3]

'We accepted with heroic credulity the proud boast that the *Titanic* was unsinkable,' the *Star* commented sadly. 'Alas!

another human illusion has proved to be in vain,' 'It is,' *The Times* observed on the following day, 'a catastrophe without parallel in the annals of shipping.' Commenting on the holocaust of millionaires, the *Daily Sketch* declared, 'The *Titanic*, like some monstrous syren, had by her beauty and ease, by her splendour and confidence, lured down to the sea men and women to whom life itself seemed subservient and obedient.'

Over every shipping office in Cockspur Street flags flew at half-mast. The entrance of Oceanic House was surrounded by a huge crowd, and a young cinematographer was busy filming the endless stream of anxious enquirers pouring through the doors. Every moment newcomers added themselves to the throng. The lines of motor-cars and carriages containing inquirers were so lengthy that those in the rear were unable to get anywhere near Oceanic House. Some of the women wore black. People moved restlessly to and fro about the large inquiry room, or sat in a sort of stunned silence on the seats. Again and again to the same inquiries the clerks returned the same negative answers. On the notice board was displayed a typewritten sheet bearing the brief announcement, '675 saved'. At intervals throughout the afternoon the meagre lists of survivors were posted up on the board as soon as they came in. These lists contained the names of first and second class passengers only. There had been scores of Londoners among the steerage passengers. As to these the invariable reply was, 'No further news at present'.

Down at Southampton the 16th was a day of grief such as had never been known in its history. The name *Titanic* was on everyone's lips. There was horror and incredulity at the news. The shock was the greater because so many people had gone to bed the night before in the belief that, at any rate, the passengers and crew were safe. Southampton was a stricken town. Under the great trees in the Avenue, up and down the High Street, and, above all, in the busy thoroughfares adjoining the river-front, anxious groups of men and women assembled to discuss the news. The Borough flag flew at half-mast above the Bargate, and the flags were at half-mast, too, over every public building in Southampton, as well as over the harbour offices and all the ships in the docks. The blinds were drawn in many a little home in Northam and Shirley, and the shutters were up in most of the shops and business premises. At least six hundred homes were affected by the catastrophe. At Northam Council School no less than 125 of the children were dependent upon parents or other relations who had sailed in the liner. Hour after hour the crowds waited outside the White Star offices and the main dock gates. Towards nightfall large numbers of women with wraps and shawls pulled loosely round their shoulders, many of them with babies in their arms and small children clinging to their skirts, swelled the throng. They stood about Canute Street in the white glare of the arc lamps, waiting for news of those who were saved. Men bit grimly on their pipes. A few of the women were quietly sobbing. From time to time scraps of conversation were heard.

'Yes, it's true,' said a woman in a weary, listless voice, 'husband and son have gone and left eleven of us. It was the first time that Arthur and his father had been at sea together, and it would not have happened if Arthur had not been out of work owing to the coal strike. He tried to get a job ashore but failed, and as he had his wife and baby to keep he signed on in the *Titanic* as a fireman. His father would not have been in the *Titanic*, but a bad leg stopped him from going in his own ship, the *Britannia*. Now they are gone and there are eleven of us. . . .'

Others presently took up the tale of woe. 'She lives nigh me in Union Street, and she has three little children. He was a fireman, and a good man at his work'. . . . 'A poor old man in Cable Street; they say he has four sons on board'. . . . 'An' there's Saunders, the shipwright over the way; he is grieving about his two sons'. . . . 'In McNaughton Street there is a girl going mad; she has only been married a month. Her husband signed on as a steward.'[4]

The long vigil continued through the night of April 16th–17th. The dawn brought no fresh news. It was not until 8 a.m. that the first intelligence concerning the officers who had been saved came through. Throughout 'the *Titanic* week' the notice-board outside the White Star offices in Canute Street was almost the centre of the town's life. 'We almost lived down there,' one of those who can recall that time has related. The crowd waiting patiently for the latest news was sometimes large and sometimes small; but it never wholly dispersed.

One after another the boats of the *Titanic* came alongside the Cunarder. Women went up the side first, mounting rope-ladders with a rope looped round their shoulders to assist them, or else were hauled up in a bo'sun's chair; the men next made the ascent, and the boats' crews last of all. Many of the lifeboats, like Boxhall's, were half empty; but a few of them were crowded, and in danger of being swamped. For the dawn wind, gradually freshening, had ruffled up a choppy sea.

The smaller children were each stowed in a bag and so hoisted safely on board. Among them was 'Bobo' Washington Dodge, still greatly enjoying his adventure, who was enchanted with this mode of ascent. 'They put me in a sack and pulled me up,' young Bobo related afterwards. 'That was lovely! I wanted them to let me down that way when we got to New York, but they wouldn't. . . .'

Among the survivors were a number of small dogs. Henry Sleeper Harper came on board the *Carpathia* with a little brown Pekinese spaniel acquired in Paris which he called Sun Yat Sen 'in honour of his country's first President'. A woman wearing a fur coat over her nightdress was nursing beneath the coat what James Bisset at first supposed was a baby, but proved, in fact, to be a small dog. 'Be careful of my doggie!' she said anxiously to the men.

The last of the lifeboats was packed with seventy-five survivors. It was fortunate for them that a good seaman was at her tiller. This was the Second Officer, Charles Lightoller, who, with many others, had clung to the upturned Engelhardt before being picked up. He trimmed the boat rather more down by the stern, and raised the bow, hoping that by keeping her carefully bow on to the sea she would continue to rise. The last few minutes were nearly too much for the overloaded craft. The *Carpathia* was heading towards them now, and rounded to about one hundred yards to windward; but around the liner's bows was a bobble that looked like swamping them and very nearly did. First one sea and then another, far heavier, lopped over the lifeboat's bows. But she rose to the following one, and then, to Lightoller's infinite relief, reached safety in the smooth water under the *Carpathia's* lee.

One after another the occupants of the boat climbed, or else were hauled up, on board the Cunard liner. Finally the officer in charge wearily scaled the ladder. As Lightoller gained the deck of the *Carpathia*, he suddenly recognized an old friend at the very same instant that the old friend recognized him. '*Hullo*, Lights!' exclaimed Dean in surprise. 'Whatever are you doing here!'[5]

This completed the tale of survivors. Altogether there were 706 souls who had escaped in the boats. More than 1,500—men, women, and children—had gone to their last account.

The *Carpathia's* passengers lined the rails as boatload after boatload of survivors came on board. They stood in solemn silence looking down on the scene below. Some of the rescued were in evening dress, while others were in their night clothes under overcoats or wraps, or else were swaddled in blankets. There were husbands without their wives, wives without their husbands, parents without their children, and children without their parents. They were escorted to the dining saloons where hot coffee, soup, and sandwiches were awaiting them.

Looking back a good many years afterwards, Captain Rostron recalls that the outstanding feature of the scene as the survivors came on board was the extraordinary silence. There was an almost total lack of excitement. It is true that in the saloon one of the rescued women burst into hysterical crying, and that later others gave way to their hopeless grief. But the great majority of the survivors suffered no physical ill-effects from the experience. Some of them recognized relatives and friends among the *Carpathia's* passengers. Colonel Gracie was greeted by Mr Louis Ogden, who was a distant connection of his. He was also welcomed by Mr and Mrs Charles H. Marshall and several other friends. They warmed him up with hot drinks and lent him clothes. Dr Washington Dodge was greeted by another prominent citizen of San Francisco, who insisted on giving up his state-room to Mrs Dodge and Bobo.

Some six hours after their nieces in the *Titanic* had sent a greeting by wireless to Mr and Mrs Marshall on board the *Carpathia*, the two girls were in one of the lifeboats watching the giant liner in her death-throes; afterwards drifting for hours in the Arctic night, until shortly after dawn, they were picked up by the Cunarder. Captain Rostron wrote:

The Marshalls knew nothing of it. They retired to their state cabin; they went to sleep. The night was calm, the sea smooth, they slept on through all the preparations that were going on on board. But among the first of the survivors who came up one of the gangways were the two nieces who a few hours before had been wirelessing from the *Titanic* to the Marshalls. While the latter had been sleeping, these young ladies had been through all the agony of the night.

It was about half-past six when the Marshalls awoke. A steward knocking on their door aroused them.

'What is it? asked Mr Marshall.

'Your nieces wish to see you, sir,' replied the steward.

No wonder he was dumfounded; hardly believing his eyes, when he opened the door and looked upon the girls, not crediting his senses as he listened to their story.[6]

Too often, alas! the story ended differently. For example, on the night of the disaster one of America's leading architects, Daniel H. Burnham, who was travelling to Europe with his wife in the *Olympic*, wrote a message of greeting to his friends, Frank Millet and Archie Butt, on board the *Titanic*, and told his steward to take it to the wireless office. Some time later the steward returned with the news that the wireless operator, without giving any reason, had declined to accept the message. On Burnham's insisting on an explanation, he was presently informed that the *Titanic* had been in collision with an iceberg, and that the *Olympic* was going to her assistance. The Burnhams thereupon made arrangements to give up their suite to their shipwrecked friends.[7] In the same way John Badenoch, the head of Macy's grocery department, who was travelling to Europe in the *Carpathia* on a business mission, at once prepared to give up his state-room to the Strauses when he heard of the accident. Before daybreak, as we know, these arrangements had been rendered nugatory.

It was some time before those emerging from the valley of the shadow of death fully realized the magnitude of the disaster. The Chief Engineer and all the other engine-room officers;

Andrews and his men from Harland and Wolff's; the maître and every one of the restaurant staff but one; the Purser and his assistants; the eight musicians; all the page-boys, lift-boys, and post-office clerks—these had perished to a man. Ismay, Sir Cosmo Duff-Gordon, and Carter found that they were the only men who remained of those who had dined in the restaurant on that fateful Sunday night. Of the men who had sat at the Purser's table Frederick K. Seward was the solitary survivor. Beesley could recognize very few of those who had gathered in the second class library on that Sunday afternoon among the survivors he met on board the *Carpathia*. All the millionaires had gone down with the ship, as had also all the clergymen. In certain cases, as with the Allisons, practically an entire family had been wiped out.

The ship's officers and all the male passengers at once gave their cabins to the survivors, and a large number of the women 'doubled up' with others so as to provide more accommodation. Many of the *Carpathia's* women passengers were soon hard at work dressmaking on behalf of the survivors. In spite of their efforts, however, some of the rescued women had to wear the night clothes and dressing-gowns in which they had left the *Titanic*. Since there were not enough berths for all the women on board, a good many of them had to sleep each night on straw palliasses in the saloons and library. The men made their beds in the smoking-room and elsewhere.

On his arrival on board the *Carpathia* Ismay had declined all offers of food and drink and asked if he could go to a room where he could be quiet. The ship's doctor at first tried to persuade him to go to the dining saloon 'and get something hot'. But Ismay still declined, and, seeing that he was suffering severely from shock, the doctor finally led him off and installed him in his own room, where he remained until they reached New York.

Soon after Ismay had been lodged in the doctor's cabin, Captain Rostron came down to see him and said, 'Don't you think, sir, you had better send a message to New York, telling them about this accident?' Ismay agreed. He wrote the message on a slip of paper—'*Deeply regret advise you* Titanic *sank this morning after collision iceberg, resulting serious loss of life.*

Full particulars later. Bruce Ismay'. Turning to the Captain, he said, 'Captain, do you think that is all I can tell them?' Rostron answered, 'Yes,' and returned to the deck.[3]

It had been decided not to tranship the survivors to the *Olympic*, or to make for the nearest port, which was Halifax, but to return to New York. About the same time, after some discussion among themselves, the *Titanic's* surviving officers came to the conclusion that it would be 'a jolly good idea' if they could get back to England in the *Cedric*, if they could only reach New York in time to catch her. Ismay thereupon dispatched another message to Franklin, signing it with his code-name. '*Very important you should hold* Cedric *daylight for* Titanic's *crew. Answer*. YAMSI.' (This was Ismay's personal signature, which he used only for his private messages.)

As usually happens with an inquiry impending, the *Titanic's* surviving officers appear to have maintained a discreet silence about certain aspects of the disaster. According to such evidence as is available, they gave away as little as possible, even to the commander and officers of the *Carpathia*.

A roll-call of the survivors having been carefully taken, the list was handed over to the wireless operator of the *Carpathia* for immediate dispatch. The list took precedence over all the private messages. To the *Olympic's* request for news of the disaster, Cottam replied, '*I can't do everything at once. Patience, please*'. However, he managed to send a brief account. He told the *Olympic's* operator that he had had nothing to eat since 5.30 the previous day. '*Please excuse sending*,' he said that evening, '*but am half asleep*.' At the same time he began sending the names of survivors, which the *Olympic* relayed to Cape Race. Cottam by this time was 'all in'; and in the afternoon he all but collapsed under the strain. A hurried appeal was sent to Bride, who was then in the ship's hospital suffering from badly injured feet and frostbite. Bride was thereupon carried up to the Marconi cabin to assist the exhausted operator, whom he relieved, watch and watch. It would appear that Cottam did most of the sending while Bride prepared the messages for him. From time to time the two were harassed by inquiries from American newspapers frantic for full particulars of the wreck. They ignored the inquiries and devoted themselves to official business and the personal messages of survivors. They had still one hundred of these personal messages to work off when the ship reached New York.

On the following day, Tuesday, the 16th, Daniel H. Burnham recorded in his diary: 'Breakfasted in our rooms. Went out and read list of *Titanic's* survivors telegraphed from the *Carpathia*, which is carrying them to New York. Frank's name is not among them, nor is Archie Butt's. My Steward is in grief; his son was a steward on the *Titanic* and has gone down. This ship is in gloom; everybody has lost friends, and some of them near relations.'[4] For the remainder of the passage the *Olympic's* orchestra ceased playing, and all concerts and dances were cancelled. The usual shipboard gaiety was completely extinguished. People conversed in low tones, and there were long silences. A large subscription was raised among the passengers and crew in aid of the victims of the disaster.

It was, perhaps, scarcely to be wondered at that certain smouldering antagonisms which had manifested themselves in the boats threatened to blaze up anew in the overcrowded *Carpathia*. There was a marked tendency to criticize the male survivors from the wreck for being alive at all. (It was for this reason that Major Peuchen took the precaution of getting a chit from Lightoller, stating that he had entered his boat in response to a direct order). Mrs J. J. Brown is supposed to have told Ismay to his face that in her home town in Colerado he would have been 'strung up on the nearest pine-tree'. Some of the women who had lost their husbands in the wreck were feeling very bitter, not altogether without reason. In the dining saloon, one night after dinner, Mrs René Harris noticed a couple from the lost liner in evening dress. They were, she says, 'a lord and lady whom I had met on the *Titanic*'. At first she supposed that they had come away from the wreck so dressed, like a number of other people. But another passenger told her that on the day before the couple had been seen on deck in sports clothes; and Mrs Harris said she later learned with no little indignation, that 'this lord and lady' had saved not only themselves, but their luggage as well. Worse was to follow. On the 17th, when Mrs Harris was sitting in a corner of the deck with some other women, she saw two members of the *Titanic's* crew approach wearing lifebelts. 'Good God!' she exclaimed. 'What has happened now?' 'Nothing, lady,' replied one of the men reassuringly. 'Someone wants to take pictures.' And just then there appeared, with their camera pointing at Mrs Harris and her companions, the 'lord and lady' from the *Titanic*. The ensuing row brought one of the officers who had been saved, Harold Lowe, on to the scene. The latter, in his usual terse style, told the pair exactly what he thought of them. . . . The snapshots were not taken.[10]

Mrs Harris was also incensed at the conduct of a certain German-American physician (characterized by another first class lady, Mrs Stengel, as 'a Hebrew doctor') who with his brother had jumped into No. 5 boat as it was being lowered; and, falling heavily on top of the unfortunate Mrs Stengel, dislocated two of her ribs and knocked her unconscious.

On Wednesday morning rumours went round among the survivors of the ice warnings which had reached the *Titanic* before the collision. By the afternoon these rumours had hardened to definite statements; and when a direct question was presently put to one of the *Titanic's* officers he admitted their truth. To their surprise and consternation the survivors then realized that the hazard of ice in their track was by no means unknown to those responsible for the navigation of the ship and that the terrible tragedy might, after all, have been avoided. It was for this and other reasons that Beesley began to prepare a letter to *The Times* which was soon to be reproduced all over the world. He worked away at it during the next two days, in odd corners of the deck and dining saloon; and on their arrival in New York he entrusted it to an Associated Press reporter. It was by far the fullest and clearest account of the disaster which had so far appeared.[11]

On the same day the *Carpathia* ran into a thick fog. During the afternoon, while she proceeded at reduced speed with her siren sounding continually, her wireless station was in communication with the U.S.S. *Chester*, to whom Bride sent a more complete list of survivors. 'If the *Chester* had had a decent operator,' Bride later complained, 'I could have worked with him longer, but he got terribly on my nerves with his insufferable incompetence.' All this time frantic inquiries were being sent out from American shore stations demanding detailed information of the disaster. From President Taft downward, some of the wealthiest and most influential men in the United States were endeavouring to get news of their relatives and friends who had been on board the *Titanic*. The messages were brought up to Rostron on the bridge. But the Master, who already had as much as he could do, paid little attention to them.

Next morning Siasconsett attempted repeatedly to exchange traffic with the *Carpathia*. 'Got MPA,' the shore operator recorded in his log, 'again offer the question, "Is Astor, Butt and Guggenheim on board?" He replies, "Astor is not aboard, the others I don't know of". . . . Call MPA and ask if he can read our signals. "Yes, I can read you O.K., but say, old man, I have not been to bed since *Titanic* went down. I have over three hundred messages." Tell him "make a try and less argument". Offer message from Mr Marconi. He gives G ["Go ahead"], clears it O.K. and gives G.' Later on the 18th, however, MPA sent 147 messages to Siasconsett and other shore stations.[12]

In New York the mood of optimism had persisted till about six o'clock on Monday evening, when news of the most alarming character came in from the Atlantic; the *Olympic* had sent a message to the effect that the *Titanic* had gone down at 2.20 a.m. and that the *Carpathia* had picked up 675 survivors; and a large crowd began to collect outside the offices of the White Star Line in Broadway. Late that night Vincent Astor drove down to inquire after his father. He saw Franklin in his office for a short time and came out weeping. The report went around that Colonel Astor was lost.

Alone among the American newspapers the *New York Times* had rightly deduced, from the sudden cessation of her wireless signals, that the *Titanic* had foundered. While other papers hesitated to commit themselves, awaiting further news, the *New York Times* made systematic preparations to gather the survivors' stories. The early editions of the paper declared that the vessel was sinking and the women and children taking to the boats. The latest edition stated that she had sunk. On the

16th when the worst fears were confirmed the paper said gravely: 'Nothing is wanting to make the disaster memorable and conspicuous among the tragedies of the sea. This surpasses all, and holds dread supremacy as the most deplorable and afflicting calamity which has ever befallen seaborne passenger travel.'[13]

The inhabitants of New York were stirred to their depths. Hundred of weeping women and men frantic with anxiety besieged the White Star offices. The police reserves had to be called out, and it was only with the utmost difficulty that the almost hysterical crowds in that part of Broadway could be held in check. Franklin, who had not left the building since the first intimation of the diasaster, was now on the verge of collapse. Little by little he revealed the terrible truth to a party of journalists who had forced their way into his office. That night the relatives and friends of the passengers motored in evening dress from the opera and the theatres to the White Star building; some of the women were sobbing unrestrainedly.

During the next few days the nation-wide outcry against the White Star Line was accompanied by irate criticism of the *Carpathia* for her long-continued silence, which infuriated the press; in their exasperation at the blank wall presented by her wireless office the staff of the shore station at Siasconsett became almost abusive; not one syllable of information could they get out of MPA despite all their pleas and appeals.[14] Even a personal enquiry from President Taft remained unanswered. Washington lay under a black pall of gloom. Flags flew at half-mast all over the United States. Wherever men gathered together, the tragedy of the *Titanic* was the only subject discussed. In New York crowds of people still hung around the White Star Company's office in Broadway. Macy's great store was closed, as were also H. B. Harris's theatres.

On the 17th an official announcement came from Washington that a special sub-committee, under Senator William Alden Smith, was to be set up by the Senate to inquire into the circumstances of the disaster. Meanwhile the United States Navy had intercepted 'Yamsi's' ingenuous telegram to hold the *Cedric*; with the result that Smith set out immediately for New York to warn Ismay that he must not attempt to leave the country. 'I made up my mind,' declared the Senator grimly, 'that Mr Ismay and the members of his crew would have to stay here and make certain explanations to the American people.'

The *Carpathia* continued obdurate to the end: on the night of the 18th, as she entered New York Harbour, she was surrounded by tugs from whose decks reporters shouted inquiries through megaphones to her unresponsive bridge. Captain Rostron had no intention of allowing the rescued passengers to be harassed by a horde of ruthless pressmen lusting for lurid details. One reporter did succeed in scrambling on board; but he was held a close prisoner on the bridge until the liner docked.

As the *Carpathia* approached New York public excitement rose to fever heat. In the vicinity of the river front a seething mass of humanity—totalling several tens of thousands of people—were awaiting the *Carpathia's* arrival in the pouring rain. From time to time the police cordons that were striving to hold the vast throng back from the river were swept aside by sheer weight of numbers. Squadrons of mounted patrolmen ruthlessly rode down detached groups of half-crazed people who were struggling to get yet closer to the pier. The women, hysterical and uncontrollable, were dealt with as harshly as the men. The tension and expectancy became almost unendurable. At last the rescue ship could be seen silhouetted against the blaze of electric signs on the Jersey shore; and the excitement redoubled. As the *Carpathia* with her escort of tugs came slowly alongside the Cunard pier, every press photographer on the quayside let off his flashlamp. Amid an explosion of magnesium 'bombs' the gangways were pushed across and the disembarkation began.

Down the gangways, before the gaze of a tense and expectant throng of relatives assembled on the pier, slowly filed the survivors of the great disaster: the rich and the poor, the distinguished and the obscure, the hale and the ailing. A large proportion of that sorrowful procession were women—including more than seventy widows. First off the *Carpathia* came Dr Frauenthal and his wife, who, without a word to anyone, quickly entered a waiting automobile and were driven away;

Mrs Cornell and her two sisters, all hatless, were met by Mr Cornell; Mrs Astor, pale-faced and silent, was met by her stepson, Vincent Astor, and the Colonel's secretary, who hurried her off in a limousine; Sir Cosmo and Lady Duff-Gordon were also among those who were recognized and reported by the watchful pressmen. Among the children and infants in the throng were young Bobo Washington Dodge, his small person swathed from head to foot in folds of white wool, jigging with delight at the blaze of magnesium flares, and the Allison baby, Travers, cradled in his nurse's arms. Last off the *Carpathia* came the steerage passengers, many of them in pitiable condition: the women frequently without wraps and the few male survivors among them poorly and insufficiently clad.

Unnoticed in the darkness, a slim, dark-haired man hurried on board the *Carpathia* and went up to the wireless cabin, where Bride was still busy at the transmitting key, his feet bound up in voluminous bandages. The man took the young operator's hand and shook it fervently. It was Guglielmo Marconi, to whose epoch-making achievement so many of the survivors owed their lives.

Chapter 15

Senator Smith

The riotous scenes enacted on the waterfront of New York on the *Carpathia*'s arrival with the survivors of the disaster was paralleled by the furious press activity which raged throughout the United States. Every important paper in the country came out with full front page stories. Day after day the screaming headlines appeared. Terrible as were the true circumstances of the catastrophe, they paled before the lurid presentation of the event by the fertile imagination of the American journalist. No report was too wild and improbable for its eager propagation by the Yellow Press. It was said that Captain Smith had been intoxicated at the time; that Murdoch in remorse and despair had shot himself on the bridge; that certain officers had fired point-blank into a crowd of terror-maddened passengers; that people in the steerage had been locked below and left to drown like rats.

The Hearst group of papers—the *New York American*, the *Boston American*, the *Chicago American*, the *Journal*, and the *Evening Journal*—with the fervent backing of the Irish, German, and other anti-British elements in the States, had by now worked themselves up into a crescendo of passionate indignation. The *Titanic* became a semi-political issue. Everything British was ridiculed and vilified, while German ships and German mariners were held up for respect and admiration. There was an insistent demand for preventative measures to make such a future disaster impossible.

Wildly exaggerated as were these effusions of the Yellow Press, there was a solid substratum of truth in some of the charges. There was no gainsaying the justice of the indictment made by the *New York Tribune*—an indictment which had also been made by the *New York American* and other less moderate journals. 'There were no preparations for an emergency,' said the *Tribune*. 'There was no drilling of the crew. There was no slackening of speed. The Captain himself did not go upon the bridge as the fatal time approached when he expected to meet ice. There was no special lookout set. As heedlessly as though no such thing as an iceberg had ever been heard of the ship went rushing to her doom.' 'On current Atlantic liners there is carried on at the same time the businesses of navigation and hotel-keeping. It does not do to mix them up. Navigation on the *Titanic*,' commented *Harper's Weekly* severely, 'seemed to have dropped into second place.' A Canadian opinion is also worth quoting. 'The *Titanic*,' declared the Ottawa *Evening Citizen*, 'had been advertised as an "express-train boat" which would leave and arrive on schedule, and with whose operation "nothing would interfere".'

From the outset American public opinion fastened on J. Bruce Ismay as the scapegoat-in-chief. Perhaps the sternest verdict of all was that passed by the great naval historian, Rear-Admiral A. T. Mahan, on the Chairman of the White Star Line. 'I hold,' Mahan wrote in the *Evening Post*, 'that under the conditions, so long as there was a soul that could be saved, the obligation lay upon Mr Ismay that that one person and not he should have been in the boat.' On the 19th Senator Rayner launched a violent attack on Ismay in the Senate as 'criminally responsible for this appalling tragedy'; he ended by actually demanding a criminal prosecution. An immense area of space in the American press was devoted to the luckless 'Yamsi', most of it totally untrue or else greatly exaggerated. He was accused of dictating to the Captain, of trying to make a record passage, and even of putting on woman's clothes in order to get into a boat.

A couple of first class ladies who had lost their husbands in the disaster and were incensed at having to 'doss down' in blankets in the Cunarder's dining saloon appear to have started these stories on their rounds.

'I know many women who slept on the floor in the smoking-room,' Mrs Lucien P. Smith declared, 'while Mr Ismay occupied the best room on the *Carpathia*, being in the centre of the boat, with every attention, and a sign on the door, "Please do not knock".' 'Better a thousand times a dead John B.

Thayer,' observed Mrs Widener bitterly, 'than a living J. Bruce Ismay.'[1]

Away in his great mansion in Philadelphia, old Peter Widener (himself a director of the White Star Line and one of the main financial pillars of the International Mercantile Marine Company) growled: 'He will have to give an account to me if George does not turn up alive. . . .'[2]

'Mr Ismay,' said the *New York American*, 'cares for nobody, but himself. He cares only for his own body, for his own stomach, for his own pride and profit. He passes through the most stupendous tragedy untouched and unmoved. He leaves his ship to sink with its powerless cargo of lives and does not care to lift his eyes. He crawls through unspeakable disgrace to his own safety, seizes upon the best accommodation in the *Carpathia* to hold communion with his own unapproachable conduct.'

On the editorial page of the same journal there was a savage cartoon of J. Bruce Ismay crouching in one of the boats, the sinking liner just visible in the background, with the caption, 'Laurels of Infamy for J. *Brute* Ismay', and the scornful inscription below: 'It is respectfully suggested that the emblem of the White Star Line be changed from a White Star to a White Liver'.

'The American press,' the British Ambassador in Washington declared, 'has been perfectly hysterical over the disaster, and has published the wildest and most untruthful statements without taking any trouble to justify the same. The particular butt has been Mr Bruce Ismay, whose conduct has been savagely criticized.'

The outcry in the American press was reflected to a lesser degree in the British. 'So far as Britain is concerned,' the *Shipping World* had remarked complacently, 'no explanation is required from an Ismay.' That might well have been the attitude of the shipping interest; but it was certainly not the feeling of the country at large. 'Someone,' *John Bull* roundly declared, 'ought to hang over this *Titanic* business.' The forceful editor of that journal, Horatio Bottomley, delivered an admirable speech in the House of Commons. Scarcely four months earlier, *John Bull* had warned its readers of the inadequacy of the life-saving equipment in the *Olympic*; observing that, if the vessel foundered, her boats would only have been able to take off about one thousand passengers, and '*2,000 souls must have gone to the bottom of the Ocean*'. Bottomley now denounced the Board of Trade for having allowed obsolete regulations to remain in force for so many years. With regard to Ismay, he had evidently been thinking along the same lines as Mahan, and summed up the matter succinctly in his editorial. 'You,' *John Bull* apostrophized Ismay, 'were the one person on board who, as Chairman of the White Star Line, had a large pecuniary interest in the voyage, and your place was at the Captain's side till every man, woman, and child was safely off the ship. The humblest emigrant in the steerage had more moral right to a seat in the lifeboat than you.'

The staider and more responsible journals in Great Britain deprecated all this flood of invective and urged the public to suspend judgment until the full facts were known. The *Morning Post*, the *Daily Chronicle*, the *Pall Mall Gazette*, and a few others demanded fair play for Ismay. It was represented by this section of the press that the latter had done all that could be reasonably expected of him, and that there was no moral obligation on him to go down with the ship.

'At the same time,' observed *Truth*, 'I cannot help regarding it as "providential" that the chairman of the company happened to be standing where he was at the moment when the last boat— or was it the last but one?—left the ship, and there were no women or children at hand to claim the place into which he was thus enabled to jump.'

The truth was, that both in the boardroom and on board ship Ismay had been accustomed to exercise all the privileges of his position; but he had not shown himself nearly so ready to shoulder its responsibilities. All the senior officers of the *Titanic*, save one, had been lost; as had also his own secretary and butler. Ismay had survived. It can be said with confidence that if, instead of taking to the boats, he had stood on the bridge with Captain Smith at the end, there would have been no such angry storm of criticism as that which now assailed the Line and its Chairman.

For Ismay this was the beginning of the end. Never again

would he stride confidently down James Street with his friend and colleague, Harold A. Sanderson, on his way to the head office of the Line at No. 30. Never again would he dominate the Board in his old high-handed style. His continued presence at the head of affairs was felt to be a handicap and embarrassment; opposition to Ismay gathered head; and the Line presently hove its Jonah overboard. As one of the principal shipping magnates of Europe, Ismay was finished. He eventually relinquished most of his business interests and withdrew to a remote corner of western Ireland.[3]

For the White Star Line also it was the beginning of the end. The reconstruction of the *Olympic* which was set in train in the ensuing months was achieved only at a ruinous cost. The influential shipping journal *Fairplay* allowed that 'the responsibility resting upon them is very great, and such as will probably entail a heavy punishment in diminished public confidence and support'. As was to be expected, a lot of passenger traffic was immediately transferred to the rival Cunard Line, whose proud boast it was never to have lost the life of a single passenger. It is worth recalling that one of W. T. Stead's friends, *à propos* of the former's spiritualistic leanings, commented gruffly, 'A pity his spirits didn't warn him not to risk that crossing—he should have travelled by Cunard'.

The *Titanic* disaster which had brought ruin to Ismay had given Captain Rostron of the *Carpathia* the opportunity of his life. 'It was then,' he declared in after years, 'that I got my feet firmly planted on the ladder of success.' The following spring he went to Washington to receive from the hands of President Taft the Congressional Medal of Honour, with the thanks of Congress—the highest tribute which the American Government could bestow. The Captain and his wife were royally fêted throughout the United States. A few years later he was appointed to command the *Mauretania*. He had become one of the most distinguished figures in the British merchant service.

The disaster brought universal fame and honour to Guglielmo Marconi. 'Those who had been saved,' the Postmaster-General said truly, 'had been saved through one man—Mr Marconi.' The London *Times*, which had been behind Marconi from the beginning, lauded him to the skies. *Punch* was another of his panegyrists. (After the rescue of several hundreds from the blazing hull of the *Volturno* the following year, Mr Punch was to congratulate Marconi with the words, '*Many hearts bless you today, sir. The world's debt to you grows fast.*') The great American inventor, Thomas Alva Edison, sent him a telegram of congratulation. It was probably the proudest moment of Marconi's career. The highest tributes were showered upon him from all parts of the world. The value and importance of the marvellous new invention had been demonstrated in a manner beyond all possible doubt.

'We owe it to patient research in a delicate and difficult branch of science,' *The Times* declared, 'that the *Titanic* was able with wonderful promptitude to make known her distress and to summon assistance. But for wireless telegraphy the disaster might have assumed proportions which at present we cannot measure, and we should have known nothing of its occurrence for an indefinite period. Many a well-found ship has in fact disappeared in those berg-haunted waters without leaving a sign to indicate her fate.'

The rapid expansion of radio communication at sea occasioned by the disaster meant vastly increased opportunities for the young operators in the service of the Marconi Marine. The demand for operators now exceeded the supply. From this time on, in fact, the wireless operator gradually came into his own; and his status and emoluments steadily improved. The Marconi Marine's shares rocketed. Formerly they had been virtually unsaleable at 10s or 12s; then, when Godfrey Isaacs took over the business side of the new enterprise in 1910, they had slowly risen; and as a result of the radio boom consequent upon the disaster they now stood at £9 and £10. In America the Marconi Company's shares also soared. The first Marconi school for wireless operators was opened in New York later in the year. The circulation of the *Marconigraph* shot up to about 20,000 weekly, an unprecedented figure—another sign of the times. Within the next few years radio components were on sale in the department stores of New York.

The night of April 14th had also given Maggie Brown the opportunity to show herself at her best and bravest. The Impossible Mrs Brown had now become the Unsinkable Mrs Brown;

she was courted by reporters and photographers; even in her home town, the social acceptance which had eluded her for twenty years was hers by right at last; the apotheosis was complete when she sat down on the right of her hostess at a dinner-party given in her honour by Mrs Crawford Hill, the reigning queen of the Thirty-Six Best Families of Denver, 'the Sacred Thirty-Six'.[4]

In reply to Senator Smith's ultimatum, Ismay had at once agreed that he and the other witnesses required should give evidence at the Inquiry. On the morning following the *Carpathia*'s return to New York, the Senator and his colleagues began their investigations. The Inquiry opened in the Waldrof-Astoria Hotel in New York; on the 22nd, however, it was transferred to Washington, where the bulk of the evidence was taken.

It was a heavy blow to British national pride; and questions were asked in the House of Commons about the forcible detention of these witnesses. But James Bryce, our Ambassador in Washington, expressed his whole-hearted approval of the compliance of Ismay and the others with the Senate's decision. 'Their offer to give evidence,' said the Ambassador decidedly, 'was the wisest course to take in view of the state of public feeling here at present.' He added, that he had instructed the Naval Attaché to attend the Inquiry.[5]

The British press expressed surprise and concern at the idea of the American Senate holding an Inquiry on one of our ships. 'The Senate was, of course, quite within its constitutional rights in doing this,' the *Shipping World* observed soberly; 'nevertheless, an Inquiry into the loss of a British ship by another Power has never before taken place.' 'Though why,' wrote Joseph Conrad wrathfully in the *English Review*, 'an officer of the British merchant service should answer the questions of any king, emperor, autocrat, or senator of any foreign Power (as to an event in which a British ship alone was concerned, and which did not even take place in the territorial waters of the Power) passes my understanding. The only authority he is bound to answer is the Board of Trade.' The *Morning Post* was doubtful about the value of an investigation conducted by such a body as the Senate Sub-Committee; and the *Pall Mall Gazette* had no confidence at all in Smith. 'There is,' commented the latter journal, 'a general consensus of opinion that the worthy Senator is not quite the man for the post, his ignorance of the sea and shipping being quite obvious.'

Ismay was the first witness to be called. He was questioned by Smith and the other Senators at considerable length. It was unfortunate for all concerned that his demeanour during the proceedings enhanced the unfavourable impression he had already made on many Americans. Ismay's manner at the Inquiry appeared affected and supercilious to the spectators and he rashly showed a good deal of amusement at the abyssmal ignorance of his inquisitors concerning certain technical matters. Smith indeed got into a terrible tangle over the problems of tonnage, registry, and marine insurance. The Inquiry was not well managed. The questions put to the witness were badly framed, disjointed, and sometimes quite irrelevant. Certain Senators made no attempt to conceal their hostility to Ismay, which he not unnaturally resented.

William Alden Smith was a man of humble origins, who, starting his political career as a page-boy in the Michigan House of Representatives, had arrived in the Senate by way of Congress and the bar. He was described by Bryce in a dispatch to Sir Edward Grey as 'one of the most unsuitable persons who could have been charged with an investigation of this nature'. Bryce said that he had discussed the Senate Committee's Inquiry with the President and that Taft had told him that the Senate would pay no attention to him; they would stand on their rights, Taft declared, and he could do nothing with them. The President was of opinion that as long as Smith thought it would keep him in the headlines the Inquiry would go on.

Within a week of the opening of the Inquiry there came a startling new development. On April 19th the *Californian* had docked at Boston. It was then given out by the Master that, on the night of the 14th, they had been about thirty miles from the scene of the disaster and had heard and seen nothing. But it appeared that among the officers and men there had been a great deal of talk, as well as long conferences in the Master's room; presently some of the talk began to get abroad, notwithstanding that Lord had told reporters that 'Sailors will say almost anything when they are ashore'; and on the 24th one of the hands, a donkeyman called Ernest Gill, went before a notary public and swore an affidavit which directly contradicted the Master's statement.

'On the night of April 14th I was on duty from 8 p.m. until 12 in the engine-room. At 11.56 I came on deck. The stars were shining brightly. It was very clear and I could see for a long distance. The ship's engines had been stopped since 10.30, and she was drifting amid floe ice. I looked over the rail on the starboard side and saw the lights of a very large steamer about ten miles away. I could see her broadside lights. I watched her for fully a minute. They could not have helped but see from the bridge and look-out.

'It was not twelve o'clock and I went to my cabin. I woke my mate William Thomas. He heard the ice crunching alongside the ship and asked: "Are we in the ice?" I replied, "Yes; but it must be clear off to the starboard, for I saw a big vessel going full speed. She looked as if she might be a big German."

'I turned in, but could not sleep. In half an hour I turned out, thinking to smoke a cigarette. Because of the cargo I could not smoke 'tween decks, so I went on deck again.

' I had been on deck about ten minutes when I saw a white rocket about ten miles away on the starboard side. I thought it must be a shooting star. In seven or eight minutes I saw distinctly a second rocket in the same place, and I said to myself, "That must be a vessel in distress".

'It was not my business to notify the bridge or the lookouts; but they could not have helped but see them.

'I turned in immediately after, supposing that the ship would pay attention to the rockets.

'I knew no more until I was awakened at 6.40 by the chief engineer, who said, "Turn out to render assistance. The *Titanic* has gone down".

'I exclaimed and leaped from my bunk. I went on deck and found the vessel under way and proceeding full speed. She was clear of the field ice, but there were plenty of bergs about.

'I went on watch and heard the second and fourth engineers in conversation. Mr J. C. Evans is the second and Mr Wooten is the fourth. The second was telling the fourth that the third officer had reported rockets had gone up in his watch. I knew then that it must have been the *Titanic* I had seen.

'The second officer added that the captain had been notified by the apprentice officer, whose name, I think, is Gibson, of the rockets.

The skipper had told him to Morse to the vessel in distress. Mr Stone, the second navigating officer, was on the bridge at the time, said Mr Evans.

'I overheard Mr Evans say that more lights had been shown and more rockets went up. Then, according to Mr Evans, Mr Gibson went to the captain again and reported more rockets. The skipper told him to continue to Morse until he got a reply. No reply was received.

'The next remark I heard the second pass was, "Why in the devil didn't they wake the wireless man up?" The entire crew of the steamer have been talking among themselves about the disregard of the rockets. I personally urged several to join me in protesting against the conduct of the captain, but they refused, because they feared to lose their jobs.

'A day or two before the ship reached port the skipper called the quartermaster, who was on duty at the time the rockets were discharged, into his cabin. They were in conversation about three-quarters of an hour. The quartermaster declared that he did not see the rockets.

'I am quite sure that the *Californian* was less than twenty miles from the *Titanic*, which the officers report to have been our position. I could not have seen her if she had been more than ten miles distant, and I saw her very plainly.

'I have no ill-will toward the captain or any officer of the ship, and I am losing a profitable berth by making this statement. I am actuated by the desire that no captain who refuses or neglects to give aid to a vessel in distress should be able to hush up the men,'[6]

Thus the donkeyman had well and truly 'blown the gaff'. Blown it with a stridency which has reverberated to the present day and started on its rounds a rancorous controversy which even now, more than a half a century later, shows no sign of ending. From the point of view of the champions and supporters of Captain Lord, Ernest Gill, the donkeyman, would seem to be Public Enemy No. 1. For, if he had not taken the initiative in the matter, the equivocal part played by the *Californian* on the night of the disaster might never have become known.

As a result of these disclosures Gill was there and then summoned to Washington to testify before the Senate Committee; and on the following day, April 25th, the *Boston American* printed the affidavit in full together with an editorial in which it was stated that Gill had repeated these allegations in the presence of four members of the crew, and, further, that they had been corroborated in a confidential communication to the *Boston American* from one of the ship's officers. The names of the four men and the officer were not disclosed.

'The *Californian* of the Leyland Line,' the journal declared, 'was the ship which was sighted by the *Titanic* but which refused to respond to her signals of distress. Captain Lord of the *Californian* thought it was some small vessel and refused to risk his ship by sending her through the ice at night to the rescue.'

The American press could now vent its wrath upon another subject besides Ismay and the White Star Line. For a while the angry headlines embraced Captain Lord and the *Californian*; and, later, they discovered yet another promising quarry in the occupants of No. 1 Emergency Boat. The papers began to publish interesting stories about the Duff-Gordons. But Ismay remained the principal scapegoat.

Smith had wisely insisted on holding the Inquiry without a moment's delay. By this means, while the survivors were still badly shaken by the catastrophe and disposed to be less cautious and reserved than they were later on, a number of significant facts, suppressions, and evasions emerged which otherwise might never have been brought to light.

For instance, Pitman mentioned that the canvas bucket for taking the temperature of the water that Sunday night was missing and that an ordinary tin bucket had been used instead. Bride was silent when asked if he knew whether Phillips had received the final ice-warning from the *Californian*.[7] Lightoller testified that the engineers and many others as well were still down below at the end and were never seen on deck at all (whereas many years later when he wrote his reminiscences he declared that they had all come up and that he had talked with some of them). Lightoller tried to make out that Ismay had been unceremoniously bundled into a boat by the Chief Officer (a statement which was refuted by Ismay's own evidence). Lightoller never breathed a word about the ice message from the *Mesaba* about which Phillips had told him while they were standing on the upturned Engelhardt.

Among other things it was established at the Inquiry that

the numbers of the passengers, especially of the women passengers, in the various boats were often exaggerated by the quartermasters and others in charge. The following is a good example of the tendency to exculpate themselves in this and other regards.

'How many did you have all told?' Senator Perkins asked the A.B. who had been put in charge of No. 1 boat.

'I would not say for certain,' Symons responded: 'it was fourteen or twenty. Then we were ordered away.'

'You did not return to the ship again?'

'Yes; we came back after the ship was gone and saw nothing.'

'Did you rescue anyone that was in the water?'

'No sir; we saw nothing when we came back.'

The Senator returned to this point some time later. 'Did you say your boat could take more?' he asked him. 'Did you make any effort to get them?'

'Yes,' said Symons. 'We came back, but when we came back we did not see anybody or hear anybody.'

'And so you made no attempt to save any other people after you were ordered to pull away from the ship by someone?'

'I pulled off,' said Symons doggedly, 'and came back after the ship had gone down.'

'And then there were no people there?'

'No, sir; I never saw any.'[8]

As will later appear, all this part of Symons's evidence was unsatisfactory, misleading, and untrue.

From beginning to end the Inquiry was vitiated by the utter lack of technical knowledge on the part of Senator Smith, who usually acted as spokesman for the Committee. Again and again the Inquiry would traverse the same ground twice—occasionally more than twice. It was Smith's almost incredible ignorance of everything pertaining to shipping and the sea which was responsible for many an impasse and fiasco in the course of the proceedings. In his examination of Lowe he got into a hopeless muddle over matters of seamanship and navigation. The fact that Bride had received the sum of $1,000 from the press appeared to worry him inordinately; he also took umbrage at the fact that the former had refused to work with an U.S.N. operator. Smith did not lack ability as a lawyer; but in the situation in which he found himself his legal knowledge and experience was of small avail. Garrulous, pompous, and naïve by turns, he was a heaven-sent subject for the cartoonist and columnist. The sheer fatuity of some of the questions he put to witnesses must have created an all-time record.

The Senator's more spectacular lapses became known on both sides of the ocean as 'Smithisms'. For example, he would particularly inquire whether the liner sank by the bow or by the head and why the passengers could not have saved themselves by taking refuge in the watertight compartments (whereon he was gleefully acclaimed as 'Watertight Smith'). When Captain Lord of the *Californian* revealed that he had stopped his engines in mid-ocean, Smith immediately wanted to know if he had *anchored* there. When Lightoller related how a funnel had crashed down on top of the throng struggling in the water, Smith asked anxiously whether it had hurt anyone. In his limitless thirst for information, Smith presently inquired what icebergs were made of. 'Ice,' explained Lowe patiently.

As the proceedings dragged on, the *Titanic* Inquiry fell into disrepute. Many Americans felt that it was making them appear ridiculous in the eyes of the world. Several of Smith's colleagues had threatened to resign. There was increasing criticism of the Senator in the press. The *New York Times* called him 'the preposterous Smith,' and inquired whether Michigan had elected him for a joke. It was rumoured in London that he had been offered an engagement at the Hippodrome. *Syren and Shipping* doubted whether he were quite sane. Many of the British witnesses were urgently needed for the forthcoming Inquiry in London. But Smith, like Pharoah of old, seemed loth to let the people go.

'In Washington,' says Lightoller, 'our men were herded into a second-rate boarding house, which might have suited some, but certainly not such men as formed the crew of the *Titanic*. In the end they point-blank refused to have anything more to do with either the Inquiry or the people, whose only achievement was to make our Seamen, Quartermasters, and Petty Officers look utterly ridiculous.'[9] In point of fact, it took the united efforts of the British Ambassador, A. S. Franklin, and Lightoller himself to restore peace.

The same writer went on to characterize the American Inquiry as a complete farce, 'wherein all the traditions and customs of the sea were continuously and persistently flouted'.

'A schoolboy would blush at Mr Smith's ignorance,' remarked the *Morning Post*. 'While Mr Smith puts his farcical questions, and flashlights are flared that photographers may get pictures of the witnesses, while outside the American Press retails the latest lie, the latest slander, about British seamen, honest Americans will feel with shame that not merely the White Star Line, but American civilization itself is on trial, and that the country is coming worse out of the ordeal than the company.'

The report of the Committee was finally presented to the Senate on May 28th. It was unexpectedly moderate and temperate in its conclusions, and to that extent came as something of a surprise to the British Ambassador, who, throughout these proceedings, had been an unsparing critic of Smith and his colleagues.

In the speech which had accompanied the presentation of the report, however, Smith (as it were) pulled out all the stops and let himself go. He spoke for over an hour to the Senators on the floor of the chamber and to the galleries above crowded with ladies in summer finery; and it was significant that not one of the Senators left the chamber till after he had finished— a compliment they rarely paid to one of their number. His speech was partly read and partly extemporized. Whatever his critics might say or think about him, there was no questioning the man's absolute sincerity. Nor can there be any doubt that Smith's speech made a strong impression on the audience, who were noticeably moved by it. The general consensus of opinion among the Senators was that some, at least, of Smith's strictures had been amply justified. Setting aside the Senator's extravagances and hyperboles, various points of the highest importance had been established.

At ten o'clock on that fateful Sunday evening the latest maritime creation was cutting its first pathway through the North Atlantic Ocean with scarcely a ripple to retard its progress. . . .

No drill, or station practice, or helpful discipline disturbed the tranquillity of that voyage, and when the crisis came a state of absolute unpreparedness stupified both passengers and crew, and in their despair, the ship went down, carrying as needless a sacrifice of noble women and brave men as ever clustered about the Judgment Seat in a single moment of passing time.

We shall leave to the honest judgment of England its painstaking chastisement of the British Board of Trade, to whose laxity the world is largely indebted for this awful fatality. Of contributing causes there were very many. In the face of warning signals, speed was increased and messages of danger seemed to stimulate her to action rather than to persuade her to fear.

Captain Smith knew the sea, and his clear eye and steady hand had often guided his ship through dangerous paths; for forty years the Storm King sought in vain to vex him and menace his craft; not once before in all his honourable career was pride humbled or his vessel maimed. . . .

The mystery of his indifference to danger, when other and less pretentious vessels doubled their look-out or stopped their engines, finds no reasonable hypothesis in conjecture of speculation; science in shipbuilding was supposed to have attained perfection and to have spoken her last word; mastery of the ocean had at last been achieved; but over-confidence seems to have dulled the faculties usually so alert.

With the atmosphere literally charged with warning signals and wireless messages registering their last appeal, the stokers in the engine-room fed their fires with fresh fuel, registering in that dangerous place the vessel's fastest speed.

At that moment the ice stole upon her hard as steel and struck her in a vital spot, while the last command of the officer of the watch, distracted by the sudden appearance of extreme danger and in his effort to avert disaster, sharply turned aside the prow, the least dangerous point of contact, exposing the temple to the blow. . . .

After severely censuring Captain Lord of the *Californian* the Senator said:

'I am well aware from the testimony of the captain of the *Californian* that he deluded himself with the idea that there was a ship between the *Titanic* and the *Californian*, but there was no ship seen there at daybreak and no intervening rockets were seen by anyone on the *Titanic*, although they were looking longingly for such a sign and only saw the white light of the

Californian, which was flashed the moment the ship struck and taken down when the vessel sank. A ship would not have been held there if it had been eastbound, and she could not have gone west without passing the *Californian* on the north or the *Titanic* on the south. That ice floe held but two ships—the *Titanic* and the *Californian*.'[10]

The verdict of the Senators was presently endorsed by public opinion generally throughout the United States. Even the more moderate section of the press was loud in its condemnation of the system and policy which it held responsible for the tragedy. 'England,' declared the *New York Times*, 'has been struck a blow in its tenderest and proudest spot. The mistress of the seas is indicted alike in its governmental administration and its seamanship, upon which the primacy of the island depends.' Several American papers urged the United States no longer to trust to foreign shipping regulations.

Across the ocean, an influential section of the British press continued to be either critical or hostile. 'Although the report sounds sensible,' said the *Daily Express*, 'Senator Smith's grotesque oration deprives it of much of its value.' 'Senator Smith,' the *Daily Mirror* observed, 'has again made himself ridiculous in the eyes of British seamen. British seamen know something about ships. Smith does not.' The *Daily Mail* compared Smith's speech with Martin Chuzzlewit's programme oration and said that 'the Senator had buried a grave and terrible event beneath a mountain of foolish fustian'. 'The whole speech,' declared the *Morning Post*, 'in fact is totally lacking in the judical and unbiased spirit which should have marked such an utterance. Throughout it is animated by the desire to strike a sensational note, and to find occasion for lavish and indiscriminate censure.' The standpoint of *The Times*, for which there was much to be said, was that it was the whole system of modern transatlantic travel, rather than any particular individual or individuals, that was to blame. 'Great liners are every day going at full speed across the danger zone of the Atlantic, and so long as nothing happens the public only encourages them in the most effective of all ways to go yet faster if they can. The postal authorities of all nations are eager for the rapid transit of their mails, and do not particularly inquire into the conditions under which rapidity is secured. Business men become eloquent over a few hours' delay, and people bent only on pleasure are in no less hurry.'

But there were a number of journals which took another point of view. The *Daily News* admitted that some of the conclusions arrived at in the report were irresistible and very disturbing. G. K. Chesterton, writing in the *Illustrated London News*, was one of the first to point out that, if the American attitude to the catastrophe was open to criticism, so, no less, was the British. 'It is perfectly true, as the English papers are saying, that some American papers are what we should call both vulgar and vindictive; they set the pack in full cry upon a particular man; that they are impatient of delay and eager for savage decisions; that the flags under which they march are often the rags of a reckless and unscrupulous journalism. All this is true; but if these be the American faults, it is all the more necessary to emphasize the opposite English faults. Our national evil is exactly the other way: it is to hush everything up; it is to damp everything down; it is to leave every great affair unfinished, to leave every enormous question unanswered.' *John Bull* had likewise no illusions about the probable result of an official inquiry in this country. 'We need scarcely point out that the scope of such an inquiry is strictly limited by statute, and that its sole effect will be to shelve the scandal till public feeling has subsided. *What* a game it is!' The *Review of Reviews*, which, it will be remembered, had lost its great editor in the disaster, was another that refused to join in the general outburst against Smith. 'We prefer the ignorance of Senator Smith to the knowledge of Mr Ismay!' the journal frankly admitted. 'Experts have told us that the *Titanic* was unsinkable—we prefer ignorance to such knowledge!' It was of opinion that the American Inquiry had been of the greatest public value—'It has given us an example of energetic action, a mass of fact and opinion has been brought out, and all the more effectively because there was the minimum of delay.' 'It is right that the whole truth should be known,' the *Economist* declared, 'and every reflecting person should be grateful to the American Senate for its prompt and searching inquiry.'

The Inquiry had drawn attention to the over-hasty inspection of the ship during her trials by the Board of Trade; to the wretched inadequacy of her life-saving apparatus—a fault arising directly from the antiquated regulations of the Board of Trade and the parsimonious instincts of shipowners; to the perfunctory and insufficient inspection on sailing day; to serious weaknesses in the construction of the vessel—the watertight compartments that were not, in point of fact, watertight at all; to the failure to supply the look-outs with binoculars; to the likelihood that Ismay's presence on board had something to do with her very high speed in the ice region; to the mismanagement in the loading and lowering of some, at least, of the lifeboats. The Inquiry had exposed the over-confidence of all concerned: above all, that of the Master, Captain Smith, since, despite all the warnings of ice in the vicinity that were coming in, the *Titanic* had been running at a higher speed than at any previous stage of the voyage. Finally, the Inquiry had focused attention on the failure of the *Californian* to respond to signals of distress 'in accordance with the dictates of humanity, international usage, and the requirements of the law'.

Chapter 16

The British Inquiry (1)

An observer at all familiar with the general operation of a British Official Inquiry involving, among other things, the conduct of a Department of State, might well have forecast, within reasonable limits of accuracy, what course that Inquiry was likely to follow.

It was only to be expected that the Inquiry would be directed towards the lessons to be learned from the disaster rather than the strict apportionment of blame; and that the really important and influential personages concerned would be dealt with very leniently. Certain of the more embarrassing issues might be conveniently sidetracked. At the same time, in view of the recent outcry in America, some awkward points would have to be handled cautiously. In the circumstances, certain strictures on both the Board of Trade and the White Star Line were probably inevitable. Many years after the principal professional witness at the Inquiry put his finger on the crux of the matter with unerring accuracy and summed up his own approach to these investigations with engaging candour.

'A washing of dirty linen,' Lightoller declared, 'would help no one. The B.O.T. had passed that ship as in all respects fit for sea, in every sense of the word, with sufficient margin of safety for everyone on board. Now the B.O.T. was holding an inquiry into the loss of that ship—hence the whitewash brush. Personally, I had no desire that blame should be attributed either to the B.O.T. or the White Star Line, though in all conscience it was a difficult task, when handled by some of the cleverest legal minds in England, striving tooth and nail to prove the inadequacy here, the lack there, when one had known, full well, and for many years, the ever-present possibility of such a disaster. I think in the end the B.O.T. and the White Star Line won.'[1]

Lord Mersey, formerly President of the Probate, Divorce, and Admiralty Division of the High Court, was appointed Commissioner to inquire into the wreck of the *Titanic*. He was a man of long and varied legal experience, who had also represented the Exchange Division of Liverpool from 1895 to 1897; and he had been on the Committee which whitewashed Dr Jamieson after the famous raid. His son, Captain the Hon. Clive Bigham, acted as secretary at the Inquiry.

On May 3rd the court began to sit in the London Scottish Drill Hall at Buckingham Gate, near the St James Park station of the District Railway. At the far end of the large hall, hung with sombre, dark maroon curtains, was the dais on which the Commissioner and his assessors were to sit. The dais was fronted by a broad sounding-board, for the accoustics of the place were very bad. In the centre of the hall were the tables for the counsel and press reporters. The witness stand was to the right of the dais and also covered by the sounding-board. Behind it stood a huge half-model of the *Titanic* with a white mark below its first funnel to indicate the point at which the vessel first struck the ice. The model, together with a great chart of the North Atlantic, occupied nearly half one side of the drill hall. The remaining space was filled with seats for the spectators, who also sat in the galleries.

Sir Rufus Isaacs (the Attorney-General), K.C., Sir John Simon (the Solicitor-General), K.C., Mr Butler Aspinall, K.C., Mr S. T. Rowlatt, and Mr Raymond Asquith appeared for the Board of Trade. Sir Robert Finlay appeared with a phalanx of supporting counsel for the White Star Line. Mr Thomas Scanlan appeared for the National Sailors' and Firemen's Union, Mr Clement Edwards for the Dockers' Union, Mr Harbinson for the third class passengers, Mr Henry Duke, K.C., for Sir Cosmo and Lady Duff-Gordon, and Mr C. Robertson Dunlop for the owners, Master, and officers of the *Californian*.

The Inquiry into the loss of the *Titanic* took place in the midst of one of those brilliant London seasons which preceded the First World War. The sense of drama was heightened by the contrast. Inside, through the narratives of eye-witnesses, was enacted, day by day, the slow, relentless unfolding of a tragedy unparalleled in the annals of the sea. On to the witness-stand advanced, one after the other, many of the principal *dramatis personae*: the men from the crow's nest in their seamen's jerseys, the firemen who had seen the water flooding into the hold through the breach opened by the iceberg, the quartermasters who had been on duty at the time of the collision, the stewards who had roused the passengers from their beds, and the officers who had paced the bridge on that memorable Sunday. Outside flowed on the busy life of London. The streets of the West End were gay with their striped summer awnings and window-boxes overbrimming with flowers. Already the lilacs and laburnums were coming into blossom. It was remarked that May was almost as warm as midsummer. The fashionable world was pouring into town, and the hotels were filling up. There were large attendances at Hurlingham and Ranelagh, and plenty of strollers in the Parks. On the 14th the King held his fourth Court at Buckingham Palace. On the same day there was a Benefit Performance at the Royal Opera House, Covent Garden, in aid of the *Titanic* Relief Fund.

From where they sat in court the ship's officers took note of their natural adversaries, the 'law sharks', with experienced mistrust. Mindful of their certificates, it behoved them to be careful—very careful indeed. Throughout all the intricacies of the Inquiry, they must remember they had to make the best case for themselves, the ship, and the Company. There was a well-tried stratagem which was usually resorted to on such occasions. That was to answer each question as it was put, with the utmost brevity, *and to say no more*. . . . Those beggars in the frock coats and shiny toppers would nobble an honest sailorman just as soon as look at him. If you gave them an inch, they would certainly take an ell. Don't let them lead you on. Give nothing away. Shut up like an oyster when necessary. . . .

The early stages of the Inquiry were chiefly concerned with the evidence of the look-out men, the quartermaster at the wheel, and the men in the stokehold; with the clearing away, loading, and lowering of the boats, and the actual sinking of the *Titanic*. All the matters under review were gone into in considerable detail. The first witnesses were Archie Jewell, a

9 The Boat Deck (*Photo: Popper*)

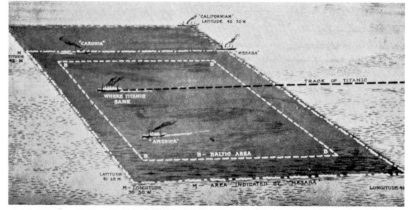

10 'The Fatal Oblong' (*Photo: Sphere*)

The *Rappahannock* in the icefield

11 C. H. Lightoller, Second Officer

Samuel Hemming, Lamp-trimmer

1. MR. V. CLARKE, OF LIVERPOOL.   2. MR. F. C. TAYLOR, OF CLAPHAM.
3. MR. G. KRINS, OF BRIXTON, SOMETIME OF THE RITZ HOTEL ORCHESTRA.   4. MR. W. HARTLEY (BANDMASTER), OF DEWSBURY.   5. MR. W. T. BRAILEY, OF NOTTING HILL.
6. MR. J. HUME, OF DUMFRIES.   7. MR. J. W. WOODWARD, OF HEADINGTON, OXON.

12   The Ship's Orchestra (*Photo: Illustrated London News*)

13 London hears the news (*Photo: Radio Times Hulton Picture Library*)

Captain Stanley Lord
(*Photo: Illustrated
London News*)

Children putting in pennies
(*Photo: Radio Times Hulton Picture Library*)

14 The witnesses from the *Californian* (*Photo: Illustrated London News*)

Lord Mersey (*right*) and his secretary arriving at the London Scottish Hall for the *Titanic* Inquiry. (*Photo: Radio Times Hulton Picture Library*)

15 The *Titanic* Inquiry. J. Bruce Ismay on the witness Stand (*Photo: Illustrated London News*)

16 *Titanic* off Queensland

look-out, and another A.B., Joseph Scarrott. Their narrations began with the clang of the alarm from the crow's nest. Scarrott's account of the rescue of some of the persons struggling in the water beside his boat caught the imagination of all the audience. They could almost see the mass of corpses floating in the ice-cold sea. One of the women listening burst into tears. Lord Mersey and his assessors were visibly moved. The Inquiry became even more interesting as its investigations continued, and witness after witness came forward to contribute his or her evidence. Sometimes the proceedings were humdrum and pedestrian in tempo, sometimes they were lively and dramatic to a degree. Sometimes the court was crowded with spectators, sometimes the attendance, apart from those whose duties obliged them to be there, was distinctly meagre. The accoustics of the hall, as has already been said, were very unsatisfactory, and it often happened that a witness was almost inaudible and had to be told to speak up.

In the course of the Inquiry there were certain days which were of outstanding interest.

On May 14th there was a larger attendance of the general public at Scottish Hall than at any of the previous sittings of the court. In anticipation of the appearance of Sir Cosmo and Lady Duff-Gordon a large number of fashionably dressed women had occupied seats in the hall; later in the day a good many men also dropped in and stood at the back of the seats. But the announcement was made that the Duff-Gordons had not yet returned from America, and the *Californian* evidence would be heard instead.

On his arrival at Scottish Hall Captain Stanley Lord was promptly 'snapped' by a press photographer. He was a tall, well-built man with a high forehead and distinctly autocratic features, attired in the customary shore-going rig of a British shipmaster, with bowler hat and tightly rolled umbrella. Under his arm he carried the ship's log.

The officers of the *Californian* and Cyril Evans, the wireless operator, who had brought his *procès verbal* with him, and Ernest Gill, the donkeyman, together with a few other members of the crew, were also present in court that day.

The questioning of Captain Lord by the Attorney-General

Sir Rufus Isaacs—one of the greatest advocates of his day—on the subject of the rockets sighted from the bridge of the *Californian* was close and sustained. It was followed with intense interest by everyone present. Captain Lord was not disposed to be communicative; his replies were noticeably terse and sometimes grudging; and this reticence inevitably provoked, not only the Attorney-General and the other counsel, but also the Commissioner, to further probing and still more pointed questions. The purpose of this questioning was to establish the fact that the rockets sent up by the unknown steamship lying in the vicinity of the *Californian* on the night of April 14th were not, and could not possibly have been, other than regular distress signals. Again and again Sir Rufus returned to this point.

'What did you think it was firing rockets for?'

'When? I did not know anything about these rockets until seven o'clock the next morning.'

'But you saw one fired?'

'I heard of one rocket. I did not see it fired.'

'You heard of one.'

'Yes.'

'That was before you went to the chart-room?'

'No, at a quarter past one.'

'Were you on deck then?'

'No.'

'Did you remain in the chart-room when you were told that a vessel was firing a rocket?'

Captain Lord said that he had remained in the chart-room, Sir Rufus, mystified by this apparent unconcern on the Captain's part, pressed him:

'I do not understand you. You knew, of course, that there was danger in this field of ice to steamers?'

'To a steamer steaming, yes.'

'You knew there was danger?'

'Yes.'

'That is why you stopped?'

'Yes.'

'And you knew also that this vessel, whatever it was, that you say had stopped?'

'Had stopped, yes.'

'What did you think this vessel was firing rockets for?'

'I asked the Second Officer. I said, Is that a company's signal? and he said he did not know.'

'Then that did not satisfy you?'

'No, it did not.'

'I mean whatever it was did not satisfy you that it was a company's signal?'

'It did not, but I had no reason to think it was anything else.'

At this point the Commissioner intervened with a number of inquiries of his own. He tried to find out the reasons for Captain Lord's continued inaction, which appeared to him inexplicable.

'That seems odd,' he observed to the Captain. 'You know that the vessel that was sending up this rocket was in a position of danger?'

'No, my Lord, I did not.'

'Well, danger if she moved.'

'If she moved, yes.'

'What did you think the rocket was sent up for?'

'Well, we had been trying to communicate with this steamer by Morse lamp from half-past eleven, and she would not reply.'

'This was a quarter past one?'

'Yes, we had tried at intervals from half-past eleven.'

'What did you think he was sending up a rocket for?'

'I thought it was acknowledging our signals, our Morse lamp. A good many steamers do not use the Morse lamp.'

'Have you ever said that before?'

'That has been my story right through—my impression right along.'

The Attorney-General resumed his examination. He pointed out that on the face of the evidence there must have been a strong presumption that the signals made by the other vessel were, in fact, distress signals.

'Just let me put this to you,' he said, 'When you asked him whether it was a company's signal he said he did not know. That would not satisfy you?'

'No.'

'Was it then you told him to Morse her and find out what ship it was?'

'Yes.'

'After the white rocket had been sent up?'

'After the white rocket had been sent up.'

'And did you tell him to send Gibson, the apprentice, down to let you know his reply?'

'Yes.'

'You did?'

'I did.'

'What was the message that Gibson brought down to you then?'

'That morning? I did not get it, not to my knowledge. I never got it.'

'You had seen the rocket or you heard of the rocket?'

'Yes.'

'You want to know what the rocket is?'

'Yes.'

'And you have failed?'

'Yes.'

'Then you say to him that Gibson was to come down and tell you what the result of the Morse signalling was?'

'Yes.'

'And then, I suppose, you remained in the chart-room?'

'I remained in the chart-room.'

So they were back where they started. They were once more up against a blank wall. Why was Captain Lord so extraordinarily reluctant to come out of the chart-room *and see for himself?* No reasonable explanation of this long-sustained inaction was ever to be forthcoming.

'Then, so far as you were concerned, you did not know at all what the rocket was for?'

'No.'

'And you remained in the chart-room?'

'Yes, I remained in the chart-room.'

'And you did nothing further?'

'I did nothing further myself.'

'If it was not a company's signal, must it not have been a distress signal?'

'If it had been a distress signal the officer on watch would have told me.'

Sir Rufus repeated:

'I say, if it was not a company's signal, must it not have been a distress signal?'

'Well, I do not know of any other signals but distress signals that are used at sea.'

'You do not expect at sea, where you were, to see a rocket unless it is a distress signal, do you?'

'We sometimes get these company's signals which resemble rockets; they do not shoot as high and they do not explode.'

'You have already told us that you were not satisfied that was a company's signal? You have told us that?'

'I asked the officer, was it a company's signal?'

The relentless questioning continued. Sir Rufus said:

'Then you were not satisfied it was a company's signal? You did think it was a company's signal?'

'I inquired, was it a company's signal.'

'But you had been told that he did not know?'

'He said he did not know.'

'Very well, that did not satisfy you?'

'It did not satisfy me.'

'Then if it was not that, it might have been a distress signal?'

'It might have been.'

'And you remained in the chart-room?'

'I remained in the chart-room.'

'Expecting Gibson, the apprentice, to come down and report to you?'

'Yes.'

'Gibson did come down?'

'So I understand.'

'But you know perfectly well that he came?'

'I know now.'

'Did you know then?'

'I did not.'

'I think you told us you heard Gibson open and close the door?'

'Yes.'

'And you said, What is it?'

'Yes.'

'And he said nothing?'

'He did not say anything.'

No other explanation. Captain Lord spoke as if it were a perfectly ordinary occurrence for a young apprentice to enter the Master's room in the dead of night, and then go away without saying a word.

'And you were expecting him to come down and tell you what the meaning of the rocket was?'

'But in the meantime I was asleep.'

The Commissioner interjected: 'Yes, but you were not asleep—at least, I suppose not—when you said to the boy, "What is it?"'

'I was wakened up by the opening of the door—the banging of the door.'[2]

The Commissioner presently put a question about this mysterious vessel which had been watched for hours by several on board the *Californian* and which Captain Lord still maintained was *not* the *Titanic*.

'Is the result of your evidence that you cannot suggest the name of any other passenger steamer that was in the neighbourhood of your vessel about midnight on April 14th?'

'No, I cannot.'

'You cannot suggest any other steamer that sent up rockets at one o'clock or between one and two in the morning of Monday, April 15th, except the *Titanic*?'

'No, I have not heard of any.'[3]

Later Scanlan, who represented North Sligo in the House of Commons, rose to cross-examine the Captain. For many years a journalist, he had recently been called to the Bar and was a clear and forcible speaker. He now endeavoured to ascertain why Captain Lord had not used his wireless to discover the identity of the unknown vessel and the reason for the rockets having been sent up.

'Would it not have been quite a simple thing for you at that time when you were in doubt as to what was the name of the ship, and as to what was the reason of her sending up rockets, to have wakened up your Marconi operator and asked him to speak to this ship?'

'It would if it had worried me a great deal,' was the Captain's rejoinder, 'but it did not worry me. I was still thinking of the company's signals.'

'At all events, now in the light of your experience', said Scanlan, 'would it not have been a prudent thing to do?'

'Well, we would have got the *Titanic*'s signals if we had done.'

'If you had done, you would, in all probability, have got the message from this vessel?'

'No, I do not think so. I am of opinion that steamer had not got wireless at all.'

'What reason have you for thinking that this steamer, a steamer which you say was, at all events, as big as your own, had not got wireless?'

'At eleven o'clock when I saw her the operator told me he had not got anything only the *Titanic*. I remarked then, "That is not the *Titanic*", judging from its size and the number of lights about it; and if he only had one ship, then it was not the *Titanic*. I do not see how he could still have that ship.'

'But as a mere matter of precaution, when you were in doubt and left word that someone was to come down to your cabin and give you a message, would not it have been a proper thing to have tried the experiment?'

'Well, I was waiting for further information. I had a responsible officer on the bridge who was finding this out for me.'[4]

The question which must have arisen in everyone's mind just then was, what on earth was the use of having a responsible officer on the bridge who was finding this out if the Master proceeded to lie down and go to sleep in the chart-room, so that when the apprentice came down with the 'further information' he could not take it in properly and promptly went to sleep again.

The Attorney-General recurred to the message, given by young Gibson to Captain Lord in the chart-room, from the Officer of the Watch. He said:

'I want to put this to you. Did not the boy deliver the message to you, and did not you inquire whether they were all white rockets?'

'I do not know; I was asleep.'

'Think. This is a very important matter.'

'It is. I recognize that.'

'It is much better to tell us what happened, Captain?'

'He came to the door, I understand. I have spoken to him very closely since. He said, I opened my eyes and said, "What is it?" and he gave me the message; and I said, "What time is it?" and he told me, and then I think he said I asked him whether there were any colours in the light.'

'That is what the boy said to you. You have questioned him a good many times since?'

'Yes, I have questioned him since.'

'Is he still an apprentice in your ship?'

'He is.'

The Commissioner said: 'Is he telling the truth?'

'Is the boy telling the truth?'

'Yes.'

'I do not know. I do not doubt it for a moment.'

The Attorney-General pressed this point. He said to the witness:

'Just think. You say you do not doubt it for a moment. Do you see what that means? That means that the boy did go to the chart-room to you. He did tell you about the rockets from the ship and you asked whether they were white rockets, and told him that he was to report if anything further occurred.'

'So he said. That is what he said.'

'Have you any reason to doubt that is true?'

'No; I was asleep.'

'Then do you mean you said this in your sleep to him, that he was to report?'

'I very likely was half-awake. I have no recollection of this apprentice saying anything to me at all that morning.'

'Why did you ask whether they were white rockets?'

'I suppose this was on account of the first question they asked, whether they were company's signals.'

'Do just think!'

'Company's signals usually have some colours in them.'

'So that if they were white it would make it quite plain to you they were distress signals?'

'No, I understand some companies have white.'

'Do really try and do yourself justice!'

'I am trying to do my best.'

'Think, you know. Mr Lord, allow me to suggest you are not

doing yourself justice. You are explaining, first of all, that you asked if they were white rockets, because companies signals are coloured. I am asking you whether the point of your asking whether they were all white rockets was not in order to know whether they were distress signals? Was not that the object of your question, if you put it?'

'I really do not know what was the object of my question.'

'And you think that is why you asked about it?'

'I think that is why I asked about it.'[5]

It was apparent by this time that the Master of the *Californian* firmly believed that, at every point and judged from every aspect of the situation, he had a perfectly valid reason for either taking, or not taking, any particular course of action; and nothing whatever could shake that belief. At the crucial moment, it seemed, he has simply gone to sleep in the chartroom and consequently, could not be held responsible for whatever had transpired during this period of unconsciousness or semi-consciousness.

Mr C. Robertson Dunlop, on behalf of the owners, Master, and officers of the *Californian*, did his best for his clients; but he was unable to make out much of a case.

'If,' he asked the Captain, 'you had known at 1.15 that the *Titanic* was in distress, could you have navigated with any degree of safety at night through the ice?'

'It would be most dangerous,' was the reply. 'I do not think we should have got there before the *Carpathia* did.'

Now, compared with the *Californian*, the *Carpathia* was nearly six times the distance from the *Titanic* when she received warning of the disaster. The Captain's reply did nothing to dissipate the very, very bad impression which his evidence had made upon the court.

It was now the turn of the apprentice to give evidence. Young Gibson came on to the witness-stand and was sworn. He gave his name, age, occupation, and address. Sir Rufus presently questioned him closely about what had happened on the bridge after his return on deck at 12.55 a.m.

'You have told me that the Second Officer said to you that the ship had fired five rockets?'

'Yes.'

'Did he tell you anything else about what he had been doing while you had not been there?'

'He told me that he had reported it to the Captain.'

'Did he tell you what the Captain had instructed him to do?'

'Yes.'

'What was it?'

'To call her up on the Morse light.'

'Did he tell you whether he had tried to call her up on the Morse light?'

'Yes.'

'What had been the result?'

'She had not answered him, but fired more rockets.'

'Did you see her fire these further rockets?'

'I saw three rockets.'

'Did the Second Officer tell you of any more than the five?'

'No.'

'Then as far as the report to you went he told you of five before you came back at five minutes to one?'

'Yes.'

'And after that you saw three more yourself?'

'Yes.'

'How soon was that after you had come back at five minutes to one?'

'As soon as I went on the bridge at five minutes to one. I called her up as soon as the Second Officer told me.'

'You called her up on the Morse?'

'Yes.'

'And she did not respond to you?'

'No.'

'And then you saw these rockets?'

'Yes.'

'Give me an idea of the time—would that take long, or was it at once?'

'Well, I called her up for about three minutes, and I had just got the glasses on to her when I saw her fire the rockets. That was the first one.'

'The first of the three?'

'Yes.'

'You say you had just got the glasses on to her. Did you see it through the glasses?'

'Yes.'

'How did you see the second?'

'With the eye.'

'What colour rockets were they?'

'White ones.'

'When you got your glasses on the vessel and saw the first rocket going up through them, could you make out the vessel at all?'

'No, sir, just her lights.'

For some moments the court was hushed and still as they all thought of the great ship in her death-agony sending up rocket after rocket in the desperate hope that help would come to her in time. Imposed on the sunlight of the radiant May morning, as it were, was a vision of two puzzled men on the bridge of the *Californian*, standing there under the glittering stars, looking out across the dark waters at the distant rockets. . . .

'When you saw the first of these three rockets through your glasses,' Sir John went on, 'did you report what you saw to the officer?'

'Yes.'

'Did he tell you whether he saw the second or the third rocket?'

'Yes, sir.'

'Was he using glasses, too?'

'No.'

'He saw it with his naked eye?'

'Yes.'

'What happened after that?'

'About twenty minutes past one the Second Officer remarked to me that she was slowly steaming away towards the south-west.'

'Had you remained on the bridge from the time you saw these three rockets until then?'

'Yes.'

'Had you been keeping her under observation?'

'Yes.'

'Looking at her with your glasses from time to time?'

'Yes.'

'What had you noticed between one o'clock and twenty minutes past one, looking at her through your glasses?'

'The Second Officer remarked to me, "Look at her now; she looks very queer out of the water; her lights look queer." '

'Did he say what he meant?'

'I looked at her through the glasses after that, and her lights did not seem to be natural.'

The audience grasped the situation in all its tragic significance; again a breathless silence fell on the court, and a vision of the stricken vessel, slowly sinking, rose before them all. Sir John continued:

'Looking at her through your glasses, what was there that you could see of her which made you think that?' Do you mean that her masthead light was not immediately over the other lights?'

'No, sir.'

'What was there to show you?'

'Her lights did not seem to look like as they did do before when I first saw them.'

The Commissioner asked: 'What was the difference?'

Sir John said: 'Could you describe them at all, Gibson?'

'No, sir.'

'You have told us what the officer said to you. Do you think yourself when you looked at her through the glasses that something was wrong.'

'We had been talking about it together.'

The Commissioner said: 'I should very much like you to tell me what you had been saying to the officer?'

'He remarked to me that a ship was not going to fire rockets at sea for nothing.'

A ripple of excitement went round the court. The spectators, listening intently and leaning forward in their seats, felt themselves nearer to the awful tragedy of April 14th than ever before. Gibson's evidence had created a sensation.

'I daresay you agreed with him?' went on Lord Mersey.

'Yes.'

'What took place after that between you and him?'

'We were talking about it all the time, sir, till five minutes past two, when she disappeared.'[6]

Herbert Stone, the *Californian's* Second Officer, was examined by Scanlan. He was a short, thick-set man in his middle twenties. The counsel asked him a number of questions leading on to the matter of the rockets.

'Did you obtain a certificate from the Board of Trade as a mate?'

'As a first mate in steamships, yes.'

'Was that certificate given to you after examination?'

'Yes.'

'When did you obtain that certificate?'

'Last December twelvemonth.'

'Is not part of the subjects of examination the signals of distress and the signals to be made by ships wanting a pilot?'

'Yes, the articles.'

'I suppose before you sat for that examination, you read something about signals?'

'I learned them.'

'Do you mean to tell his Lordship that you did not know that the throwing up of rockets or shells, throwing stars of any colour or description, fired one at a time at short intervals, is the proper method for signalling distress at night?'

'Yes, that is the way it is always done as far as I know.'

'And you knew that perfectly well on the night of the 14th of April?'

'Yes.'

The implication of these admissions was self-evident, even to landsmen. The excitement of the audience quickened as the inquiries continued. The Commissioner asked Stone:

'The very thing was happening that you knew indicated distress?'

The unfortunate Second Officer saw both the force and hazard of the question. In vain he tried to temporize, and his embarrassment became more pronounced; but Lord Mersey would not have it.

'If that steamer had stayed on the same bearing after firing these rockets—' Stone ventured.

'No,' said Lord Mersey sternly, 'do not give a long answer of that kind. Is it not the fact that the very thing was happening which you had been taught indicated distress?'

'Yes,' was the unwilling reply.

'You knew it meant distress?' resumed Scanlan.

'I knew that rockets shown at short intervals, one at a time, meant distress signals, yes.'

'Do not speak generally. On that very night when you saw those rockets being sent up you knew, did you not, that those rockets were signals of distress?'

'No.'

It was apparent that the Commissioner was not prepared to extend the same degree of forbearance to the Second Officer of the *Californian* that he had previously granted to the Master. He observed sharply to Stone:

'Now do think about what you are saying. You have just told me that what you saw from that steamer was exactly what you had been taught to understand were signals of distress. You told me so?'

'Yes.'

'Well, is it true?'

'It is true that similar lights are distress signals, yes.'

'Then you had seen them from this steamer?'

'A steamer that is in distress does not steam away from you, my Lord.'[7]

The Second Officer clung to this line of argument and was not to be shifted. As it was the only possible defence he had, it was scarcely to be wondered at. But his reasoning failed to impress the court. It was all too clear that neither the Master in the chart-room nor the O.O.W. on the bridge had reacted to the rockets in a proper seamanlike manner. For rockets had been used at sea as distress signals from time immemorial. Failure to respond to this most urgent appeal for aid was about the most heinous offence of which a mariner could be guilty.

In court, his officers had done their best for Captain Lord. Outside, in the luncheon interval, however, they were a good deal less reticent about the commander's responsibility for what had happened; and presently, in response to the angry reproaches of the wife of one of the *Titanic's* officers, they frankly admitted that distress signals had been seen that night from the *Californian*: but they said they had been unable to get Captain Lord to bestir himself; in fact, they were unmistakably afraid of him.

The Third Officer, Charles Victor Groves, now occupied the witness-stand. Groves, who had served for some time in the P. & O. as a junior officer without a certificate, had gained his second mate's certificate the previous year. He was examined by the Solicitor-General.

'When did you go on watch?'

'At eight o'clock.

'The Captain states that he was on the bridge at eleven o'clock,' said the counsel, 'and was there until 11.30.

'I say he was not, replied the witness.

'You say he was not?'

'Most emphatically.'

Groves presently related how he had gone down to the chartroom on the lower bridge and knocked on the door and informed the Master that a steamer was approaching on their starboard quarter. 'Captain Lord said to me, "Can you make anything out of her lights?" I said, "She is evidently a passenger steamer coming up on us." '

'Did you say why she was a passenger steamer?' said Rowlatt.

'Yes. I told him that I could see her deck lights and that made me pass the remark that she was evidently a passenger steamer.'

'How many deck lights had she?' asked the counsel. 'Had she much light?'

'Yes, a lot of light. There was absolutely no doubt her being a passenger steamer, at least in my mind.'

'Could you see much of her length?'

'No, not a great deal; because as I could judge she was coming up obliquely to us.'

Groves went on to relate how at about 11.45—one bell had been struck just then, he recollected, to call the middle watch—the lights of the distant steamship appeared to go out; and he supposed that they had been switched off for the night.

'I want to ask you a question', said Rowlatt. 'Supposing the steamer whose lights you saw turned two points to port at

11.40, would that account to you for her lights ceasing to be visible to you?'

'I quite think it would.'

The officer was later examined by the Solicitor-General on the subject of the scrap log.

'You had come on duty, in one of the watches,' said the counsel; 'would you come up at four o'clock in the morning?'

'No, about 6.50. That is on the Monday morning.'

'That is what I mean. Then when would you come on duty and be the officer of the watch and have to keep the scrap log?'

'It is my duty between eight and twelve under ordinary conditions.'

'By that time you had heard the news about the *Titanic?*'

'Yes.'

'Knowing that, did you not look back in the scrap log and see what entries had been made by your colleague between midnight and 4 a.m.'

'No, I did not.'

'It would be on the very next page, would it not? You turn over the page, I suppose, when you get to midnight?'

'Yes, we finish a page when we get to midnight.'

'You would have only to turn back one page and see the record made by the officer of the watch from midnight to 4 a.m. as to what he had seen?'

'Yes.'

'And you did not do it?'

'No, I did not do it.'

The Solicitor-General paused. 'We had better get the Chief Officer, I suppose.'

'Yes,' agreed the Commissioner; and, turning to Groves, he said, 'If you had been on the bridge instead of from eight to half-past twelve, from twelve to four, and had been keeping the scrap log-book and had seen a succession of white rockets with stars going up from this vessel which you speak of or from the direction of this vessel, would you in the ordinary course of things have made a record of the fact in your scrap log?'

'Most decidedly, that is what the log-book is for.'

'So I should have thought. Then it would have been the

business of the man who had charge of this book to record these facts?'

'I think so, my Lord.'

'Who was he?'

'Mr Stone was on watch.'

'And, therefore, if Mr Stone did what you think was his duty, this scrap log which was thrown away, or which, at all events, cannot be found, would contain a record of these rockets having been seen?'

'Yes, my Lord, but it is not my duty to criticize a senior officer, though.'[8]

The court was now beginning to get some insight into the peculiar state of things that obtained on board the *Californian*. It was not only the oral testimony of several of her officers that was open to question. Even more, it was the fact that the *Californian's* log contained absolutely no reference to the eight rockets which had been sighted during the night of April 14th;[9] and the scrap log into which such remarks should have been entered had unaccountably disappeared. So far as the ship's log was concerned, the night had—apparently apart from the ice—passed peacefully and uneventfully. There was nothing at all in the 'Remarks' column to suggest what had been happening.[10]

The Chief Officer, G. F. Stewart, was now closely questioned concerning the absence of any mention of the incidents of the night of April 14th, especially of the rockets sighted, in the official record he had himself copied from the scrap log.

'Now, I should like you to follow this,' began the Solicitor-General. 'As far as your memory serves you, did you enter into that log-book everything that you found on the scrap log sheet?'

'Yes.'

'You observe there is nothing at all in your log book about seeing distress signals?'

'Yes.'

The Solicitor-General pressed him on this point.

'Give us your views,' he urged. 'Supposing you were keeping the scrap log in a watch when you were in ice, and supposing you saw a few miles to the southward a ship sending up what appeared to be distress signals, would not you enter that in the log?'

The witness appeared embarrassed. 'Yes—I do not know.'

Again the Commissioner intervened. He rapped out:

'Oh, yes, you do!'

'Yes, I dare say I should have entered it,' admitted Stewart reluctantly, 'but it was not in our scrap log-book.'

'How do you account for it not being there?'

'I do not know, my Lord.'

'It was careless not to put it in, was it not?

'Or forgetful,' said Stewart defensively.

'Forgetful?' exclaimed Lord Mersey. 'Do you think that a careful man is likely to forget the fact that distress signals have been going on from a neighbouring steamer?'

'No, my Lord.'

'Then do not talk to me about forgetfulness.'

The Commissioner subsided into frigid silence while the Solicitor-General continued with his examination.

'The scrap log-book is intended to be kept at the time, is it not, as the things happen?'

'Yes, sir,' the witness replied, 'but they generally write them up at the end of the watch.'

'And you were there at four o'clock at the end of the watch?'

'Yes.'

'And Mr Stone told you then at four o'clock that he had seen these signals?'

'Yes.'

The Commissioner said: 'And they had been sending messages to the Captain about them?'

'Yes.'

The Solicitor-General said: 'Three times?'

'Yes.'

'And you were just going to take over the ship for the next watch and take charge of this same sheet of paper?'

'Yes.'

'Did it not occur to you that it was odd that there was nothing entered on the scrap log-book?'

'I did not notice the scrap log-book at that time.'

'You made entries on the same sheet of paper between four and eight o'clock, did not you?'

'Not till eight o'clock.'

'At eight then?'

'Yes.'

'Did not you notice it then?'

'I noticed there was nothing there.'

'Then you did at eight o'clock notice there was nothing in the scrap log-book about what had happened between midnight and four?'

'Yes.'

'And you have told us, in your view, it would be right to make such entries?'

'Yes.'

'Did you ever speak to the Second Officer about it?'

'No.'

'Never?'

'No.'

The Commissioner added: 'Or to the Captain?'

'No.'

'Or to anybody?'

'No, my Lord.'[11]

When Stewart at last quitted the witness-stand, a strong suspicion had taken root in the minds of those present that something of a 'fiddle' must have occurred concerning the log of the *Californian*. The replies given by the Chief Officer, were, to say the least of it, unsatisfactory.

The eight rockets seen from the bridge of the *Californian* at approximately the same time as eight rockets were fired from the *Titanic* were the crucial point in the eyes of the Court. There was no longer room for doubt that the *Californian* had, for all practical purposes, ignored these rockets. Whatever the Master's excuse, that was what had actually occurred. Though he positively denied that the unknown vessel was or possibly could be the *Titanic*, it did not alter the fact that *he had failed to take proper action in response to signals of distress.*

Chapter 17

The British Inquiry (2)

The Duff-Gordon affair at last came up on Friday, the 17th.

For some time past strong rumours had been circulating concerning the proceedings of one of the *Titanic's* smaller boats, No. 1 Emergency Boat. It will be recalled that no other boat went away with so few passengers or with a larger proportion of the ship's crew. This boat, which could well have taken about thirty more passengers, was said to have deliberately rowed away from the vicinity of the wreck and from the agonized appeals for help. It was further said that the crew had been bribed by some of the passengers; as a result of which No. 1 boat had become known as 'the Money Boat'. The rumours centred on Sir Cosmo and Lady Duff-Gordon, who, in consequence, had asked to be allowed to give evidence to clear themselves of these imputations.

The affair had excited so much interest that the two tiers which ran round the large hall were filled with spectators and the floor of the hall was also crowded. The seats assigned to the press were fully occupied. Two German princes, relatives of the Royal Family, were given seats in front of the places assigned to the counsel. Count Benckendorf, the Russian Ambassador, was also present. In striking contrast to all the fashionably attired spectators there was a party of the *Titanic's* stewardesses, dressed in black, as well as a number of elderly men and women in mourning who had attended the Inquiry from the start.

Just as Gill, the donkeyman, had 'blown the gaff' in the case of the *Californian* incident, so did a fireman named Hendrickson make certain allegations with regard to No. 1 boat which led to the whole matter being thoroughly investigated. The dramatic narratives of members of the crew were followed with intense interest by all in the court. Hendrickson stated that the cries of the people struggling in the water, only two hundred yards away, could be heard clearly by everyone in the boat; that he had proposed going back to their assistance, and that Sir Cosmo and Lady Duff-Gordon, together with another of the passengers, had strongly opposed the suggestion; that no more was said about going back, and that the men continued to row away from the wreck.

The drama of No. 1 boat intensified with the cross-examination of Hendrickson by Henry Duke, K.C., M.P., the counsel for the Duff-Gordons. Duke was a tall man of commanding presence; a slow and deliberate speaker, and a formidable cross-examiner. Hendrickson, however, stood the cross-examination very well, his testimony being corroborated by that of another fireman in the boat.

'I cannot understand this,' the Commissioner interposed. 'Was there any discussion on board this boat as to whether you should go to these downing people—any talk?'

'No,' replied Henrickson, 'only when I proposed going back, that is all.'

'Do you mean to tell me that you were the only person that proposed to go back?'

'I never heard any others.'

'And to whom did you speak?'

'Anyone there who was listening.'

'Did you speak to everybody?'

'I spoke to everyone there; I shouted out in the boat.'

'Now tell me what each person said.'

'These people I have mentioned before, I have told you what they said.'

'Well, tell me again,' said the Commissioner.

'They said it would be too dangerous to go back we might get swamped.'

'Who said that?'

'Sir Duff-Gordon.'

'Did anyone else say it.'

'No; his wife as well, that was all.'

The Commissioner went on: 'What did Symons say?'

'He never said anything.'

'And after these two people said it would be too dangerous what did you say?'

'I never said any more.'

'Then am I to understand that because two of the passengers said it would be dangerous you all kept your mouths shut and made no attempt to rescue anybody?'

'That is right, sir.'[1]

The examination of the quartermaster who had been in charge of 'the Money Boat' provided one of the most entertaining episodes of the day's sitting. This quartermaster, George Symons, had been accounted a good and dependable man by Lightoller. Be that as it may, he had scarcely distinguished himself during the night of April 14th; though whether this was due to some inherent weakness in his character or whether to mistaken deference to those he regarded as his betters will never be known. Among other things, the interesting fact came to light that a small sum of money had recently changed hands . . . and a loud burst of laughter greeted Symons's ingenuous objection to saying anything at all about a certain visit he had received from the Duff-Gordons' solicitor on the grounds that 'what took place in a man's own home was no business of anybody'. Symons's version of events on the fateful night of the 14th differed materially from Hendrickson's.

'After I left the ship I gave the order to pull away. We were pulling very hard; we were pulling very steady; a moderate pull. After I gave that order we pulled away I should say about two hundred yards, and I told them to lay on their oars, just a little while after that, after I saw that the ship was doomed, I gave the order to pull a little further and so escape the suction.'

Symons described how her lights forward had all disappeared and Sir Rufus said:

'Then when you saw her like *that*, what was the next thing that happened?'

'Being the master of the situation,' said Symons glibly, 'I used my own discretion. I said nothing to anybody about the ship being doomed, in my opinion. I pulled a little further away to escape, if there was any suction. A little while after that we pulled a little way and lay on the oars again. The other boats were around us by that time, and some were pulling farther away from us. I stood and watched it till I heard two sharp explosions in the ship.'

Later Sir Rufus asked him:

'When you saw the *Titanic* go down did you hear any cries from the people that went down with the boat?'

'Yes.'

'Did you try to rescue them?'

'I thought at the time, being master of the situation, it was not safe in any case to go back at that time.'

'But,' inquired Sir Rufus, 'apart from going back to the ship, you could have gone back, could you not, some way to pick up persons, without going into the seething mass of people?'

'The thing is those people, I suppose, would be together when they go down.'

'But they do not all stop long?'

'No, that is true. They do not stop together as a rule.'

'You were there with ample room?'

'Yes; we had room, say, for another eight or a dozen more in the boat. I do not know what the boat's complement is.'

'The boat's complement is forty, and you had twelve.'

'If there were forty in that boat there would not be room.'

'What?'

'I think myself if there were forty in that boat practically when the sea rose in the morning it would not be safe.'

'The sea did not rise. If the sea had risen I dare say it might have been so; but we are speaking of a calm night. The sea was quite calm at this time. You quite understand you were to be ready to go back if called?'

'That is right.'

'Do you tell my Lord,' said the Attorney-General, 'that you determined, without consultation with anybody, that you would not go back?'

That was an awkward one for Symons. Once more he fell back on his stock phrase. He replied:

'I determined by my own wish, as I was master of the situation, to go back when I thought that most of the danger was over.'

'What?'

'I used my own discretion, as being master of the situation at the time, that it was not safe to have gone back at that time until everything was over.'

Later the Commissioner said: 'I am not satisfied at all.'

Sir Rufus went on:

'Now, I want to know a little more about that. Was the question raised about your going back to the people who were shrieking at this time?'

'None whatever.'

'Do you mean to tell my Lord that nobody ever mentioned, amongst the people that you had in that boat, going back to try to save some of the people who were in the water drowning?'

'I never heard anybody of any description, passengers or crew, say anything as regards going back. Had there been anything said I was almost sure to have heard it.'

'You mean nothing was said, either by you or anybody?'

'I used my own discretion.'

'You have told us that several times,' said Sir Rufus acidly. 'I understand that you used your discretion, and that you were master of the situation; we have got those phrases. What I am asking you about now is whether at that time you heard anything said by anybody in the boat about going back.'

'None whatever.'

One last awkward point was raised, to which the unfortunate Symons had to reply.

'You said in America,' the Commissioner reminded him, 'to Senator Perkins that you had fourteen to twenty persons in the boat?'

'I thought I had,' said Symons defensively; 'I was in the dark.'

'You were not in the dark when you gave that evidence', said the Commissioner drily.[2]

Monday, May 20th, might well have been accounted 'the Duff-Gordon day'.[3] For some time before the sitting opened motor-cars were driving up to the entrance of Scottish Hall, one after the other, for all the world as if some brilliant society function were afoot. (The wife of one of the *Titanic's* officers bought herself a new hat for the occasion.) Once again the place was filled with distinguished visitors, including Prince

Albert of Schleswig-Holstein, Lady St Helier, Lady Middleton, and, of course, Mrs Asquith. Fresh arrivals were constantly crowding in through the doors. There was a lively buzz of conversation. Those who were well disposed to the Duff-Gordons came to support them; and those who were not came —well, to see how they got on.

Lord Mersey took his place on the dais. There was a rustle of dresses and a scraping of chairs as the fashionable throng settled themselves expectantly for the show. Every place in the hall was occupied. Some of the spectators even overflowed into the press seats. On this day men were in the minority. The large hall was gay with white blouses and flower-decked hats. Some of the women took off their hats and jackets (the day was warm though dull), others adjusted their opera glasses. The general effect was strongly suggestive of a matinée audience, waiting for the curtain to go up. For one afternoon, at least, the Wreck Commissioner's Court had become part of the London season. To judge from the look on the Commissioner's countenance he did not at all approve of the transformation; but there was nothing he could do about it.

Lady Duff-Gordon, looking pale but quite self-possessed, sat with bowed head while her husband was giving his evidence. She was the subject of a good many curious glances. In front of her sat the Duff-Gordon's counsel, Henry Duke, wary and alert. Sir Cosmo was a handsome man of soldierly bearing with a marked resemblance to the Emperor William II. His demeanour at the outset of the ordeal was easy and self-assured; as time went on, however, he began to look older and considerably less confident. Scanlan examined him.

'Is it your evidence,' said the counsel, 'that while the cries of the drowning people were heard after the *Titanic* sank there was no conversation whatever between you and your fellow passengers and between you and members of the crew?'

'I said that after the *Titanic* sank there was a dead silence.'

From the start an accusatory note was apparent in the line that the counsel was taking. It really seemed as if more than a suggestion of 'militancy', of class antagonism, of the passionate party warfare of those years, were creeping into the Inquiry. Resentful murmurs began to be heard from the spectators in the gallery as the relentless examination continued. Sir Cosmo had noticeably lost a good deal of his former ease and confidence.

'When the people were crying out for help,' Scanlan remarked, 'were you all mute in the boat?'

'I think as soon as that occurred the men began to row at once.'

The Commissioner asked him: 'And, as I understand, to row away from the cries?'

'I presume so, my Lord; I do not know why.'

Sir Cosmo then categorically denied that his wife had objected to their going back for fear of the boat being swamped or that he had supported her in this.

Later Harbinson rose to cross-examine Sir Cosmo. Once again the accusatory note was unmistakable; once again there was the suggestion of class warfare; and the tension in the court increased. On one occasion Lord Mersey reminded the counsel pointedly: 'Your duty is to assist me to arrive at the truth, not to try to make out a case for this class against that class.' It was not easy for this particular counsel to please Lord Mersey; Harbinson was acting on behalf of the third class passengers; and, what made matters worse, Harbinson was an Irishman. Dozens of his clients and fellow-countrymen had perished in the disaster. Sometimes his feelings got the better of him. He began to question Sir Cosmo about his famous promise to present each member of the boat's crew with £5.

'Was not this,' he inquired, 'rather an exceptional time, twenty minutes after the *Titanic* sank, to make suggestions in the boat about giving away £5 notes?'

'No, I think not,' replied the witness. 'I think it was a most natural time. Everything was quiet; the men had stopped rowing; the men were quite quiet lying on their oars doing nothing for some time, and then the ship having gone I think it was a natural enough remark for a man to make, "I suppose you have lost everything?" '

By this time the whole court was following the evidence with almost painful attention and expectancy. Once again it was as if the present were forgotten, and the tragedy were being re-enacted in their mind's eye; their thoughts were of the little band of survivors in No. 1 boat, adrift on the dark waters in that terrible first half-hour after the *Titanic* had gone down, and the anguished cries from the wreck were gradually growing fainter and fewer, until they finally died away into silence.

'Would it not have been more in harmony with the traditions of seamanship that that should have been the time that you should have suggested to the sailors to have gone and tried if they could rescue anyone?'

'I have said that I did not consider the possibility—or rather I shall put it that the possibility of being able to help anybody never occurred to me at all.'

'That is to say,' the counsel went on, 'would I accurately state your position if I summed it up in this way, that you considered when you were safe yourselves that all the others might perish?'

'No, that is not quite the way to put it.'

The Commissioner suddenly intervened. 'Do you think,' he asked the counsel with some indignation, 'a question of that kind is fair to this witness? The witness's position is bad enough. Do you think it is fair to put a question of that kind to him? I do not!'[4]

The friends and supporters of the Duff-Gordons had been becoming increasingly restive during the cross-examination of Sir Cosmo. At this point they gave full vent to their feelings. There was a spontaneous burst of applause from all parts of the hall, which Lord Mersey made no attempt to suppress.

It was now the turn of the lady. A murmur of excitement went round the crowded hall as Lady Duff-Gordon came forward to be sworn. As she mounted the witness-stand she took off her white gloves and repeated the words of the oath in a firm, clear voice. 'Lucile' was, as usual, elegantly dressed. Instead of the becoming toque she had worn on her previous appearance in court, she was now wearing a large black picture hat which admirably set off her small, rather plaintive face. Standing there in front of the great model of the *Titanic*, she appealed, consciously or unconsciously, to every chivalrous instinct in the male.

Examined by the Attorney-General, she gave a detailed account of the way in which No. 1 boat was loaded. (Incidentally, it is interesting to note how the character of the witness, as so often happened at this Inquiry, came out in the evidence.) The fashionable audience leaned forward to look and listen.

'After the three boats had gone down, my husband, Miss Franks, and myself were left standing on the deck. There were no other people on the deck at all visible and I had quite made up my mind that I was going to be drowned, and then suddenly we saw this little boat in front of us—this little thing [*pointing on the model*]—and we saw some sailors, and an officer apparently giving them orders and I said to my husband, "ought we not to be doing something?" He said, "Oh, we must wait for orders," and we stood there for quite some time while these men were fixing up things, and then my husband went forward and said, "Might we get into this boat?" and the officer said in a very polite way indeed, "Oh certainly, do; I will be very pleased." Then somebody hitched me up from the deck and pitched me into the boat and then I think Miss Franks was pitched in. It was not a case of getting in at all. We could not have got in, it was quite high. They hitched us up in *this* sort of way [*indicating*] into the boat and after we had been in a little while the boat was started to be lowered and one American gentleman got pitched in while the boat was being lowered down.'

The Attorney-General presently asked: 'Did you hear anything said about suction?'

'Well, perhaps I may have heard it,' she replied, 'but I was terribly sick; and I could not swear to it.'

'I am asking you about something which I only know from your statement to your solicitor. Did you hear a voice say, "Let us get away"?'

'Yes, I think so.'

'Did you hear it said, "It is such an enormous boat; none of us know what the suction may be if she is a goner"?'

'Yes, I heard them speaking of the enormous boat. It was the word "suction" I was not sure of. I see what you mean.'

'It is not what I mean, Lady Duff-Gordon,' responded the Attorney-General. 'It is what you are said to have said to your solicitor.'

'Well, I may have said so.'[5]

When Lady Duff-Gordon stepped down from the witness-stand, there was a general rustling and scraping preparatory to the departure of many of the audience. So far as they were concerned, the show was over.

During the rest of the afternoon session of the 20th the witness-stand was occupied by Lightoller.

He was the sole survivor among the senior officers of the *Titanic*. It was a miracle, indeed, that his own life had been spared. 'E.J.', Wilde, Murdoch, Moody, O'Loughlin, Simpson, McElroy, Barker, Denison, and every one of the engineers—all had perished. Long ago, Lightoller had boasted to his chum sister, '*I'll* never be drowned' . . . but he had been near enough to it, in all conscience, at 2.10 a.m. on the night of the wreck. Another thing Lightoller knew he had to be profoundly thankful for was that he had refused the chance of going away in a boat and had purposely stepped back on board the sinking ship. He had taken his chance and had lived to tell the tale.

Because he was the only surviving watch-keeping officer, the brunt of the attack would necessarily fall upon him. None knew better than Lightoller what perils confronted him at the hands of some of the ablest lawyers in London. The case for the defence was all too vulnerable at a number of points. There was the question of all the reports received about ice to the westward; of the high speed at which the vessel had been running; of the visibility; of the look-out kept on the bridge and in the crow's nest; of the adequacy of the life-saving equipment on board, and of the number of hands available for getting the boats away. Above all, he was apprehensive that a direct question would be put to him about the means of egress from the steerage to the Boat Deck—which, as he was perfectly well aware, would, if answered truthfully, be very awkward for his Company.[6]

Hour after hour he stood up to the skilful probing enquiries of Sir Rufus Isaacs, Sir John Simon, Mr Scanlan, Mr Edwards, and all the rest of them. Lightoller, in fact, proved himself as useful to his Company at the Court of Inquiry as he had on the bridge. That the White Star Line came out of the Inquiry as well as it did was largely due to him. He occupied the witness-stand throughout the latter part of the 20th and the whole of the 21st. Hundreds of questions were put to him and received unhesitating replies. Scarcely ever did anyone score off Lightoller, while he continually discomfited his opponents. Taken all in all, it was an amazing performance.

When Lightoller gave an account of his escape from the sinking liner, how he was nearly sucked down into the funnel, how he was blown clear just in the nick of time, how he managed to grab the rope which was trailing from the upturned Engelhardt, and how he eventually succeeded in hoisting himself up on its flat bottom, he was heard with breathless interest by the whole court.

The audience craned forward in their seats to catch every syllable of the narration of this sturdy, bronzed, stern-faced sailor with his deep, powerful voice and confident air as he spoke of the grim realities of life and death, in striking contrast to the black-coated, pale-faced lawyers who questioned him. He looked exactly what he was, the experienced Western Ocean mail boat officer; and his ready responses carried conviction.

As regards all the warnings from other ships, Lightoller could only recall the ice-report shown him by Captain Smith at 12.45 p.m. on Sunday, and mentioned by him to the First Officer when the latter returned to the bridge after luncheon. He said he had no recollection of any other.

'When a liner is known to be approaching ice,' Lord Mersey inquired, 'is it usual to reduce speed?'

'I have never known speed to be reduced,' Lightoller replied without hesitation, 'in any ship I have ever been in, in fair weather.'

Scanlan's subsequent endeavour to establish the charge of excessive speed was casually, not to say contemptuously, refuted by this witness.

'What I want to suggest to you,' said the counsel, 'is that it was recklessness, utter recklessness, in view of the conditions which you have described as abnormal, and in view of the knowledge you had from various sources that ice was in your immediate vicinity, to proceed at $21\frac{1}{2}$ knots?'

'Then all I can say,' rejoined Lightoller, 'is that recklessness applies to practically every commander and every ship crossing the Atlantic Ocean.'

'I am not disputing that with you,' said Scanlan, 'but can you describe it yourself as other than utter recklessness?'

'Yes.'

'Is it careful navigation in your view?'

'It is ordinary navigation, which embodies careful navigation.'

'Is this your position then: that even with the experience of the *Titanic* disaster, if you were coming within the near vicinity of a place which was reported to you to be abounding in ice, you would proceed with a ship like the *Titanic* at 21 knots?'

'I do not say I should.'

'At night time, and at a time when the conditions were what you have described as very abnormal, surely you would not go at $21\frac{1}{2}$ knots?'

'The conditions were not apparent to us in the first place; the conditions of an absolutely flat sea were not apparent to us till afterwards. Naturally I should take precautions against such an occurrence.'

'And what precautions would you take if you would not slow up or slow down?'

'I did not say I would not slow up.'

'Cannot you say whether you would or not?'

'No, I am afraid I could not say right here what I should do. I should take every precaution whatever appealed to me.'

After some further argument Scanlan said:

'I do not think anything would convince you that it was dangerous that night.'

'I have been very much convinced that it was dangerous,' was the unruffled reply.

'I mean that the conditions you have described were dangerous.'

'They proved to be,' said Lightoller equably.

'What I want to suggest is that the conditions having been so dangerous, those in charge of the vessel were negligent in proceeding at that rate of speed?'

'No,' replied Lightoller.[7]

Scanlan gave it up. . . .

Lightoller did not budge from the position he had taken up throughout the Inquiry. To proceed at full speed under such conditions, he declared, was the uniform practice in the North Atlantic trade. This was corroborated by the testimony of many experienced mariners. One after another a long procession of mail boat commanders mounted the witness-stand and testified to that effect: John Pritchard, 'Bertie' Hayes, William Stewart, Alexander Fairfull, Andrew Braes, and many others. Not even if warning were received of an ice-field ahead would speed be reduced—not, in fact, till the ice was actually *seen*. So long as the weather was clear and a good look-out kept one could rely on seeing ice at a sufficient distance to avoid it. Not one of these witnesses had ever come so close to an iceberg on a perfectly clear night that he was unable to clear it.

Why, then, had the *Titanic* not sighted the iceberg in time? It was clear from the evidence that the warning had only come from the crow's nest when the berg was no more than a few hundred yards distant. There could be no argument about that. The question naturally arose, why had it not been seen at a far greater distance? When the possibility of local haze was raised, Lightoller rejected it in the most positive manner. He said that he had seen no haze himself; and he insisted that it would have been observed as easily from the bridge as from the crow's nest. Questioned by the Solicitor-General on this point, the witness fell back on an argument which he developed with considerable skill.

'It is difficult to come to any conclusion,' Lightoller informed the Court. 'Of course we know now the extraordinary combination of circumstances that existed at the time, a combination that would not again happen in a hundred years. It is extraordinary that they should all have existed on this particular night; everything was against us, everything.'

Lord Mersey inquired what these circumstances were.

'Well, in the first place there was no moon,' said Lightoller, 'then there was no wind, not the slightest breath of air, and the most extraordinary circumstance of all was that there was no swell. Had there been the slightest degree of swell there would have been such a movement of water that I have no doubt the berg would have been seen in plenty of time to clear it. The sea was as smooth as the top of a table or a floor; it was most extraordinary, and ninety-nine men in a hundred who cross the Atlantic would not be able to call in mind any such smooth sea.'

'Did the swell get up afterwards?'

'Yes, almost immediately. I had not been on the collapsible boat more than half an hour before a swell was distinctly visible. In the morning there was quite a breeze.'

'Was there any other circumstance?'

'Well, the berg into which we ran must have been, in my opinion, a berg that was very shortly before capsized. That would leave most of it that had been below the water above it, and practically all black ice, or it must have been a berg broken from a glacier with its blue side towards us. And even in that case there would still have been the white outline that Captain Smith spoke about, and no matter how dark the sky is you can see this in time to clear it, provided it is not cloudy. On this night there was not a cloud in the sky, every star was visible, and therefore there would have been a certain amount of reflected light from the ice. Had it been field ice it would have been very visible, and you would have been able to see it two miles away. Had it been a normal iceberg, with three white sides, we could have easily made it out $1\frac{1}{2}$ to 2 miles away. The only way I can account for not seeing it is that it was probably a berg overturned, as they frequently are, and thus bringing most of that part that had been in the water above the water and exposing a dark surface.'

'Do these circumstances, in your opinion, account for the men on the look-out not seeing it before?'

'Yes.'[8]

There was a fallacy here: but it was never exposed at the Inquiry. The professional seaman, on his own ground, sure of himself, discoursing of affairs with which he was intimately familiar, enjoyed a decisive advantage over his legal opponents. Lightoller, in fact, had it all his own way. The 'law sharks' had no chance against him. In the end the ingenious argument of 'abnormal circumstances'—or, as Sir Robert Finlay put it, 'an extraordinary concatenation of events'—was, despite Lord Mersey's evident misgivings, reluctantly accepted.

The *Titanic* Inquiry was not the only notable sideshow on Monday, May 20th; on that same day the libel action which the First Lord of the Admiralty, Winston Churchill, was bringing against a certain periodical in defence of his honour—ever a sensitive point with politicians—had attracted a good many interested spectators. In the ensuing weeks the stream of distinguished and distinguishable people that filed into Scottish Hall became gradually thinner; though the reports of the Inquiry still filled long columns in the newspapers. What might be called the *Titanic* legend had by now taken firm hold of the public imagination. Subscriptions continued to pour into the Relief Fund. Children were taken to see the lifelike model of brave Captain Smith at Madame Tussaud's. It would be wrong, however, to suppose that the gaiety of the Season was greatly affected by the disaster. After the first stunning shock of '*Titanic* week', life went on as usual. Early each morning troops of horsemen and horsewomen cantered light-heartedly under the elms in Rotten Row. In the warm summer evenings strollers in the Royal Parks could be heard humming snatches of the langourous waltz melodies from Franz Lehar's operetta, *Gypsy Love*, which had its opening night at Daly's on June 1st. There was a new musical comedy by Paul Rubens, *The Sunshine Girl*, at the Gaiety. The Pavlova matinées at the Palace were drawing enormous audiences. A play by John Galsworthy, *The Silver Box*, had excited a good deal of discussion. On Court nights, the long line of carriages moved slowly through the throng of interested spectators assembled in the Mall. The Season was remarkable for the number of dances that were given. Night after night the strains of waltz or ragtime might be heard coming from some great house in Mayfair or Belgravia. The Derby on June 5th was followed by the King's Birthday, Ascot Week, Henley Regatta, the Eton and Harrow match, and, finally, Goodwood. In Parliament, the stormy debates on the Welsh Disestablishment Bill gave place to those on Irish Home Rule.

In the latter part of June, the counsel delivered their final addresses, which summarized the main points at issue. Above all, there was the question of the Captain's responsibility. Lord Mersey said he was very anxious not to fix blame on a man who could not be there, unless it was very clearly proved; and he wanted to consider everything that could reasonably be brought to light concerning his conduct. He said that if the Captain had followed the same practice as other experienced masters on this route, it would be a very difficult thing indeed for one to say he was guilty of negligence.

The Commissioner's obvious desire to exculpate the late Captain Smith automatically played into the hands of Sir Robert Finlay. For if 'E.J.' were not to be held responsible for the collision, neither could his clients, the White Star Line, be held culpable either. Sir Robert proceeded to press home his advantage.

'I shall ask the court,' he said, 'to say that there has neither been negligence nor error of judgment, and I shall submit on behalf of these officers that they did what was right under the circumstances, and that no blame of any sort or kind is attributable to anybody.'

Scanlan, on the contrary, attributed the disaster to the lack of proper seamanship and skill in navigation, with an utter disregard of the warnings which had been given and of the duties incumbent upon them under the peculiar weather conditions which prevailed at the time. He enlarged on the inadequacy of the life-saving equipment on board the *Titanic* and the want of proper boat-drill. He declared that the Board of Trade was much more to blame than the shipowners. With regard to lifeboats, he said that they were quite a neglected department in a ship. The reason he suggested was that there was no money in lifeboats.

Edwards also stressed the 'grave negligence' in navigation. He said Mr Ismay had taken it upon himself to arrange with the Chief Engineer at Queenstown, without the Master being informed, that there should be a turn of speed on Monday and Tuesday. Again he inquired, why should the *Baltic's* marconigram have been given to Mr Ismay at all? This showed conclusively that the Master, in handing the marconigram to the managing director of the Company, recognized the special and peculiar position the latter held on board the *Titanic*. In practically ignoring the special warning of the ice-reports, and by proceeding at such a speed, the Master or Mr Murdoch was guilty of reprehensible negligence. He went on to say that the Board of Trade had been entirely wrong in all these years in dealing with the question of watertight compartments and watertight decks.

Harbinson, as counsel for the third class passengers, had had rather a stormy passage throughout the Inquiry. The Commissioner from the outset had not concealed his opinion that a special spokesman for the steerage passengers was neither necessary nor desirable. On several occasions Lord Mersey had plainly disliked the line he was taking; and had made that dislike very clear. Harbinson's conclusions, like those of Scanlan and Edwards, were diametrically opposed to those of the counsel for the White Star Line.

'The first proposition, my Lord,' he declared, 'that I desire to submit is that this calamitous accident, this disaster, was not the outcome of an inevitable accident. By "inevitable accident", my Lord, I mean an accident which could not possibly have been prevented by the exercise of ordinary care, caution or skill, and any suggestion to your Lordship will be . . . that if proper and seamanlike care had been exercised this very deplorable disaster could have been avoided.'

Harbinson showed himself no less critical of the Board of Trade, whose lax and lethargic attitude to safety measures at sea had, in his opinion, been largely responsible for the inadequacy of the life-saving equipment on board the *Titanic*. (Amongst other peculiar things which had come to light in the course of the Inquiry, the discovery had been made that the Archbishop of Canterbury was, *ex officio*, a member of the B.O.T.)

'I wish to say,' he observed, 'that the Board of Trade has got eyes and many ears, but it does not seem to have any brains. . . . And although it gets information from all sides it does not seem to be able to digest it, to assimilate it, or to apply it; and if, as the result of this awful tragedy, the Board of Trade could be modernized, and made, as it were, the reflex of the living, throbbing and palpitating life of this country, then I should think, at all events, appalling, world-wide as this calamity has been, my Lord, it will have borne some fruit.'[9]

The growing prolixity of that Grand Old Man of the British

Bar, Sir Robert Finlay, was becoming, in his latter days, somewhat an embarrassment to his colleagues. The present occasion was no exception. When he rose to address the court on behalf of the White Star Line, he went on, not for hours, but for days. From June 25th to 28th he was able to demonstrate, at any rate to his own satisfaction, that there had been no negligence on the part of the ship's officers; that experience had shown that it was perfectly safe to proceed, at night, at full speed through the ice region in clear weather; that Ismay's conduct on the night of the disaster had been beyond reproach; that the number of boats carried by the *Titanic* was far in excess of that stipulated by the Board of Trade regulations; that good discipline had prevailed among the passengers, and that the lack of proper boat drill had had nothing to do with the loss of life. As politicians like to say, he left no stone unturned and no avenue unexplored; and, like Tennyson's brook, he looked like going on for ever. As his views, apparently, were so closely in accord with those of the Commissioner, this did no harm; and, before he had finished his address, Lord Mersey and Sir Robert Finlay were almost purring at each other.

'May I,' said Sir Robert, 'just in general terms recall to your memory that Mr Ismay repeatedly travelled by these boats, and travelled as an ordinary passenger in the Company, and he never occupied any other position except that of an ordinary passenger. Of course he was in charge of the Company, and in a sense that would mark him out from the passengers, and in that respect he was not an ordinary passenger, but it did not affect in one degree the relations to the ship of a man of Captain Smith's standing. I hope I may dismiss all the attacks that have been made upon Mr Ismay as unfounded and having no relation to the facts. Your Lordship will recollect what I said about the question of speed, that there was no intention to make a record passage.'

'You need not dwell upon that,' was Lord Mersey's rejoinder. 'I am satisfied that no record passage was being made.'

'The White Star Line have really never gone in for great speed, because all their vessels are vessels of comparatively low speed.'

'You need not trouble about that.'

'I am extremely sorry,' Sir Robert observed, 'I have been so long.'

'Please do not think,' said Lord Mersey reassuringly, 'that you have not been of the greatest assistance to me.'[10]

In his final address, on June 28th, Dunlop, the counsel for the owners, Master, and officers of the *Californian*, declared that the court had no jurisdiction to pass any censure on Captain Lord. In the event, however, his objection was overruled by the Commissioner.

A few days afterwards the court considered the crucial issue of Captain Smith's responsibility when in the known vicinity of ice. The various positions which had been plotted on the chart showed that the *Titanic* was driving straight into the danger zone with ice to the north, and ice to the south, of her track. Though most of the reports related to the north, the general drift of the ice was southward, and the place where the liner sank was well within the area of danger. These facts had been clearly established in the course of the Inquiry and made a profound impression upon the court.

In his summing-up, Lord Mersey observed that with the knowledge of the proximity of ice which the Master had two courses were open to him. One of these was to stand well to the southward instead of shaping a westerly course; and the other was to reduce speed materially at nightfall. In the event he did neither. Why had he maintained course and speed? The answer was to be found in the evidence. It was shown that for many years past the practice of liners using this track when in the vicinity of ice at night had been in clear weather to keep the course, maintain the speed, and trust to a sharp look-out to enable them to avoid the danger. It was said this practice had been justified by experience, no casualties having resulted from it. But the event had proved the practice to be bad. Its root was probably to be found in competition and in the desire of the public for quick passages rather than in the judgment of navigators. But unfortunately experience appeared to justify it. In face of the practice and of past experience it could not be said there had been negligence; and in the absence of negligence it was impossible to fix Captain Smith with blame.

'It is,' Lord Mersey declared, 'however, to be hoped that the last has been heard of the practice and that for the future it will be abandoned for what we now know to be more prudent and wiser measures. What was a mistake in the case of the *Titanic* would without doubt be negligence in any similar case in the future.'[11]

Chapter 18

Negligent Navigation

The Inquiry into the loss of the *Titanic* had lasted for thirty-six days, in the course of which ninety-eight witnesses had been examined and more than 25,600 questions asked; it was the longest and most detailed Inquiry ever held by a Wreck Court; and the general impression was that the last word had been said about the disaster.

'It is difficult to suppose, for instance,' commented the *Daily Telegraph* on July 31st, 'that any court which had to inquire into the question of the responsibility of the owners of the ship would disregard the expression of opinion of Lord Mersey and those who sat with him. The report having, in effect, acquitted them of all blame, it is not likely that any attempt will be made hereafter to establish the contrary.'

That was where the *Daily Telegraph* was wrong. Undaunted by the power and resources of the big battalions which would assuredly be ranged against him, a small farmer from County Cork, named Thomas Ryan, who had lost a son in the disaster, had the temerity to challenge this verdict, and presently took the matter to law. It was the first of several actions successively brought to recover damages for the death of persons who had lost their lives while passengers in the *Titanic*.

The case of Ryan v. Oceanic Steam Navigation Company opened on June 20th, 1913, before Mr Justice Bailhache and a Special Jury. The plaintiff, Thomas Ryan, sued the defendants, the Oceanic Steam Navigation Company, otherwise the White Star Line, to recover damages for the death of his son, Patrick Ryan, who lost his life while in the defendants' vessel, the *Titanic*, owing to the negligence of the defendants' servants. Mr Campbell, K.C., and Mr Scanlan appeared for the plaintiff; and Mr Duke, K.C., and Mr Maurice Hill, K.C., and Mr Raeburn for the defendants.

Thus action was joined once more on the crucial issues of the disaster. The case was fought on much the same evidence, and with many of the same witnesses. But the atmosphere of the King's Bench was very different from that of the Scottish Hall: there was no model of the lost liner dominating the scene, no throng of fashionably attired spectators; there was none of the emotionalism, none of the almost theatrical touches which had characterized the Inquiry. The legal attitude to all these matters was calm, detached, shrewd, and analytical. As the arguments, examinations, and cross-examinations proceeded, the inherent weakness of the case for the owners and officers of the *Titanic* began to appear. The vulnerable points of the defendants' case came under strong and continuous attack: whereas at the Inquiry Lord Mersey, though obviously doubtful and uneasy, had not cared to probe too deeply. The professional reputation of poor 'E.J.' was no longer regarded as sacrosanct, nor could his owners find safe shelter behind it.

Mr Campbell opened his case with the assertion that the question of negligence they had to consider was one of degree, and he could conceive no case in which the admitted facts more conclusively proved gross negligence than the present. They could have gone more south and avoided the ice, or slowed down. What happened? The enormous obstacle was not seen by any official on the ship until they were within five hundred yards of it. The vessel travelled that distance in thirty-seven seconds, and, having failed to take any precautions, nothing could then be done. They had not abated the full speed of the vessel through the danger zone, and although they saw the berg five hundred yards away they were unable owing to the speed of the ship to deflect it so as to pass safely by. Why was not the iceberg detected before? He believed it could be established that the berg could have been seen a mile away. Why was it not seen? There was no increase that night in the number of the lookout. It consisted of two men in the crow's nest and an officer on the bridge—the ordinary watch in perfect weather on a safe route. The grave omission was this. These icebergs looked on from a height were not easy to detect as if you were on a plane with them. There should have been a stemhead look-out, who would have seen the berg without having to look down on it from above. The look-out men had look-out glasses from Belfast to Southampton, but at Southampton they were taken from them. They would say that if they had had glasses they could have detected the ice much sooner than they did. . . . The defendants were in this dilemma. Assume their case was that the conditions were so unfavourable that they could not see a berg until it was quite close, what was their excuse for not reducing speed? If, on the other hand, the conditions were so favourable that they could see the berg easily, why did they not see it? The omission to do so was damning evidence of negligence.[1]

Mr Duke, in opening the case for the defendants, said that what was relied on here was not that Captain Smith and the other officers of the *Titanic* fell into some error of judgment, but that they were guilty of a lack of proper ordinary and reasonable care. That was an appalling proposition. Captain Smith was as fine and capable and high-minded a seaman as ever sailed the seas. The men who were involved had been the pick of the merchant service of this country. The *Titanic* was the finest product of modern shipbuilding.

It was said that the Captain had been warned of the presence of ice and had disregarded the warnings. Every warning had in fact been taken into account. That day and every day the rule was that such a notice should be fixed up in a conspicuous position for those concerned to see. That had been done. The survivors would tell the jury what had been done; how the course had been worked out and the probable position of the ice ascertained.

It was said that in these circumstances that it was negligent to maintain this speed. Captain Smith and each one of the officers was responsible for the safety of this ship; yet it had not occurred to any one of them they were not doing the proper thing in keeping on this speed. Where were the seamen of any position or responsibility who said that it was a negligent thing to navigate the Atlantic in these circumstances at that speed? The jury would be told by his witnesses that in the presence of ice the safest course was to keep a sharp look-out and to go ahead at full speed and get out of the ice region.[2]

Examined by Campbell, Harold Bride declared that the duty

of operators with regard to messages affecting the navigation of the ship was to take them to a responsible officer; that such telegrams had priority over private messages; that if he had received an important ice-report he would have passed it on immediately. He added, that was his practice and Phillips's as well.[3]

Stanley Herbert Adams of the *Mesaba* also gave evidence. He said that he had received no reply to the ice warning he had sent the *Titanic* from his Captain. It had been acknowledged by the operator on duty in the ship's wireless station; that was all. As to whether the telegrams had been taken up on the bridge or not, there was no conclusive evidence either way.[4]

Joseph Scarrott, A.B., said that he had been in the duty watch at the time of the collision. His duty was to 'stand by' for any orders that were given. Campbell asked him:

'Would a man at the stemhead have a better opportunity of look-out than a man in the crow's nest?'

'That would depend upon the atmosphere,' was Scarrott's reply. He said that he thought the iceberg could have been seen for about one thousand yards from the crow's nest.

'Would powerful glasses assist you?'

'I prefer glasses,' said the witness.

He testified that he had heard conversation among the crew that night to the effect that they were expecting ice.

Reginald Robinson Lee was examined by Mr Campbell with regard to the visibility at the time of the collision. He said that conditions that night were not favourable for a clear view. Part of the berg was above the haze. When he sighted the berg he did not think he could see the lower part of it below the haze. If the whole berg had been enveloped in haze he could not have seen it so soon.

'From the time you saw the berg,' Campbell asked, 'was it possible to avoid it?'

'Half a minute more,' replied Lee, 'would have been enough to avoid it.'

He said that the berg faced the ship with its dark side. He had seen a berg which presented its dark side when off St John's, Newfoundland. The reason he had not seen this berg before was because it presented its dark side; he thought he might have sighted it some minutes earlier if it had presented the ordinary white appearance of ice; it was higher than the foc'sle—it was as high as the boat deck. He said that he had not known the North Atlantic without a swell before this occasion. The sea was quite smooth. It was most unusual; it was an oily sea. The consequence was that there was no 'lipper of water' around the iceberg when it loomed ahead; if there had been it would have made breakers and they could have seen it. In the normal condition of the sea in the North Atlantic he would have sighted the iceberg earlier. Two or three hours after he left the ship, Lee added, a breeze sprang up.[5]

Lee's evidence was strongly controverted by Lightoller, who once again spoke up in defence of the Western Ocean mail boat tradition of navigation. He said if he had seen the haze spoken of by the look-out man he would have reported it to the Master, and, if necessary, reduced the speed of the ship on his own initiative. He had reason to doubt the evidence given by the look-out men as to the existence of haze. He did not believe there was any haze. The reasons why the iceberg was not seen earlier were as follows. There was no moon. There was no ripple. The black side of the iceberg faced the ship. There was no swell. If the iceberg were seen five hundred yards away he did not think that the collision was inevitable. If the helm had been whipped over and one of the engines put astern, he said, the *Titanic* might possibly have cleared the berg.

However, Lightoller was obliged to admit that he could not remember whether he had actually passed on Captain Smith's order to Murdoch about their having to slow down 'if it became in the slightest degree hazy'.

Cross-examined by Campbell, Frederick Fleet, the other look-out who had been in the crow's nest at the time of the collision, said he saw the haze for about a quarter of an hour before the impact. It was right ahead of him, he said, he could have picked up the object soon enough to have given notice in time to avoid the accident.[6]

The evidence of Captain E. G. Cannons, of the Atlantic Transport Company, called as an expert witness on behalf of the defendants, was of special interest and importance. Cross-examined by Campbell, it appeared that Captain Cannons, in the same circumstances, would not, after all, have acted in the same way as Captain Smith. Captain Cannons declared that he had received as many as four messages a day regarding ice, but that it was an unusual occurrence. If all the five marconigrams mentioned in the case had been received by responsible officers, they would have indicated a particularly dangerous area. If he knew he was approaching such an area, he would take the precaution of slowing up, although he knew the night was clear. The *Mesaba* report was more alarming than the first three. Assuming that he had received it, he would, if nothing were sighted, have navigated his vessel to the first longitude mentioned at full speed, having everybody on the alert, and would then have eased up. With his own ship, whose speed was 16 knots, if he saw a berg right ahead he could alter her course so as to avoid it in sixteen seconds.

Captain Cannons further testified that in the neighbourhood of an abundance of ice the atmosphere had a tendency to become hazy or foggy. He said that icebergs sometimes turned turtle and came up again. It was a sight which once seen was never forgotten. When the berg came up the ice was a bluish colour, but after exposure to the air it became white again.[7]

The importance of Captain Cannon's evidence was, first, because of its implied criticism of the Western Ocean mail boat school of navigation; and, secondly, because it tended to corroborate the evidence of a number of witnesses who had testified to the existence of haze in the vicinity of 41° 46′ N., 50° 14′ W. on the night of the disaster. So far as the present case was concerned, it put a different complexion on affairs.

The other masters declared that they would have acted in the same way as Captain Smith. Captain Pritchard, formerly of the Cunard Line, when examined by Duke testified that he could stop the *Mauretania* running at 26 knots in three-quarters of a mile, and could alter course in ten seconds. Captain Hayes said that he had had long experience of the Atlantic crossing. In clear weather in the ice region it was his practice to maintain his course and full speed. He said that when he received reports of ice in clear weather his practice was to carry on the ordinary routine of the ship. The danger in the ice region was not a danger of ice, but a danger of fog. In clear weather a berg could be seen from five to six miles away at night. He said that he had been an officer under Captain Smith for five or six years, and that the latter was a careful navigator, who never took a risk, or in his opinion, came to an unwise decision. He also knew Mr Murdoch, who had been an officer under him, and said that he was a capable, efficient, and zealous officer.[8]

In his closing speech, Duke fell back on the same line of defence, in its essentials, as had been successfully employed at the Inquiry. He maintained that the evidence which had been given showed conclusively that on a dark night an iceberg could be seen at a distance of four miles, and according to the rules of conduct on the sea employed by prudent seamen those in charge of the *Titanic* were justified, when the look-out was set, in proceeding on the assumption that a berg would be visible at that distance. The range of sight for ordinary eyes was four miles. The turning circle of the *Titanic* was 440 yards. Where was the imprudence, with a sufficient look-out and a ship perfectly under control, of going within four miles of an iceberg which you could avoid in two seconds? Here was a well-found ship capable of facing and meeting those perils of the sea which had to be looked for in the North Atlantic. Care was exercised in the setting of the look-out and in the observance of the course and speed of the vessel. He maintained attention had been given to the dictates of experience, and it was impossible that the jury should hold the defendants, by their servants, guilty of negligence or find that Captain Smith or Mr Murdoch had failed in their duty. That, in essence, was the counsel's defence against the charge of negligence.[9]

In his reply, Campbell dealt with the question whether any haze on the night of the accident prevented the look-out men from having a clear view, and he submitted that there was a strong body of testimony that such was the case. Whether the *Mesaba's* message was received or not, the messages admittedly received indicated that the ship was approaching a particularly dangerous area, in which it was necessary to exercise the greatest possible care. With regard to the nature of the iceberg with which the collision took place he would assume that it was as black as the defendants' witnesses had painted it. Even in that case Mr Lightoller said that it would be visible at some distance because there would be something white about it from whatever side it was approached. In view of such evidence, how could it be said that this disaster was due to the berg being black?

The counsel referred to the fact that the look-out men were not provided with glasses, and pointed out that it was significant that one of the men had said that if he had glasses in all probability he would have been able to see the berg in time to avoid the accident. The defendants were in a dilemma. If the accident were due to the iceberg being invisible by reason of a haze, then the defendants would be negligent in proceeding at full speed, because Captain Smith himself had said, 'If there is the slightest sign of haze we must go dead slow'. If, on the other hand, there was no haze and the look-out men could have seen the iceberg earlier and did not, then that would be negligence which would render the defendants liable.[10]

In his summing up, Mr Justice Bailhache said that, with regard to the *Mesaba* message, if that had been received by a responsible officer it showed that there was ice right in front of the *Titanic*. If she ought to have slowed down on the receipt of the first three marconigrams, *a fortiori*, she ought to have done so on the *Mesaba* message. It was for the jury to consider whether that message had been received. In conclusion, the judge said that in substance nearly the whole case turned upon the question of the iceberg being black and not white, as was expected, and the jury must consider whether, in the face of the knowledge that there were occasional black bergs to be found which were difficult to see, and the fact that there was a discussion about them that night, it was negligent to run the *Titanic* at such a speed that if a black berg was met it could not be avoided. They must bear in mind that an experienced body of navigators of the highest class had said that in similar circumstances they would have acted in the same way as Captain Smith, while against that Captain Cannons had told them that if he had known there was ice in his course he would have slowed down.

The jury then retired; and after an absence of an hour and three-quarters they returned a verdict to the effect that the navigation of the *Titanic* was not negligent in regard to the look-out, but was so in respect of speed. They also found that there was not sufficient evidence to show whether the *Mesaba* message was communicated in due course to some responsible officer of the *Titanic*.[11]

Some time afterwards the Company took the case to the Court of Appeal; but it was dismissed on February 9th, 1914, Lord Justice Vaughan Williams delivering the following judgment.

'Was the ship negligently navigated in adopting the course which was adopted? There can be no doubt but that Captain Smith diverted his course and adopted the course which he did adopt by way of precaution to avoid the ice which he was warned against by marconigrams from the *Caronia* and *Baltic*, but it is said that, having regard to the terms of these messages, Captain Smith, having diverted his course to avoid the ice, had good reason to suppose that when after the diversion he approached nearer the "lane" the icebergs he was warned against had passed the "lane" in the direction of south or south-west. Against this it is said that the very diversion of the course of the ship in consequence of the marconigrams about the ice in the neighbourhood of the "lane" which constitutes the adopted course for this season of the year shows that Captain Smith at all events did not personally believe in the hard-and-fast application of the rule to maintain course and speed laid down by most of the expert witnesses. Moreover, the conversation between Captain Smith and Mr Lightoller showed that Lightoller had made calculations from which he inferred that it was likely that icebergs would be met about the time at which the collision in fact took place. This does not, to my mind, show that it was negligence to make the diversion which Captain Smith made, but it does show that he must have considered the question whether or not at the moment when he was returning to the "lane" he was not running into a dangerous region or zone. Now assuming that he had information that ought to have led him to the conclusion that he was running in such a dangerous region, Mr Lightoller was on duty at the moment of the conversation, and on the Captain's departing to his room actually ordered some precautions to be taken against collision with ice. So far as negligence is concerned, it makes no difference whether the negligence was the negligence of Lightoller or Captain Smith, or, indeed, the negligence of Murdoch, who succeeded Lightoller as the officer in charge shortly before the collision. . . . But the strength of the case against the ship rests on the knowledge or apprehension of danger which Lightoller certainly had, and Captain Smith possibly had. This inference which I draw is derived from the conversation between Captain Smith and Lightoller, and the orders given in apprehension of danger. The outcome of these considerations to my mind is that the only answer which the *Titanic* can give to the charge of negligent navigation in proceeding in the circumstances that I have narrated at full speed must be that it is the practice of ships navigated across the Atlantic by the most skilled navigators to maintain course and speed in such circumstances. But the evidence of Captain Cannons, an expert witness called on behalf of the plaintiffs, undoubtedly is capable of being understood as admitting that the circumstances may be of such a character as to require a departure by a prudent navigator from the general practice. Whether the occasion was such as to require a departure from the general practice was a question for the jury. The duty of careful navigation does not amount to a warranty against accidents causing damage in the course of the voyage; the duty of those navigating the ship is to use reasonable care. It is for the jury to find whether there has been a failure to perform this duty. If there is evidence upon which the jury may reasonably come to the conclusion that there has been such failure the verdict cannot be disturbed. To my mind it is impossible to say in the present case that there was no evidence upon which the jury might find, as they did, negligence. The diversion from the "lane" by the order of Captain Smith was itself clear evidence that he himself recognized the seriousness of the danger ahead of which he had notice, and was a recognition of the fact that even on a clear night you cannot always safely maintain course and speed in a region made dangerous by ice. The recognition of this is in fact the only excuse for the diversion from the course laid down by all the great shipping lines on November 15th, 1898.

'There is one other matter which I think is material, that is the defence that the condition of the sea and atmosphere and the failure to discover the proximity of the iceberg bring the case within the dictum of Mr Justice Bailhache in his summing up that "It is never negligence to fail to provide for the unforeseen or unforeseeable". I think that the danger in this case was neither unforeseen nor unforeseeable. There was warning, to my mind, of dangerous ice ahead, and the jury might reasonably come to the conclusion that in the circumstances a prudent master ought thereupon to have slowed down, or even to have stopped, and if the master failed to perform this duty he cannot say, "I am excused because the state of things which the ship afterwards encountered was unforeseen or unforeseeable"; as the accident might not have happened if he had slowed down.'[12]

The judgment was from every point of view well and solidly grounded, distinguishing as it did the essential from the non-essential. It was based upon a far more accurate and dispassionate assessment of the evidence than had been the case at either the American or British Inquiry. The *ex parte* testimony given by Lightoller, which had hitherto carried so much weight, was heard yet again, considered, and finally discounted. 'E.J.'s' professional reputation was no longer unblemished. The charge of negligent navigation was upheld. *The danger was neither unforeseen nor unforeseeable.* That was the crux of the matter. The whitewash so liberally applied by Lord Mersey and his assessors had been effectively swept away and something like the true facts of the case exposed to view.

Chapter 19

The Row about the Californian

For a while the Board of Trade persevered in its search for the mysterious vessel which, it was alleged, had lain on that fateful night between the *Titanic* and *Californian*. To that end extensive inquiries were set in train for 'a steamer having one black funnel with a white band which might have been in the vicinity of 41° 46′ N., 50° 4′ W., on or about 1.30 a.m. and 4 a.m. on April 15th last'.[1]

'Do you not think,' Lord Mersey had asked the *Californian's* Chief Officer in the course of the Inquiry, 'that if there had been another steamer firing rockets that night we should have heard something about it by this time?'[2]

'Your Lordship may yet,' said Mr Dunlop. . . . But his Lordship never did. From that day to this no evidence has emerged of another vessel firing rockets at about the same time that the *Titanic* fired them. All these inquiries made on behalf of the Board of Trade proved fruitless. Even at the present time conjectures are still raised about the possibility of some marine *doppelgänger* which may have sent up the rockets seen by the two men on the bridge of the *Californian*; but no proof worthy of the name has ever been adduced that such a vessel in fact existed.[3]

The Hydrographer of the Navy Department, Washington, had no doubts about the matter. The Department had prepared a chart marked '*Titanic*—Ice barrier—near-by ships', which was very carefully worked out. The Hydrographer informed the Senate Committee: 'The evidence does not indicate to me that there was any such third steamer in those waters, especially in view of the fact that no such steamer was seen by other steamers or by those in the lifeboats the following morning, and as the ice barrier, from all reports, between the reported position of the *Californian* and that of the *Titanic* was impassable to a vessel proceeding to the westward, and there is no testimony to show if such a steamer was between the *Californian* and the *Titanic* she proceeded to the eastward, the captain of the *Californian* having testified that he last saw the said steamer proceeding to the westward and being on a bearing to the westward of the *Californian*. Nothing appears in the testimony to show that the steamer so seen reversed its course and proceeded to the eastward.'[4]

Incidentally a rather intriguing point has come to light in connection with the inquiries that were made about 'wireless and other messages received' respecting the proximity of ice in the North Atlantic.[5] The owners of the vessel that had sent the warning by Morse lamp to the *Titanic* shortly before the collision, Messrs Furness, Withy and Company, actually informed the Board of Trade: 'We beg to advise you that we had no vessels in the vicinity when the disaster occurred to the *Titanic*'; and the acting Master of this vessel, the *Rappahannock*, who had himself sent the warning of the icefield ahead, was never called to give evidence at the Inquiry. The explanation may possibly lie in one of the *Titanic* files at the Board of Trade which are still inaccessible to the historian.

The crucial point, of course, is the rockets. The whole matter of discrepancies regarding bearings and timings, which was perfectly well known at the time of the disaster, pales into insignificance compared with the damning evidence of the distress signals. It is this point which altogether convinced—and, in the opinion of the present writer, rightly convinced—the Court of Inquiry. 'It has always appeared to me,' wrote a master mariner to the *Nautical Magazine* later in 1912, 'and to many others with whom I have discussed the subject, to be a mere matter of detail whether those on board the *Californian* saw the *Titanic* or they did not? They evidently saw a vessel of some sort firing rockets, a signal of danger. It was the duty of the *Californian* to have gone to her assistance. They did nothing! Whose fault it was is only known to Captain Lord and his officers. They might not have been able to get near her on account of the ice, but they might have *tried*.' 'Whether they were low rockets without an explosion, colour or trail in the sky,' observed the late Captain A. E. Smith fifty years afterwards, 'all these things were immaterial, they were rockets and obviously signals of distress.'[7]

If one endeavours conscientiously to follow the deeply involved and complicated reasoning of the pamphlet published by the Mercantile Marine Service Association, entitled, *The 'Californian' Incident*, one's head begins to reel. And small wonder. After all, it is only necessary to study the logs of the vessels engaged in certain naval operations of the past to realize how little dependence can sometimes be placed on the accuracy of times, distances, and bearings. If ever there was a case of not seeing the wood for trees, of failing to draw the inescapable conclusions from the evidence, of rejecting the essential for the inessential, we have it here. The author of *The 'Californian' Incident* ought to be a Don. . . .

Lord Mersey and his assessors were unanimously of opinion that the rockets seen by the *Californian* were those of the *Titanic*; nor would they accept Captain Lord's statement that he had heard nothing of the apprentice Gibson's message.

'There are contradictions and inconsistencies as told by the different witnesses,' the Commissioner declared. 'But the truth of the matter is plain. The *Titanic* collided with the berg at 11.40. The vessel seen by the *Californian* stopped at this time. The rockets sent up from the *Titanic* were distress signals. The *Californian* saw distress signals. The number sent up by the *Titanic* was about eight. The *Californian* saw eight. The time over which the rockets from the *Titanic* were sent up was from about 12.45 to 1.45 o'clock. It was about this time that the *Californian* saw the rockets. At 2.40 Mr Stone called to the Master that the ship from which he had seen the rockets had disappeared. At 2.20 a.m. the *Titanic* had foundered. It was suggested that the rockets seen by the *Californian* were from some other ship, not the *Titanic*. But no other ship to fit this theory has ever been heard of. . . . The ice by which the *Californian* was surrounded was loose ice extending for a distance of not more than two or three miles in the direction of the *Titanic*. The night was clear and the sea was smooth. When she first saw the rockets the *Californian* could have pushed through the ice to the open water without any serious risk and so have come to the assistance of the *Titanic*. Had she done so she might have saved many if not all the lives that were lost.'[8]

The Court of Inquiry had made a number of recommendations; but, with this single exception, had found nobody to blame for the disaster. In thus censuring the Master of the *Californian* for the part he had played, or was alleged to have played, on the night of the wreck, Lord Mersey and his assessors followed the American finding.

The Master had a very bad press. The *Review of Reviews* wanted to know whether the Board of Trade had taken any steps in the way of bringing Captain Lord, 'that thousand-fold murderer', to justice.[9] 'I fear,' growled *John Bull*, apostrophizing the accused, 'you are a remnant of an old type of skipper, and it strikes me that your officers were somewhat too timid in expressing their views to you. They should have chanced your displeasure, and pulled you out of bed. Another matter I don't like is the utter absence of any reference to these distress signals in your log-book. Was the idea to say nothing about it, had the donkeyman not split?'[10] In its first leader that day the *Daily Telegraph*, after alluding to the indictment held to have been proved against a British shipmaster, declared: 'It stands on record for all time; it calls for no comment, for the condemnation is as unmitigated in its simple severity as it is unmerciful in its stern recital of the probable consequences of this fatal lapse from the high standard of conduct on the sea, accepted by sailors everywhere as a commonplace duty which none would dare to escape even at personal peril. This portion of the report stands out as a thing apart—a horror which in the days to come will wound the human instinct of the race whenever the story of the *Titanic* is recounted. . . .'[11]

That was as far as the authorities went in the matter. No further action was taken over the *Californian* incident. Captain Lord was not hanged (though one or two periodicals roundly declared that he ought to have been); he did not lose his certificate or have it suspended; he was not even 'roughmusicked' to the burden of 'Capten, art tha sleepin' there below?' But the stigma remained. . . .

During the ensuing months Captain Lord made repeated protests both to the Board of Trade and to his professional organization, the Mercantile Marine Service Association, with a view to getting the case re-opened. But all these protests were in vain; as no one had been censured for the actual loss of the *Titanic*, no one was allowed to appeal; Lord's reputation remained under a heavy cloud; and because of the Court's finding he was presently constrained to leave the Leyland Line, in which he had served for more than fourteen years.

'My employers, the Leyland Line,' he wrote to the Board of Trade on August 12th, 'although their nautical advisers are convinced we did not see the *Titanic*, or the *Titanic* see the *Californian*, say they have the utmost confidence in me, and do not blame me in any way, but owing to Lord Mersey's decision and public opinion caused by this report, they are reluctantly compelled to ask for my resignation, after 14½ years' service without a hitch of any description, and if I could clear myself of this charge, would willingly reconsider their decision.'[12]

The reply was to the effect that as all the circumstances attending the loss of the *Titanic* had formed the subject of a searching investigation by a Court of Inquiry, the Board of Trade would not feel justified in taking any steps with regard to a re-hearing of the case.

The following year, on August 8th, 1913, Lord returned to the attack:

'By the general public the *Titanic* Inquiry is forgotten, but to me, the undeserved stigma of the *Californian* which I have to bear will always remain, unless your Dept. by opening an enquiry will give me an opportunity of clearing myself. A further hearing by an independent Court, on the evidence already submitted at the former Inquiry, is all I ask for.'[13]

The official reply brought little consolation to Captain Lord.

'With reference to your letter of the 8th August and to previous correspondence respecting the Report of the Official Inquiry held in London into the loss of the s.s. *Titanic*, I am directed by the Board of Trade to state that they have carefully considered the statements to which you refer, but, as you were informed in August last year, they are unable to re-open the matter'.[14]

Lord's endeavours to have the Official Inquiry re-opened were abandoned on the outbreak of the First World War. Despite the stigma of the *Californian*, his affairs prospered. In 1913 he was offered an immediate command in the Nitrate Producers' Steam Ship Company Limited, with whom he served during the next fourteen years. It would appear that, following the *Titanic* affair, Lord's disposition suffered something of a sea-change. He was no longer the self-assured, autocratic, overbearing character that he had been; he went softly, so to speak, throughout the rest of his time afloat. He retired from the sea, on account of ill-health, in 1927.

In his *The Truth about the 'Titanic'*, which appeared shortly after the disaster, Colonel Archibald Gracie had roundly charged Captain Lord with 'the grossest negligence' in not responding to signals of distress. Twenty-five years later Lightoller published his *'Titanic' and Other Ships*, in which he dealt pretty roughly with the *Californian*, which to the day of his death he always declared to be the 'stand-by' ship seen from the bridge of the doomed liner. It was not, however, until twenty years later still that Captain Lord, who by this time was over eighty, returned to the fray. About this time a book and a film called *A Night to Remember* (the name of the author, by a strange irony, also happened to be Lord) gave wide publicity to the drama of the sinking liner and the 'stand-by' ship.

Captain Lord thereupon appealed to the Mercantile Marine Service Association; and the case was taken up energetically, even passionately, by the General Secretary, Mr W. L. S. Harrison. The immediate result was an impasse in the Council of the Association and the resignation of the President, Captain Sir Ivan Thompson. Pamphlets were circulated giving Captain Lord's version of 'the *Californian* incident', and in 1965 the Council formally petitioned the President of the Board of Trade to order the re-hearing of that part of the Inquiry relating to the happenings on the night of the wreck on board the s.s. *Californian*.

That well over fifty years after the event and with nearly every important witness in the case dead the Board of Trade flatly refused to order a re-hearing, is understandable. Only if it could have been clearly established that Captain Lord had been 'framed' at the Official Inquiry, or that there had been deliberate suppression of vital evidence, could such a request as this be treated seriously. Even if reliable witnesses could be produced who had actually been on board some vessel in the vicinity of the *Titanic* that had fired eight rockets (*mirabile dictu*) at or about the same time as the *Titanic's* eight rockets had been sent up, there would *still* be no case for a re-hearing— since the crucial issue, of course, was the failure of a British shipmaster to go to the aid of a vessel making distress signals; that is, sending up rockets at regular intervals. As it is, these demonstrations have convinced neither the Board of Trade, nor affected the general consensus of professional opinion, which remains, as it always has been, decidedly adverse to Captain Lord.

To clear Captain Lord of the heavy charges brought against him a good many people would have to be proved wrong. That, indeed, is what has been averred. The Official Inquiries were wrong, declare the Lordites, so were the Hydrographer of the Navy Department and his staff, so was Captain Rostron, so were Lightoller, Boxhall, and Beesley, so was the Third Officer of the *Californian*, the apprentice, Gibson, and Gill, the donkeyman, so also were Bisset and the other officers of the *Carpathia*. Everyone, it would appear, is out of step but the Master of the *Californian*. . . .

Amongst other things, it has been argued by Captain Lord's apologists that the *Titanic's* position that night was incorrect. Yet the Hydrographer to the Navy Department, the British Naval Attaché, and the other Naval experts attending the American Inquiry in Washington were quite unconvinced as to a possible error in the *Titanic's* position. Moreover, on the strength of this position sent out by the *Titanic's* radio the *Carpathia* went straight to the scene of the wreck and experienced no difficulty in finding the survivors, and Captain Rostron had subsequently congratulated Boxhall on the accuracy of his calculations—'What a splendid position that was you gave us.'

Captain Lord in his appeal to the Board of Trade averred that 'a nautical man rarely makes a good witness'. Why this should be so is not very easy to fathom—provided, of course, he is truthful and honest. But the only response which this particular nautical man had made to the news that rockets were being fired in the vicinity of his ship was to turn over and go to sleep again and afterwards to excuse himself on that score in a manner reminiscent of the dashing automobilist who, in answer to the damning evidence that he was on the wrong side of the road at the time of the crash, explains triumphantly, '*I don't remember a thing about it!*'—as if that disposes of the whole unfortunate affair.

No attempt has yet been made to account for the extraordinary state of affairs that, according to the testimony of her officers, seems to have prevailed on board the *Californian*. Some of the statements made by Messrs Stewart and Stone at the Inquiry would have strained the credulity of a child of ten. (Incidentally, what Stone would sometimes say in private was very different from what Stone had said in public.) *John Bull* in the excerpt cited above was in all likelihood tolerably near the mark in suggesting that his officers were somewhat nervous of Captain Lord. There is always a natural inclination to keep on the right side of an autocratic and overbearing Master; and if the Master in question were not both autocratic and overbearing it is to be surmised that his photographs, as well as the evidence, do him a grave injustice. It is possible that Captain Lord had never encouraged his subordinates to speak their minds freely and openly. Therein may lie the true explanation of the *Californian* incident. The epitaph on quite a number of officers of both the Royal Navy and Merchant Service might very well be, *They kept their noses clean*. Some suspicion as to the reality of the situation on board the *Californian* was probably in the mind of the court when the other officers were all sent outside while Captain Lord was giving his evidence. . . .

An alternative, and less charitable, explanation of the inaction of the Master of the *Californian* on the night of the disaster was that suggested by the *Boston American*. After all, there were two obvious courses which Lord might have followed. The first was to go up on the bridge and see for himself what was happening; the second was to do what his own Chief Officer actually did when it was too late—*wake up the wireless operator*. But in either case he would have been committed to what he might regard as a most hazardous line of action—that is, a rush through the icefield in the darkness to the help of the distant steamer. By his own inaction and his own testimony, as well as that of certain of his officers, Lord had laid himself open to just such a charge, whether justified or not.

'Captain Lord,' summed up the former acting Master of the *Rappahannock*, 'was properly censured by the Court of Inquiry held at the time. Nothing can alter the known facts of the case, and the lessons to be learned from such a tragedy should never be forgotten or hushed up.'[15]

A consideration of prime importance which the Board of Trade had always to bear in mind was the necessity of keeping shipmasters fully aware of their responsibilities with regard to rendering assistance to vessels in distress. With this object in view handbills had been distributed to masters of vessels while the *Titanic* Inquiry was still in progress reminding them of the grave obligation to render such assistance.[16] The inaction of the *Californian* on the night of he tragedy was a scandal to some, a mystery to others. Nevertheless it was by no means unique. 'Here again,' Lightoller observed, 'we were to see exemplified, what has become almost proverbial at sea, that in cases of disaster, one ship, the first on the scene, will be in a position to rescue, and yet, through some circumstance or combination of circumstances, fails to make that rescue.' Something of the same muddle or misunderstanding seems to have occurred in connection with the burning of the *Volturno*.[17]

It is difficult to understand what the Council of the Mercantile Marine Service Association hoped to achieve by this campaign. The reversal *in toto* of the original finding of the Court of Inquiry was by no means to be counted on, even supposing that the Council's request had been granted. Nor is the present writer able to comprehend why the reversal of this finding should necessarily put a stop to all further criticism of 'the conduct of a British shipmaster'. The *Californian* 'myth' did not, as has wrongly been suggested, come down the years simply and solely from the verdict of the Official Inquiry. The charges against Captain Lord and certain of his officers arose out of the facts of the case, as implicit in the evidence, and were supported by the consensus of professional opinion.

Chapter 20

'The Sea Hath Spoken'

Soon after the disaster the myths began to sprout. Inevitably the *Titanic* legend captured the popular imagination. It was responsible, indeed, for a good deal of error and misunderstanding which has persisted to the present day. The legend imposed itself upon, and in large measure obscured, the true facts of the case. What actually happened on the night of April 14th is by no means the same as what is supposed to have happened.

The public—or, at any rate, the public that mattered—wanted stories of heroism and self-sacrifice; and it got them. J. L. Garvin of the *Observer* said he thought the strains of 'Nearer, my God, to Thee' were worthy to be remembered with the drums of the *Birkenhead*. *Lloyd's Weekly News* printed the hymn in full, along with the score. The opening line was inscribed on Wallace Hartley's tombstone when his body was brought home and interred in his native Lancashire. 'It was,' the *Daily Chronicle* declared, 'a fitting ending to a solemn and terrible tragedy, and could not have failed to have brought consolation to all, and helped to bring them nearer to One Who holds the sea in the hollow of His hands.' Assuredly 'Nearer, my God, to Thee' has come to stay . . . despite the fact that it was actually not that hymn at all, but 'Autumn', which was played just before the end.

The gallant behaviour of everyone concerned—particularly of the first class gentlemen—was rather overdone in the press and in the pulpit. Actually it was not quite so heroic as all that. According to some of the early newspaper accounts, the boats were almost wholly filled with women and children. This, as is evident from the statistics, was very far from the truth. In several of the boats there were more men than women. A large number of firemen and stewards were among those saved.

Several men took refuge under the boats' thwarts. One of the first class gentlemen abandoned ship with such precipitancy that he broke two of the ribs of the unfortunate lady on whom he fell. Many a *beau geste* which has been attributed to Astor and Butt is almost certainly apocryphal.[1] The fulsome tribute paid to Dives and Co. by the fashionable preachers of New York and elsewhere on the Sunday following the disaster also had its ludicrous side. In the course of a sermon in which he must have struck almost as many attitudes as Nelson's Lady Hamilton, the Reverend Doctor Ernest Stires singled out for special mention the wealthy industrialist Arthur Ryerson, praising 'the quiet smile, the gentle determination, with which he put the dearest persons of all, the girls, the boy, even the maid, into the lifeboat and watched them row away to safety'.[2] It is to be hoped that everyone in the devoted congregation— even the maid—was properly edified by these Christian sentiments. . . . The obsequies of John Jacob Astor (who had been one of the Reverend Ernest's parishioners) were distinguished by the same gestures of deferential regard and respect, not to say adulation, on the part of the local clergy. The lost lamb was received back into the fold. His rare qualities were suitably commended; his transgressions were charitably overlooked. When all is said and done, \$150 millions covers a multitude of sins. . . .

The 'perfect discipline' of the crew was similarly exaggerated. The loading and lowering of the boats was in some degree a shambles; it was not by any means well organized; and Lightoller's commendation of the Merchant Service at the expense of the Royal Navy was altogether uncalled for. The conduct in the boats of two of the trusted quartermasters, George Symons and Robert Hitchens, certainly does not suggest 'perfect discipline'.

Understandably, the part played by the redoubtable Mrs J. J. Brown has gained considerably in the telling. Maggie, indeed, had behaved splendidly that night and deserved all the credit that came her way. However, she had not, in actual fact, divested herself of most of her clothing for the benefit of others; and then, brandishing a revolver, assumed command of No. 6 boat in her corsets. . . .[3]

The story of the large black Newfoundland dog which leaped from the decks of the sinking liner into one of the lifeboats and then sagaciously proceeded to pilot that craft to the *Carpathia*, 'his joyous barks signalling Captain Rostron that he was coming', must also, alas, be rejected as apocryphal.[4]

It was too much to expect that anything like the whole truth would or possibly could be revealed at the British Inquiry. Long experience of such tribunals in this country has shown that an official Inquiry is almost invariably a whitewashing operation. It is difficult, indeed, to see how it could be otherwise. After all, what is truth? In public affairs what one regards as the truth depends very largely upon one's national, party, or other sectional allegiance. Though the professionally religious may hold up their hands in pious horror at the suggestion, there can be no question that this is what usually happens in real life; and even among their reverend selves deviation from the strict truth is not altogether unknown.

Thus at the *Titanic* Inquiry Lord Mersey exhibited an almost child-like innocence of the realities of the situation at sea. Over and over again he would swallow—hook, line, and sinker—statements which every officer in the merchant service knew perfectly well to be untrue. It did not need a Solomon to to detect some of the fallacies in the specious arguments which were seriouslyadvanced. If the *Titanic* was due in New York on the 17th and there was no intention of docking on the 16th, why was she running at a speed that must have brought her into the Hudson River long before her proper time? Then there were the standing orders of the White Star Line.[5] These not only authorized, but positively directed, the Master to avoid all risk and danger, which might have been done either by reducing speed or else by steering well to the southward of the ice. The fact that Captain Smith, a prudent and experienced commander, adopted neither of these expedients shows clearly enough what was expected of him, and what he knew was expected of him. In the same way 'E.J.' was obviously under the necessity of attending a dinner party given by such wealthy and influential passengers as the Wideners—whatever Lightoller with his tongue in his cheek might suggest to the contrary. Lord Mersey was even willing to delude himself into agreeing that Ismay was no more than an ordinary passenger on board the *Titanic*; though it is to be observed that an ordinary passenger usually pays for his passage ... and does not, as a rule, peremptorily summon the Chief Engineer to his cabin, or take over an official message from the Master.

The most appalling catastrophe in the annals of the sea was comfortably attributed to 'a combination of circumstances that never occurred before and never can occur again'; at a later date, at the unveiling of the memorial to Captain Smith, it was blandly described as 'one of those unforeseen contingencies which are inseparable from life at sea'. 'Never before,' the papers declared, 'had ice been encountered so far south' (exactly the same observation had been made when the *Arizona* struck ice in the same region more than thirty years before). 'By the mysterious will of God,' said a Bournemouth vicar, 'the ship struck an iceberg.' *Populus vult decipi et decipiatur*. It was almost as if the British public desired to be humbugged.

Well-known diarists like Arnold Bennett and Wilfrid Scawen Blunt incorporated the myth in their entries for April, 1912. Historians also lapped it up. 'And now the sea,' declaimed R. H. Gretton, 'calling up its terrors, had drifted an iceberg across her track in the night, and engulfed her in a few minutes.' A more misleading description of the great disaster could hardly be written. Of the danger of ice ahead there had, in fact, been ample warning: it was neither 'unforeseen nor unforeseeable'; and after the collision, so far from foundering in a matter of minutes, the *Titanic* had remained afloat for more than two and a half hours. 'What suspicions emerged at the Inquiries,' ended this most gentlemanly historian, 'of human failure in the crisis of the disaster may be left now unexplored.'[6]

However, in the end a kind of rough justice was done.

Though press comment in America had been decidedly hostile to Ismay, it was not so in this country; at the Inquiry he had been ably defended by counsel, and at first he appeared to have carried the day. 'There is no observation of an unfavourable nature to be made from any point of view upon Mr Ismay's conduct,' Sir Robert Finlay had declared. 'There was no duty devolving upon him of going to the bottom with his ship as the captain did.' To all outward appearance the

Chairman of the White Star Line had left the court without a stain on his character. Officially he was cleared, exonerated, and exculpated in every possible way. *But his colleagues on the Board threw him out and he had to live in Connemara. . . .*

In the same way the White Star Line also had apparently been vindicated at the Inquiry. Their servants, the Master and officers of the *Titanic*, had been cleared of the charge of negligent navigation. They had made a mistake, it was admitted; but only a mistake. So far from being censured by the Commissioner, Captain Smith had become almost a national hero. The united efforts of Finlay and Lightoller had worked miracles for the Company. *But in the law courts the Company had lost the case. . . .*

For the past twenty years and more it had been the custom in the North Atlantic trade to discount the hazards of the ice region. There had been plenty of evidence at the Inquiry to demonstrate that the normal procedure, in the fast passenger steamships, was to maintain course and speed, during the hours of darkness, so long as the weather remained clear. *But the practice now stood condemned; the shipping lanes were fixed well to the southward of the danger zone, and an International Ice Patrol was set up. . . .*

Scanlan's endeavours to prove that the life-saving equipment on board the *Titanic* was utterly inadequate and that there were not nearly enough seamen to launch and man the lifeboats were controverted by the opposing counsel and deprecated by the Commissioner. *But these points were fully and frankly admitted in the measures subsequently taken to amend the regulations. . . .*

It is safe to say that it is improbable in the extreme that the full truth about the *Titanic* disaster will ever be known; there are not a few important points which have never been resolved, and are never likely to be resolved; nevertheless, enough evidence has by now come to light to enable us, with confidence, to establish the main chain of causation.

The *causa causans* may be said to have been the influence of great wealth upon the North Atlantic passenger traffic. The *Titanic* was essentially an appeal to the class, growing larger every year, that had more money than it knew what to do with. For upwards of half a century the largest, swiftest, and best-appointed vessels in the world had plied on the trade-routes between Europe and North America. Almost every year had seen a steady advance in point of size, speed, reliability, and comfortable accommodation. Luxuries, undreamed of by one generation, were taken entirely for granted by the next. It was the ever-increasing demand for first class accommodation of the most spacious and costly character imaginable that had led to the construction of these enormous, fast, luxurious liners which were travelling Grand Hotels provided with everything the heart could desire, 'except', as the *Labour Leader* drily remarked 'an adequate supply of lifeboats'.

The perennial danger of ice in these waters had been known to seamen for centuries, as is amply clear from successive editions of the sailing directions. In the course of the nineteenth century, through this cause, an unknown number of ships had been lost without a trace. Less than twenty years before the *Naronic*, bound from Liverpool to New York on her maiden voyage, had mysteriously disappeared in the vicinity of the Banks—it was believed that she struck an iceberg during a heavy snowstorm; the *Alleghany*, the *State of Georgia*, and the *Huronian* had likewise 'gone missing'. Moreover, there had been a good many hairbreadth escapes. In the autumn of 1879 the Guion liner *Arizona*, then the largest ship afloat, had run bows on against an iceberg off the Banks and had sustained such severe damage that she only just managed to crawl into Halifax.[7] In later years the *Portia*, *Saale*, and *Normannia* had struck ice; and the *City of Rome* and *Columbia*, though running at reduced speed, had also collided with ice.

During the first week of April, 1912, the track used by the North Atlantic trade had been seriously obstructed by bergs and field-ice. Only a few days before the disaster both the *Germania* and the *Empress of India* had altered course to avoid the ice-field. The Cunard liner *Carmania* reported that for some hours she had been in grave danger. For nearly thirty-six hours the commander of the Allan liner *Tunisian* had hardly quitted the bridge. The French liner *Niagara* had been holed twice beneath her water-line and had had several of her plates buckled. (This occurred in approximately the same region as that in which the *Titanic* sank. The *Niagara* had actually sent out an SOS.) There were also several smaller vessels, the s.s. *Dura*, *Lord Cromer*, and *Armenian*, which had reported dangerous experiences in this region and suffered more or less serious damage.

As a general rule, when the ice reached so far to the south-ward and eastward, it would be honeycombed, half melting, and on the point of disintegration. In this particular April, however, the ice reports coming in showed a different condition. Ships were reporting 'glacial ice, hard as steel and blue in tint, which shows that it does not contain air and will travel far before it melts'.[8]

It is significant that when, some forty minutes after receiving the last of the ice warnings sent that night, the *Titanic* crashed into an outlying berg of the ice-mass which was encompassing the *Californian*, the great liner was actually to the *westward* of some of the ice reported.

It is not, perhaps, generally realized that the express steam-ships of the rival Cunard Line had a reserve of speed which the White Star liners did not possess. If the former for any reason had to slow down, they could always hope to make up the lost time later. In the case of the slower White Star liners this could not be done. Had the *Titanic* later run into fog and been obliged to slow down, the ensuing delay, added to that caused by running at reduced speed in the ice region, would have thrown out her schedule.

During the Inquiry the *Nautical Magazine* had commented acidly on the '*cautious*, *prudent*, and *ever-watchful* system of navigation' enjoined by the White Star Line's regulations in view of the known 'secret pressure put upon masters to keep up speed and make passages'.

Masters in the Atlantic service would be only too thankful if this caution were the recognized procedure in the trade; *but it is not*. Of course, Captain Smith has the blame put upon him, but we seamen know perfectly well how the case stood and we should fancy that Lord Mersey with his long experience of the Law Courts must have had a shrewd suspicion as to the real state of things. But Captain Smith must be blamed, in our opinion most unjustly; he had enough responsibilities upon his shoulders without the added burden of Mr Ismay's presence, and every one of us would sooner have our owner's room than his company, particularly upon a first voyage. There is enough secret pressure put upon masters to keep up speed and make passages as it is, and the presence of an autocrat on board does not tend to ease that pressure. No master would go at full speed if expecting to meet with ice unless he were obliged; personally it is nothing to him. But Captain Smith was a paid employee of Mr Ismay. "He made a mistake, a very grievous mistake," is Lord Mersey's way of putting it.[9]

In making these observations the *Nautical Magazine* no more than voiced the sentiments of many an indignant master mariner who dare not openly say what was being thought and said in the privacy of the officers' quarters on board the larger passenger liners. The truth of the matter is that these regulations were only a cloak to cover the Company, should an accident occur. It was never intended that the commander should rigorously abide by them. On the contrary, he was expected to keep to schedule, with a view to saving the tide and docking on time. This is implicit in the fact that the Chairman of the White Star Line saw—without protest—the formal instructions of his Company deliberately broken when, on the night of April 14th, the *Titanic* steamed at high speed through a region of the ocean where ice was being everywhere reported—i.e. under potentially hazardous conditions. This high speed was maintained, moreover, even with the icefield right in her track, and in spite of the *Rappahannock's* urgent warning.

In this connection it should be observed that, during the Inquiry, in reply to a suggestion from Lord Mersey that commanders would sometimes hold on through fog at full speed, Sanderson had declared: 'The man who told you that is either extremely ignorant or most vicious. Such a thing is never done. The logs of other vessels can be obtained'.[10]

It was not, however, because such things were never done that the logs were silent on this important point; but rather because such entries were purposely excluded from the record. Senior officers knew very well what was expected of them.[11]; and their juniors were warned to keep their mouths shut or risk dismissal. Many of these ships escaped disaster by good fortune rather than by prudent navigation.[12] An experienced Master once told the present writer that, during this period, the aggregate of 'near misses' that occurred would have probably filled a family Bible. . . .

In fact, not only at the time of the *Titanic* disaster, but also for long before, and for long afterwards (as the unfortunate 'cod-bankers' knew to their cost), liners continued to run at high speed through the blinding fog off the Newfoundland banks,[13] and not infrequently ran down fishing schooners and dories. Such a thing is never done, indeed! The crews of the Brixham smacks and Mounts Bay luggers could also tell a different story. Again and again, in the vicinity of the Lizard, Wolf, and Bishop Rock, fishing vessels have been within an ace of being sent to the bottom by some 'Ram-you-damn-you liner' driving on at a rate of knots in thick weather. It is not so many years since that the *Energetic*, a Mounts Bay fishing vessel, was run down in this manner by a fast steamship with the loss of nearly every man on board; and about the same time another fishing vessel, the *Amelia* of St Ives, was also lost, without a single survivor.

'I do not want to make surmises,' Sir Ernest Shackleton had remarked at the Inquiry, 'and I do not want to lay down any particular rules, but there is a general feeling amongst people at sea that you have to make your passage. If you do not make your passage it is not so good for you.'[14]

Masters, therefore, for the most part faced the risk of collision as a matter of course. But not all. There were some who for days had found themselves unable to sleep after hearing the crunch of a dory stove in by the liner's bows at dead of night . . . and who did not think it right to run such risks on account of the necessity of keeping to schedule. That is why a certain number of first-rate officers would not enter the mail boat service at all or left it after some such experience as that related above.

Any suggestion that the wireless apparatus in use at this time was crude and untrustworthy may be dismissed as false and unfounded. Radio in 1912 was *not*, as has quite wrongly been suggested, 'an erratic novelty'. On the contrary, the transmitting and receiving apparatus fitted on board these liners was efficient, reliable, and well-tried. It was not the wireless equipment of the *Titanic* and *Californian* which was at fault. It was the human element that failed.

Bride, preoccupied with his accounts spread out on the operating-table, failed to take down the ice-report sent out by the *Californian* in the afternoon of April 14th. Later on Phillips became so absorbed in the backlog of lucrative private traffic with Cape Race that, contrary to regulations, he put on one side a message affecting the navigation of the ship, 'just until I squared up what I was doing before sending it to the bridge'[15] (In the event, the casual phrase 'just until' meant something like two hours). On board this great liner there was a whole army of stewards and stewardesses, as well as a smaller, but very adequate, attendance of 'gentlemen's gentlemen', ladies' maids, children's Nannies, governesses, etc.: *but there was no one to take that vital message to the Officer of the Watch*. There was much to be said for Phillips and Bride. Overworked, underpaid, and deprived of their fair share of rest and recreation, these operators were, if the truth were known, subject to much the same secret pressure as that put upon the commander. Luxury came before safety.[16] As has already been said, Evans made no further attempt to warn the *Titanic* of the ice-field which encompassed the *Californian* after he had bungled the business in the first instance—instead, he had closed down his station and turned in, though emergency conditions prevailed. Neither in the *Titanic* nor in the *Californian*, in fact, was due regard paid to this urgent matter of the successive ice warnings.[17]

In view of the hazards entailed through the *Titanic's* high speed when entering the ice region there was need for the utmost vigilance. Additional look-outs should have been put on and all ice-reports carefully scrutinized. In point of fact, as we know, this was not done. The look-outs were not increased, and the commander's casual handling of the *Baltic* telegram almost passes belief. It apparently did not occur to Captain Smith that night, as it had to Captain Rostron, to send for 'Sparks' and make inquiries about the ships within range. If Captain Smith had done this, it is possible that he might have heard about the *Mesaba* message. The keenness and vigilance which characterized the *Carpathia* were in striking contrast to the laxity and over-confidence which obtained in the *Titanic* and the lack of proper liaison between her wireless station and the ship's officers.

The crucial question of the visibility at the time of the collision was never cleared up satisfactorily at the Inquiry. In order to cover the Master and the O.O.W. against the charge of negligent navigation, it was necessary for Lightoller to deny the existence of any haze: the look-outs had, nevertheless, testified that there *was* haze: and several other witnesses had given testimony to the same effect. At night, it is sometimes very hard to know whether there is haze or not. There may, conceivably, have been something like the phenomenon known as 'a Swatow mist' which gives an observer the impression that there is a clear horizon when, in fact, the visibility is restricted to half a mile or less.[18] Surface haze may sometimes be seen from the crow's nest when it would be invisible from the bridge. Even Lightoller had ultimately to admit the possibility of local haze in the vicinity of ice. The disappearance of the binoculars usually kept up in the crow's nest was another link in the causal chain.[19]

The conditions of visibility and sea being as they were on the night of the 14th, it was hazardous in the extreme for a vessel of the size of the *Titanic* to proceed at $22\frac{1}{2}$ knots. The huge liner was slow to respond to the movement of her rudder. Her turning-circle was necessarily a wide one.[20] Moreover, there was a perceptible interval between the moment when the look-outs actually sighted the iceberg ahead and when the O.O.W. ordered the helm to be put over. The cumulative time-lag proved fatal to the *Titanic*.[21]

It was shown at the Inquiry that the structural strength of the *Titanic* was by no means proportionate to her size. She possessed no inner skin like the *Mauretania* and other large liners; nor was she really divided by watertight compartments, but only partly divided; for, though the other watertight bulkheads were carried up to D Deck, the transverse bulkhead abaft of No. 4 boiler room, for some inexplicable reason, stopped at E Deck. But for this inadequate sub-division the *Titanic* might have remained afloat. None of the additions to the sub-division which were desirable would have added seriously to the cost of the vessel; but they would undoubtedly have decreased the capacity of her passenger accommodation.

Arising out of this point was the attempt, in certain quarters, to discover a scapegoat in the First Officer. It occurred at both the American and British Inquiries, and also in the press. It now appeared that the *Titanic* was only unsinkable provided that she charged an obstruction end on, and that Murdoch, therefore, ought coolly and deliberately to have steered for a head-on collision with the berg.

This suggestion not unnaturally excited a certain amount of derisive comment among Murdoch's professional brethren. 'We shall have presently,' Joseph Conrad observed scornfully, 'in deference to commercial and industrial interests, a new kind of seamanship. . . . When in doubt try to ram fairly—whatever's before you. . . .'[22]

In point of fact, Murdoch appears to have done everything that was prudent and possible in the circumstances; there was little chance, indeed, for the *Titanic* to have avoided the collision during the very brief interval that elapsed between the look-outs sighting the iceberg and the fatal impact. And Murdoch, as we have seen, was the last man in the Line likely to lose his head in a moment of emergency.

In 1912 the safety regulations of the Board of Trade were hopelessly out of date. They bore little relation to the realities of the situation. The regulations, made in 1894, stipulated that 'vessels over 10,000 tons' must carry sixteen lifeboats of a stated total capacity, as well as a number of rafts or floats. There were now vessels at sea of several times that tonnage; but the regulations remained unchanged. There were consequently not nearly sufficient lifeboats for the number of passengers and crew carried in the largest class of modern liner. Though all the legal requirements would have been fully met if the *Titanic* had provided boats and rafts for rather less than one thousand persons, at the same time she was actually certified by the Board of Trade to carry more than 3,500 persons. The explanation of this extraordinary state of things may probably be found, first, in the normal British official inertia and, second, in the fact that the Board of Trade was unduly influenced—not to say dominated—by the shipping interest. To quote *Syren and Shipping*:

There cannot be the slightest doubt that if the vessel had been provided with sufficient boats to carry all the people on board her not a single life need have been lost. The chief culprit, of course, is the Board of Trade, that Department having allowed regulations made eighteen years ago, when the largest liner afloat was of about 12,000 tons, to continue in force in these days of floating towns. Mr Sydney Buxton's statement in the House on Thursday last only serves to make matters worse. The Board have been tinkering with the subject in the time-honoured fashion, but, of course, nothing has been *done*. Had not this world-shaking tragedy arrived to galvanise them into activity they would doubtless have gone muddling on for years, 'considering', and 'investigating' and 'pigeon-holing' *ad nauseam*.[23]

It was the firm belief that the *Titanic* was unsinkable that probably accounts for the more than casual attitude of her officers and petty officers to boat assignments and boat drill. The consequence was that boats were sent away half-empty, and there was more than twice as many first class gentlemen in them as third class children. Of all those persons who still remained on board the *Titanic* when she foundered, only about a dozen were picked up by the eighteen boats in the vicinity. The boats of the *Titanic*, insufficient though they were, should have taken 53 per cent of all on board: whereas the number of those rescued was only 32 per cent.

With the best will in the world, the officers were unable to perform their duty efficiently. They were confronted with unmanageable numbers; the life-saving equipment was utterly inadequate—and there had been no proper boat drill. Notwithstanding that conditions of weather and sea were ideal, and that there was ample time for taking to the boats, the results fell a long way short of what might reasonably have been expected. Unaware of the urgency of the danger, a large number of the passengers at first showed marked reluctance to quit the *Titanic*. Their unwillingness to leave was strengthened by the assurance of the officers that in response to their distress call ships were hurrying to the rescue and would be alongside in an hour or two. Very few of them had any idea of the extent of the damage the ship had sustained. Some of the women refused to leave their husbands, others had practically to be thrown into the boats. This attitude of mind, as Conrad has pointed out, appears to have originated in the myth of the *Titanic*'s unsinkability.

All the people on board existed under a sense of false security. How false, it has been sufficiently demonstrated. And the fact which seemed undoubted, that some of them actually were reluctant to enter the boats, when told to do so, shows the strength of that falsehood. Incidentally, it shows also the sort of discipline on board these ships, the sort of hold kept on the passengers in the face of the unforgiving sea. These people seemed to imagine it an optional matter. Whereas the order to leave the ship should be an order of the sternest character, to be obeyed unquestioningly and promptly by everyone on board, with men enough to enforce it at once, and to carry it out methodically and swiftly[4]

Though there are no grounds for supposing that there was any official discrimination between the various classes of passengers, the statistics show all too clearly that the first class fared favourably indeed compared with the others. The men in the second class came off worst of all. (This was probably the result of the second and third classes being lumped together in the boat assignments.) All but a handful of the women in the first class were saved: and of this handful nearly all had chosen to remain on board of their own free will.

When all is said and done, the root cause of the great tragedy was simply bad seamanship. It has been argued by Conrad and others that the want of proper and seamanlike care on the part of those responsible for the navigation of the *Titanic* may justly be attributed to the demand for rapid and luxurious travel and the readiness of the principal shipping companies to satisfy that demand. But all this is in no way invalidates the former conclusion. Bad seamanship still remains bad seamanship, whatever the motivating cause.

Once more one's thoughts recur to Bjarni Herjólfsson and his crew who were the first, in their small vessel, to traverse the Western Ocean. That the science of shipbuilding and the art of navigation had progressed immeasurably since the days of the Vikings is beyond question or doubt. That 'E.J.' was a better seaman than Bjarni Herjólfsson, however, is by no means so certain. Bjarni Herjólfsson, at least, never believed that his ship was unsinkable. . . .

The loss of the *Titanic* was, surely, a classic case of that overweening pride and arrogance which provokes the wrath of the gods, known to the Greeks of old as *hubris*. The new liner was the largest, most magnificent, and most sumptuously appointed vessel which had ever put to sea. 'The greatest skill of the designer, the best materials procurable, the greatest care of the ablest mechanics of one of the greatest shipbuilding yards in existence, were employed to turn out this final triumph of the brain and hands of man.'[25] She was the pride of the British merchant service. She was the ship which 'God Himself could not sink'. It was not only the pampered heirs of the Gilded Age who thought, felt, and spoke in this foolish, boastful way. Even professional seamen, it appeared, were in thrall to *hubris*. Of a truth, the brag was one of the prime causes of the fatality. On his own admission the trusted and experienced 'E.J.' actually seems to have believed that the modern Atlantic liner was for all practical purposes unsinkable. He had certainly acted as if she were. . . . The point was made in a deeply moving sermon preached by the Bishop of Winchester in St Mary's Church, Southampton, on the Sunday following the disaster. 'When,' asked the Bishop, 'has such a mighty lesson against our confidence and trust in power, machinery, and money been shot through the nation? . . . God grant that we and our sister nation of America may take to heart and profit by the lesson. The *Titanic*, name and thing, will stand for a monument and warning to human presumption.' It would, indeed. The appalling tragedy was to be a lesson, not only to church-going folk ashore, but to seamen of all nations, in the years to come. For at sea the price of safety, then as now, must be unceasing vigilance. Notwithstanding her immense proportions and luxurious appointments—her restaurants, her 'millionaire suites', her electric lifts, her Turkish Baths, her squash court, her trellised verandahs, and the rest—the *Titanic* was still a ship. Every link in the chain of circumstances which had led up to her destruction was attributable, in one way or another, to disregard of this fact. Certain ancient lessons of the sea had been forgotten, and had to be learned anew. *Ait enim mare.*

References and Notes

ABBREVIATIONS

Am. Inq.   *The 'Titanic' Disaster*: Report of the Committee on Commerce, United States Senate.
Beesley   Lawrence Beesley, *The Loss of the 'Titanic'* (1912).
Bisset   Captain Sir James Bisset, *Ladies and Tramps* (1955).
Br. Inq.   *Report on the Loss of the 'Titanic'* (*S.S.*) H.M.S.O., 1912.
Gracie   Colonel Archibald Gracie, *The Truth about the 'Titanic'* (1913).
Lightoller   Commander C. H. Lightoller, *'Titanic' and Other Ships* (1935).
M.   Minutes of the *'Titanic'* file at the Board of Trade.
P.V.   *Procès-verbal*, or wireless log-book.
Rostron   Captain Sir Arthur Rostron, *Home from the* Sea (1937).

Chapter 1
    [1] C. Hamilton Ellis, *The South-Western Railway* (1956), p. 17.
    [2] Q. Harvey O'Connor, *The Astors* (1941), p. 277.
    [3] *Letters of Archie Butt*, ed. L. F. Abbot (1924), p. xxiv.

Chapter 2
    [1] Beesley, p. 11.
    [2] Shan F. Bullock, *Thomas Andrews, Shipbuilder* (1912), pp. 59–61.
    [3] *Ib.* p. 60.
    [4] Frank Bustard, *What happened to the White Star Line* (MS. Liverpool City Library); Wilton J. Oldham, *The Ismay Line* (1961), *passim*.
    [5] Originally a double line of boats had been contemplated for the *Titanic's* boat deck similar to that which had recently been fitted in the *Edinburgh Castle*. Welin davits had been installed in the *Titanic*, which would have permitted of two or even of four boats upon one set of davits; but in the end a single line was found sufficient to meet the requirements of the Board of Trade. It appears that Ismay was in the main responsible for the final decision. See *Br. Inq.*, Nos. 21280–1; *Engineering*, July 1st, 1910.

[6] *Shipbuilder*, Vol. VI (1911), Special Midsummer Number; *Engineering*, May 26th, 1911; *Southampton Times; Hampshire Advertiser; Hampshire Independent; Bournemouth Daily Echo; Isle of Wight Observer;* private information.

[7] Filson Young, *Titanic* (1913), pp. 33–4.

[8] *New York Times*, April 20th, 1912.

[9] *Engineering*, Vol. 91, p. 531.

[10] *The Ismay Line*, p. 175.

[11] Satterlee, *J. Pierpont Morgan* (1929), p. 530.

[12] Bisset, p. 250.

[13] Lightoller, pp. 218–19.

[14] Private information.

[15] *Ib*.

[16] Lightoller, p. 219.

[17] Jack Binns had made his name a few years before as operator of the 15,000-ton White Star liner *Republic*. When in 1909 that vessel was rammed in a fog by the Italian liner *Florida* near the Nantucket lightship, a distress call from Jack Binns brought another White Star liner, the *Baltic*, to the scene of the accident in the nick of time. For some years past the international distress call had been CQD: henceforth Jack Binns, who had remained at his post until everyone was safely off the sinking ship, was generally known as 'CQD Binns'. See Karl Baarslag, *SOS* (1937), pp. 42–62.

[18] R. A. Fletcher, *Travelling Palaces* (1913), pp. 139–40.

[19] Local press, as *supra*; Lightoller, p. 218.

[20] Lightoller, p. 214; private information.

[21] G. W. Bowyer, *Lively, Ahoy* (1937); *Southern Evening Echo*, June 21st, 1967; private information.

[22] Private information.

[23] Beesley, pp. 15–16.

[24] Private information.

Chapter 3

[1] Lightoller, p. 220; Beesley, pp. 16–20; Bisset, pp. 69–70.

[2] René Harris in *Liberty Magazine*, April 23rd, 1932.

[3] *Lively, Ahoy*; private information.

[4] It is to be remembered that this was many years before the introduction of the New Helm Orders. Under the Merchant Shipping Act of 1932, which came into force on January 1st, 1933, the past indirect system of helm or steering orders was no longer permissible. Thenceforward the order 'STARBOARD' was only

to be given when it was intended that the wheel, the rudder blade, and the head of the ship should go to starboard; 'PORT' was only to be given when it was intended that the wheel, the rudder blade, and the head of the ship should go to port. But, in 1912, the former indirect system of helm orders was still in use.

5 *Southampton Evening Echo*, June 21st, 1967.

6 *Thomas Andrews, Shipbuilder*, pp. 61–2.

7 Walter Lord, *A Night to Remember* (1957), p. 158.

8 *Am. Inq.*, pp. 584–5.

9 Richard O'Connor, *Down to Eternity* (1957), p. 35.

10 Caroline Bancroft, *The Unsinkable Mrs Brown* (1963), *passim*.

11 Walter Lord, *The Good Years* (1960), p. 270.

12 *Q. Shipping World*, May 15th, 1912.

13 *Thomas Andrews, Shipbuilder*, p. 61.

14 *Le Matin*, April 11th, 1912.

15 *Q.* Estelle Stead, *My Father* (1913), p. 342.

Chapter 4

1 *Cork Examiner, Cork Constitution, Irish Times, Freeman's Journal.*

2 Beesley, p. 24.

3 Private information.

4 Beesley, p. 25.

5 *Am. Inq.*, p. 393; *Br. Inq.*, Nos. 17507–12.

6 *Ib.* pp. 24–5.

7 The oscillatory discharge of a condenser forms the essential foundation of all wireless transmitters and receivers. To emit, or to absorb, electro-magnetic radiation on an effective scale it is necessary to open out the plates of the condenser to form what is known as an open oscillatory circuit. During the 1890s Marconi devised such a circuit; and thereafter progressively extended the range of his communications.

8 *Marconigraph*, May, 1912; private information.

9 *SOS*, p. 20.

10 Though practically all Marconi marine stations were equipped with magnetic detectors at this time, crystal detectors were standard with the German Telefunken Company, Marconi's main rival, who used a cartridge-type silicon-gold combination, as well as certain other combinations, of proved efficiency. The Navy also had discarded magnetic for crystal detectors, after finding that the latter could be adequately protected from gunfire vibration by special shock-absorbing mountings. Marconi's first standard crystal receiver was designed by the late Captain H. J. Round in 1914.

[11] *Surrey Times*, April 20th, 1912; private information.

[12] *Marconigraph*, May, 1912.

Chapter 5

[1] Washington Dodge, *The Loss of the 'Titanic'* (1912), p. 4.

[2] Archibald Gracie, *The Truth about the 'Titanic'* (1913), p. 5.

[3] Beesley, p. 39.

[4] *Thomas Andrews, Shipbuilder*, pp. 63–4.

[5] Q. Edith Harper, *Stead the Man* (1914), p. 244.

[6] *Daily News*, April 20th, 1912.

[7] *New York Herald*, April 20th, 1912.

[8] *Letters of Archie Butt*, pp. xxvi–xxvii.

[9] Q. Wolf and Fleming, *Rosenbach* (1960), p. 76.

[10] The actual certificate would follow later.

[11] Lightoller, p. 204.

[12] *Ib.* p. 261.

[13] *Nautical Magazine*, Vol. 87, p. 483. This is corroborated by an important statement in the *Newfoundland and Labrador Pilot* (1907 ed.), p. 29; and also by the fact that, on the same route, there is no significant difference between passages made nowadays *with the aid of radar* and those made fifty and sixty years ago.

[14] *Atlantic Monthly*, May, 1910, p. 582.

[15] 'How many of the missing bankmen meet their end in this way,' the *St John's Herald* (Newfoundland) had observed on August 28th, 1906, 'can only be conjectured, but certain it is that far more are sunk than are reported to the world. Frequently the steamer's people scarcely know what has happened when such a catastrophe occurs to the accompaniment of a midnight storm, so slight is the shock of impact on her huge hull, and with spectators few at these times, and look-outs and watch-officers having every reason to escape inquiry and possible punishment, the temptation to hurry on and make no alarm is usually yielded to. . . . So frequent are these collisions, that the recent comic papers had a rather ghastly joke about a tourist returning to America and bemoaning the uneventful passage, as the ship "ran down only one fishing smack, don't you know" '. In this connection a letter addressed to *The Times* on April 20th, 1912, by James J. Page, of the Bengal Pilot Service, is worth quoting: 'In November, 1907, I wrote to the President of the Board of Trade calling his attention to the high speed at which Transatlantic steamers are navigated through fog. I instanced the Marconigrams published in the Press the previous September of a giant liner "emerging from the dense fog which had enveloped her

for the past sixteen hours in which speed had frequently to be reduced to 19 knots". I contended it would be "very doubtful if those on board such a vessel . . . going at 19 knots, would even know should they run down a small craft, and the course of any vessel going at such a speech in thick weather may well be termed murderous".' See also *Atlantic Monthly*, August, 1910, p. 288.

[16] In an interview with some journalists about this time, 'E.J.' had declared in his usual sanguine style: 'Of course there have been winter gales and storms and fog and the like in the forty years I have been on the seas; but I have never been in an accident worth speaking of . . . I never saw a wreck. I have never been wrecked. I have never been in a predicament that threatened to end in disaster of any sort' (*Q. The Sinking of the 'Titanic'*, ed. Logan Marshall (1912), p. 234).

[17] Private information.

[18] This information was given to the present writer by Captain Edwin Jones, 'Chang' Jones, as Murdoch used to call him (in his younger days the former had been in the China coasting trade), who went on to say that shortly afterwards he left the bridge and went down on the saloon deck, where he met a passenger who had apparently witnessed the whole affair. 'Well, that was a narrow escape,' gasped the latter. 'Wasn't that ship close!' 'What ship?' asked Jones coldly. A pause. The other man stared at him in blank amazement. 'Do you mean to say,' he said incredulously, 'you didn't see a big ship just now? Why, she nearly ran us down!' Jones thereupon gave it as his opinion that the ship the passenger thought he had seen must have been the *Flying Dutchman* . . . after which he hurried back on to the bridge and warned the O.O.W. that there had been a witness. 'For God's sake,' said Murdoch, 'go and tell Bertie' [Captain Bertram Hayes, then Master of the *Arabic*]. In such cases, as has already been said, the official policy was to hush the matter up.

[19] Lightoller, *passim*.

[20] *Am. Inq.*, p. 369.

[21] Private information.

[22] *Marconigraph*, June, 1911.

[23] Thus on the morning of Saturday, the 13th, the *Titanic* relayed part of the news service for the benefit of the *Minnehaha*. (*Minnehaha* P.V.).

[24] A notice would be posted up in the foyers, smoking-rooms, and elsewhere on board to the effect that messages might be sent to such and such a vessel up to a certain hour.

[25] Phillips was 'on' from 8 p.m. to 2 a.m., and Bride from 2 a.m. to 8 a.m. During the rest of the twenty-four hours their duties were variable to suit each other's convenience. As a rule Phillips was generally on duty until 2 p.m., after which Bride took over. They relieved each other at meal-times.

[26] *Marconigraph*, June, 1911.

[27] Thus a few weeks before Phillips, then senior operator in the *Oceanic*, had recognized the distinctive 'style' of the operator at Cape Race (Newfoundland) and had inquired what Gray was doing at MCE. Gray, recently transferred from Glace Bay (Nova Scotia), countered by asking what Phillips was doing at sea again; and the latter told him that he had been appointed to the *Titanic* on her maiden voyage in April, and was eagerly looking forward to this experience.

[28] *SOS*, p. 30.

[29] Frustration was the mother of bad language. It was not to be wondered at that the axiom arose, 'You can't be a radio operator and remain a Christian!' Over and above the official abbreviations of the 'Q' code there existed a long list of others – invitations, exhortations, imprecations, profanities, and obscenities, which a good many operators had 'at their finger tips' and which could not possibly be quoted. Some of the foreign operators were renowned for their objugatory powers over the ether, '*God-damned Slaby Arco*', one incensed German operator shot off at another attached to a rival system, '*rotten louse and hump-backed monkey*!' There had been times, indeed, when such exchanges on the high seas had been followed by a furious affray when one day the antagonists had happened to come face to face on the waterfront or in some 'dive' ashore. Such liberties, however, were not permitted by the Marconi Marine. See *ib.* p. 37.

Chapter 6

[1] René Harris in *Liberty Magazine*, April 23rd, 1932.

[2] J. B. Thayer, *The Sinking of the S.S. 'Titanic'* (1940), p. 13.

[3] *Am. Inq.*, p. 1100.

[4] *Marconigraph*, September, 1911; *Year-Book of Wireless Telegraphy* (1913), p. 559.

[5] *Travelling Palaces*, p. 243.

[6] *Am. Inq.*, p. 772.

[7] *Star*, April 22nd, 1912.

[8] *Travelling Palaces*, pp. 252–4.

[9] *A Night to Remember*, p. 5.

[10] *Titanic*, pp. 48–9.

[11] *Thomas Andrews, Shipbuilder*, pp. 55–6.

[12] *Travelling Palaces*, pp. 116–9.

[13] Lightoller, pp. 258–61.

[14] *Ib.* p. 221.

[15] In accordance with the practice in the express White Star steamships, senior officers did four hours on and eight hours off. The Chief Officer's duty was from 2 to 6 a.m. and p.m.; the Second Officer's, from 6 to 10 a.m. and p.m.; the First Officer's, from 10 to 2 a.m. and p.m. The junior officers did four hours on and four hours off; they would stand the 'dogs' in the evenings so that their watches altered every day.

[16] The longitude was found by calculating the difference in degrees of arc between Greenwich time and the ship's time. Greenwich time was known from the chronometers on board. The ship's time was calculated from the altitude of the sun or a star, and the known latitude. To compute the longitude it was necessary to find the hour angle, or ship's time, by spherical trigonometery. The sides of the spherical triangle were represented by the polar distance (difference of declination from 90°), the zenith distance (from the true altitude), and the co-latitude (its difference from 90°). The ship's hour angle was the angle at the pole between the two sides of the triangle representing the polar distance and the zenith distance.

[17] The inherent fallibility of dead reckoning can be readily gauged from the following example. A few years before the *Bovic* had made a passage which was for long legendary in the White Star Line. It was claimed that she steamed from Tuskar to Nantucket in eight days without sights, running on dead reckoning; and she made a very good landfall. Against this notable achievement, however, is to be set the fact that her Master, *still relying on his dead reckoning*, subsequently piled up, first, the *Suevic* on the Maenheere Rocks off the Lizard, and, second, the *Highland Hope* on the Burlings. In dead reckoning chance, rather than skill, is usually the determining factor. Even in the hands of the ablest and most careful navigator too much trust ought not to be put in D.R. Thus on the present voyage, when it became urgently necessary to know the *Titanic's* exact position, it was found that her dead reckoning position was seriously in error.

[18] *East Coast of the United States Pilot*, Part I (1909), p. 34; *Nova Scotia and Bay of Fundy Pilot* (1911), p. 15. Cf. *Syren and Shipping*, January, 1910, p. 159.

[19] *New York Times*, April 20th, 1912.

Chapter 7

[1] *Am. Inq.*, pp. 963–4.

[2] *Empress of Britain* P.V.

[3] *Br. Inq.*, Nos. 18387–95, 18644–55, 19000–4.

[4] *Travelling Palaces*, p. 142.

[5] Beesley, p. 33.

[6] *Ib.* 40–45.

[7] *Travelling Palaces*, p. 154.

[8] Beesley, pp. 46–8.

[9] Private information.

[10] *A Night to Remember*, p. 158.

[11] *Thomas Andrews, Shipbuilder*, p. 64.

[12] *Am. Inq.*, p. 772.

[13] *The Sinking of the S.S. 'Titanic'*, p. 13.

[14] Gracie, p. 127.

[15] *Ib.* 4–5; *Toronto Globe*, April 19th, 1912.

[16] Beesley, pp. 52–4.

[17] *Am. Inq.*, pp. 791–1101.

[18] *Br. Inq.*, No. 16791.

[19] *Ib.* p. 343; No. 15689.

[20] After some discussion between Captain Smith, Wilde, and Boxhall, they decided that 'Paris' denoted the longitude of the French capital and allowed for the difference in longitude between Paris and Greenwich. 'E.J.' stood by the Fourth Officer when he was marking the positions of the ice with a cross. Boxhall observed that these positions were of no use to them as they lay well to the north of their track. The Captain considered the report from the *Touraine*; then he glanced at the chart and was satisfied.

[21] *Br. Inq.*, No. 16099.

[22] *Ib.* p. 825.

[23] *Ib.* No. 16176.

[24] *Am. Inq.*, pp. 963–4; *Br. Inq.* Nos. 18828–40.

[25] *Ib.* No. 16122.

[26] *Ib.* No. 8943. This message had been offered to the *Titanic* earlier; it had not been taken because Bride was busy with his accounts – which, as he afterwards explained, had been made up for Saturday, but not for Sunday. And also, he added, because it used to take some time to start up the motor and alternator, 'it not being advisable to leave them working, as the alternator was liable to run hot'.

[27] *Ib.* Nos. 15310–7.

[28] The course had been S. 62° W. true until 5.50 p.m.; it was

then altered to S. 86° W. true—that is, N. 71° W. by the steering compass.

[29] *Br. Inq.*, Nos. 15984–8.

[30] *Ib*. Nos. 17704–9.

[31] That part of the advancing power of the screw which, for various reasons, is lost is called the slip. Slip is greatest with the vessel going ahead, or astern, from stop.

[32] *Br. Inq.*, No. 15173.

[33] *Am. Inq.*, p. 450; *Br. Inq.*, Nos. 13593–5.

[34] *Ib*. Nos. 16221, 22052.

[35] *Olympic* P.V. This 'freaky reception', or fading, may be ascribed to the Northern Lights, which are known to have a considerable effect on radio propagation (and were certainly seen that night). Atmospherics had been 'coming on bad' for some time. The tendency of static charge to build up in the *Titanic's* large aerials and rigging, intermittently discharging into the air on reaching a certain level of potential, would be exaggerated under the frost conditions that obtained. Interference due to this and also to the ship's generating and lighting installation would be superimposed on the natural static, or X's, in the atmosphere. Jamming, as has been said, was almost endemic in the traffic lanes.

[36] *Br. Inq.*, Nos. 22022–88; Lightoller, pp. 222–3.

[37] The Nord-deutscher Lloyd liner, *Prinz Friedrich Wilhelm*, heard the *Titanic* transmitting dozens of messages to Cape Race. '*MGY arbeitet fast ununterbrochen mit MCE: MGY zeichen sterben teilweise weg*' ('*Titanic* works almost continuously with Cape Race: *Titanic's* signals die away at times').

[38] *Am. Inq.*, p. 1035; M 24939.

[39] Private information.

[40] *Br. Inq.*, Nos. 8988–9020.

Chapter 8

[1] *Br. Inq.*, Nos. 13611–35.

[2] *Ib*. Nos. 16925–32.

[3] *Ib*. Nos. 13656–71.

[4] *Ib*. Nos. 11339–40.

[5] Gwyn Jones, *The Norse Atlantic Saga* (1964), pp. 64, 147; G. J. Marcus, '*Hafvilla:* A Note on Norse Navigation', *Speculum*, Vol. XXX, pp. 603–4.

[6] Lightoller, p. 223; *Br. Inq.*, No. 13676.

[7] *Ib*. Nos. 13682–95.

[8] *Ib*. 937.

⁹ *Ib.* Nos. 13707–24.

¹⁰ *Ib.* Nos. 16918–22, 22022–88; Lightoller, pp. 222–3.

¹¹ *Br. Inq.*, Nos. 15737–51.

¹² Captain A. E. Smith's letter to the *Daily Telegraph*, April 7th, 1962; private information.

¹³ *Am. Inq.*, p. 902; *Br. Inq.*, Nos. 8988–9020.

¹⁴ *Ib.* Nos. 2401–8, 17250–73.

¹⁵ *Ib.* Nos. 1027, 13734, 15353, 15355, 17275–80, 17299–326.

Chapter 9

¹ *Br. Inq.*, Nos. 15358–77; *Nautical Magazine*, Vol. 181, p. 262.

² *Br. Inq.*, No. 13734; Lightoller, p. 227.

³ *Br. Inq.*, pp. 32–4.

⁴ Lightoller, p. 229.

⁵ 'I worked on the 7.30 position to 11.46 on speed and course'— J. G. Boxhall in *Nautical Magazine*, Vol. 181, p. 263.

⁶ *Journal of Commerce: Report of the 'Titanic' Inquiry* (1912), p. 267.

⁷ The following account of the part played by the two wireless operators that night is based on Bride's interview with the *New York Times*, his official letter to the Company, and the evidence given at the American and British Inquiries.

⁸ *Morning Post*, April 29th, 1912.

⁹ *Thomas Andrews, Shipbuilder*, p. 67; *New York Herald*, April 20th, 1912.

¹⁰ *Ib.* pp. 69–70.

¹¹ *Harper's Weekly*, April 29th, 1912.

¹² Beesley, pp. 83–4.

¹³ *Br. Inq.*, Nos. 15394–400.

¹⁴ *Ib.* Nos. 15404–14.

¹⁵ Lightoller, pp. 233–4.

¹⁶ *Ib.* p. 237.

¹⁷ *Am. Inq.*, pp. 277–8; *Br. Inq.*, No. 15034.

Chapter 10

¹ Beesley, pp. 54–5.

² *Ib.* pp. 72–3.

³ *Ib.* pp. 79–80.

⁴ *Ib.* (1929 ed.), pp. 66–7. This was probably James Moody, the Sixth Officer, who was among those lost.

⁵ *Ib.* (1912 ed.), p. 161.

⁶ *New York Times*, April 20th, 1912.

⁷ *Am. Inq.*, p. 1107.

[8] *Ib*. pp. 1149–50.

[9] *Ib*. p. 804.

[10] *St Ives Times*, May 10th, 1912.

[12] Beesley, pp. 76–7.

[11] *Daily Graphic*, April 20th, 1912.

[13] *Le Matin*, April 19th, 1912.

[14] Lightoller, p. 240.

[15] *Ib*. p. 241.

[16] *Am. Inq*., p. 655.

[17] At the American Inquiry, Lightoller gave evidence that Ismay was hustled into one of the boats by Wilde, the Chief Officer. Jack Thayer's version of this incident is rather different and probably a good deal nearer the truth. 'A large crowd was pressing to get into them [the boats]. No women were around as far as I could see. I saw Ismay, who had been assisting in the loading of the last boat, push his way into it. It was really every man for himself.'

[18] *Thomas Andrews, Shipbuilder*, p. 73.

[19] Katherine Burton, *Harry Widener* (1939).

[20] *Am. Inq*., pp. 990–1004; Gracie, p. 27.

[21] *New York Sun*, April 22nd, 1912.

[22] Lightoller, p. 243.

[23] *Ib*. pp. 245–6.

[24] *The Sinking of the S.S. 'Titanic'*, p. 22.

Chapter 11

[1] Lightoller, pp. 247–50.

[2] *Ib*. p. 250; Beesley, p. 115.

[3] Gracie, pp. 71–2.

[4] Beesley, pp. 121–2.

[5] Lightoller, p. 250; private information.

[6] *Am. Inq*., p. 659.

[7] *Q*. Gracie, p. 169.

[8] Cape Race P.V.; private information.

[9] *Am. Inq*., pp. 1134–9; *Br. Inq*., pp. 65–8; *SOS*, p. 78.

[10] Lightoller, p. 234.

[11] *Virginian* P.V.

[12] *Olympic* P.V.

[13] Cape Race P.V.

[14] *Carpathia* P.V.

[15] *New York Times*, April 20th, 1912.

[16] Lightoller, pp. 251–2.

[17] Beesley, pp. 135–6.

The Maiden Voyage

Chapter 12

[1] *Br. Inq.*, Nos. 8988–9020.
[2] *Am. Inq.*, p. 903; private information.
[3] *Ib.*
[4] Captain McMillan in *Journal of Commerce*, March 16th 1968.
[5] *Br. Inq.*, Nos. 7483–510, 7829–66, 7880–96, 7948–56.
[6] *Ib.* Nos. 7552–72.
[7] *Ib.* No. 7971.
[8] The Leyland liner *Californian* continued to distinguish herself
during the rest of the morning of the 15th. Captain Lord, as will
later be seen, failed to discover a single body in the vicinity of the
wreck; and the *Californian's* wireless signals jammed the transmissions of other ships. The operator of the *Baltic* recorded wrathfully in his log-book: 'Sigs MPA [*Carpathia*] . . . unable to work
owing to insistent jambing by MWL [*Californian*] who is talking
all the time . . . MWL persists in talking to SBA [*Birma*]; such
remarks as 'Do you see a four-masted salmon pink smoke stack
steamer around, etc. Impossible for us to work MPA . . . Sigs MPA
but can do nothing for jambing by MWL and SBA who are carrying
on long irrelevant conversations . . . MWL still monopolizing the
air with his remarks. Carrying on conversations with every station.
MPA is trying to send me message but communication out of the
question owing to MWL . . .'. (*Baltic* P.V.). The *Baltic* later threatened to report MWL for 'jambing' [jamming].

Chapter 13

[1] Bisset, p. 276.
[2] *Ib.* pp. 277–8.
[3] *Br. Inq.*, p. 65, Nos. 17090–109.
[4] Rostron, p. 57.
[5] Bisset, pp. 278–9.
[6] *Ib.* p. 279.
[7] *Am. Inq.*, pp. 19–21; Rostron, p. 63.
[8] Bisset, pp. 279–80.
[9] *Ib.* p. 281.
[10] *Ib.* p. 283.
[11] *Ib.*
[12] *Ib.* pp. 286–7.
[13] Beesley, pp. 199–201, 210–11.
[14] Bisset, p. 291.
[15] *Ib.* p. 296.

Chapter 14

[1] *Southampton Times; Hampshire Advertiser; Hampshire Independent,* April 16th–23rd, 1912.

[2] *Daily Telegraph,* April 16th, 1912.

[3] *Times,* April 17th, 1912.

[4] *Daily Mail Overseas Edition,* April 20th, 1912.

[5] Private information.

[6] Rostron, pp. 73–4.

[7] Charles Moore, *Daniel H. Burnham* (1921), ii, pp. 154.

[8] *Am. Inq.,* p. 961.

[9] *Daniel H. Burnham,* pp. 154–5.

[10] René Harris in *Liberty Magazine,* April 23rd, 1932.

[11] Beesley, pp. 147–8.

[12] Siasconsett P.V.

[13] The handling of the *Titanic* story by Carl Van Anda, managing editor of the *New York Times,* must be accounted one of the most brilliant journalistic achievements of the era. It gave that journal a lead over its rivals which it has never relinquished. See E. A. Weeks, *The Open Heart* (1956), pp. 97–8; *Down to Eternity,* pp. 154–6.

[14] A rumour was circulating to the effect that Cottam and Bride were engaged in taking the baseball scores during the return to New York.

Chapter 15

[1] *Am. Inq.,* p. 1150; *New York Herald,* April 20th, 1912.

[1] *San Francisco Chronicle,* April 19th, 1912.

[3] Ismay was succeeded as President of the International Mercantile Marine Company and Chairman of the White Star Line by his colleague, Harold A. Sanderson; but shortly after P. A. S. Franklin was appointed President of the International Mercantile Marine Company. See *The Ismay Line,* pp. 218–25.

[4] *The Unsinkable Mrs Brown,* pp. 36–7.

[5] M 12178.

[6] *Am. Inq.,* pp. 710–1.

[7] *Ib.* p. 902.

[8] *Ib.* p. 573.

[9] Lightoller, p. 255.

[10] *The 'Titanic' Disaster: Speech of Hon. William Alden Smith* (May 28th, 1912).

Chapter 16

[1] Lightoller, p. 257.

[2] *Br. Inq.,* Nos. 6897–954.

³ *Ib.* Nos. 6999–7000.

⁴ *Ib.* Nos. 7090–4.

⁵ *Ib.* Nos. 7280–94.

⁶ *Ib.* Nos. 7476–533.

⁷ *Ib.* Nos. 8022–37.

⁸ *Ib.* Nos. 8503–64; private information.

⁹ The log of the *Californian* for the first watch begins: 'Eight p.m., light wind; small swell; clear weather. Midnight, calm and smooth sea; clear weather; ship surrounded by ice' (*Am. Inq.*, p. 720). No mention at all of the rockets seen from the bridge in this or the following watch.

¹⁰ The column headed 'Remarks' is the wide column on the right-hand side of the log-book in which are entered details of the weather and sea, any vessel signalled, any land, derelict, or ice sighted, etc. All these items are entered, either at the time or at the end of the watch, by the O.O.W. in the scrap log, or rough log-book, usually in pencil. In due course they are copied out neatly in ink in the official log-book.

¹¹ *Br. Inq.*, Nos. 8721–52.

Chapter 17

¹ *Br. Inq.*, Nos. 5141–53.

² *Ib.* Nos. 11501–730.

³ The mounting tension and excitement in the Court of Inquiry on May 20th can best be appreciated by studying the press accounts of the proceedings that day which was one of the most important in the Inquiry. The *Pall Mall Gazette*, *Westminster Gazette*, *Daily Telegraph*, *Daily News*, *Daily Mail*, and *Daily Mirror* are especially informative.

⁴ *Br. Inq.*, Nos. 12647–68.

⁵ *Ib.* Nos. 12875–95.

⁶ While they were at Belfast Lightoller and Moody had together explored the route leading from the steerage quarters up to the Boat Deck. As a result of this experience they realized that the difficulties and distance involved were so great that there would be little chance for the third class in the event of a sudden emergency.

⁷ *Ib.* Nos. 14414–25.

⁸ *Ib.* Nos. 14197–209.

⁹ *Ib.* p. 738.

¹⁰ *Ib.* pp. 812–13.

¹¹ *Ib.* p. 30.

Chapter 18

[1] *Times*, June 21st, 1913.

[2] *Ib.*

[3] *Ib.*

[4] *Ib.*

[5] *Ib.*

[6] *Ib.* June 24th, 1913.

[7] *Ib.* June 24th–25th, 1913. Further light is shed on the crucial factor of visibility at the time of the impact by a letter addressed to the Board of Trade, during the Official Inquiry, by Captain J. E. Sargent, a Master of wide experience in large cargo and cattle steamships. Captain Sargent declared that large bergs were frequently enveloped in haze; he recalled that on one occasion when the weather appeared quite clear he was close on three bergs before seeing them. 'The crow's nest in modern large steamers at night time is not a good place to keep a look-out for ice. The blue Arctic ice and the water, being practically the same colour, looking down from such a height they cannot be seen' (M 14378). See also Captain Sir Ivan Thompson's letter to the *Daily Telegraph*, April 14th, 1962.

[8] *Ib.* June 25th, 1913.

[9] *Ib.* June 26th, 1913.

[10] *Ib.*

[11] *Ib.*

[12] *Ib.* February 10th, 1914.

Chapter 19

[1] M 10226.

[2] *Br. Inq.*, Nos. 13682–95.

[3] It is not a little ironical that the Mercantile Marine Service Association, which later was so strongly to champion the cause of Captain Lord, in the original report of the disaster in its journal, *The Reporter*, stated that 'the *Californian*, which had seen the rockets, but had erroneously assigned them to another vessel (which had passed out of sight to the South-West while she lay stopped on account of ice), also steamed at daylight to the locality indicated by wireless signals for assistance, lat. 41° 46′ N., long. 50° 14′ W. She arrived too late to be of service' (M.M.S.A., *The Reporter*, Vol. 37, p. 806).

[4] *Am. Inq.*, pp. 1118, 1120.

[5] M 10226, 16309–11, 14701, 14912, 15478, 15589, 17046–8, 17374, 17554, 17686, 18225, 18975, 19155, 19782.

[6] M 17449.

[7] Private information. This point, which is of vital importance, was clearly established at the British Inquiry.

[8] *Br. Inq.*, pp. 45–6.

[9] *Review of Reviews*, Vol. 46, p. 168.

[10] *John Bull*, April 27th, 1912.

[11] *Daily Telegraph*, July 31st, 1912.

[12] *Q. The 'Californian' Incident* (1965), p. 50.

[13] *Ib.* pp. 51–2.

[14] M 24407.

[15] Captain A. E. Smith's letter to the *Daily Telegraph*, April 7th, 1962. Cf. John C. Carrothers and Walter Lord in the March and August, 1968, issues respectively of the *U.S. Naval Institute Proceedings*.

[16] M 25042.

[17] Lightoller, p. 235.

Chapter 20

[1] It would seem that one Jony Yates, gambler and con. man, was as much to the fore in assisting the women and children as any of the millionaires.

[2] *New York Tribune*, April 21st, 1912.

[3] Gene Fowler, *Timber Line* (1933).

[4] *Sinking of the 'Titanic'*, ed. Logan Marshall (1912), pp. 125–6; *A Night to Remember*, p. 164.

[5] The standing orders of the White Star Line are quoted at length in *The Ismay Line*, p. 283.

[6] R. H. Gretton, *A Modern History of the English People*, III, p. 69.

[7] Though the *Arizona's* bows were completely stove in her collision bulkhead had held. The accident occurred in clear weather and with a calm sea; but a heavy cloud rising across the ship's bows made it difficult to distinguish objects in time to avoid them. During the ensuing years the lesson of the *Arizona* was apparently forgotten. The fact is, there was always a tendency to underestimate the danger of ice. In any case, the *Arizona* was only a 5,000-ton ship, running at scarcely 15 knots: a fact to which she probably owed her escape from total disaster.

[8] *New York Times*, April 20th, 1912.

[9] *Nautical Magazine*, Vol. 88, p. 240.

[10] *Br. Inq.*, No. 19320.

[11] In the course of his letter to *The Times*, April 20th, 1912, quoted above, Captain Page recalled a statement made by Admiral de Horsey to the *Daily Mail*: 'I recall to mind, many years ago, when

giving evidence at the Society of Arts before a Committee on the subject of speed in a fog, that certain captains of liners, on being assured that their names would be kept secret, stated that it was their practice to maintain high speed in a fog as being safer for their own ship, and because compliance with the rule of reduced speed would cause such delay of mails and passengers as would lead to their company's dispensing with their services and appointing less conscientious commanders'. Page recalled that the British Government had refused point-blank to take any action; Lloyd George (then President of the Board of Trade) holding the view that 'as I am not aware that any sufficient reasons have been adduced for altering it, I would not propose to take any steps in that direction'.

[12] There is a good deal of truth in Pepys's shrewd comment, that 'it is by God Almighty's providence and great chance, and the wideness of the sea, that there are not a great many [more] misfortunes and ill chances in Navigation than there are. . . .' (*The Tangier Papers of Samuel Pepys*, ed. E. Chappell, p. 127.)

[13] Many years after the *Titanic* disaster, a certain steamship was running at high speed in thick weather, when a Dutch liner suddenly swept past, missing her by inches. The fog was so dense at the time that those on the steamship's bridge could see nothing of the other vessel but one of her boats hanging in the davits. The Master gasped at the apparition and immediately ordered the junior (the future Commander W. C. A. Robson) not to breathe a word of what he had seen—not even to the officers out on the other wing of the bridge; then he went below for a stiff peg. . . . It is scarcely necessary to add that, even so, *speed was not reduced*.

[14] *Br. Inq.*, No. 25098.

[15] Lightoller, p. 223.

[16] G. J. Marcus, 'Disaster at Sea', *Sunday Telegraph*, April 8th, 1962.

[17] Such deficiencies and irregularities as may have occurred in certain ships' stations on the night of the disaster never became a matter of public knowledge. Evans indeed was strongly criticized by other operators for turning in at a time *when emergency conditions prevailed*. He may well have received some sort of reprimand in private: but no overt action was ever taken. After all, the Marconi Marine Company had profited greatly from the *Titanic* affair and had no mind to spoil its public 'image'. It never admitted to any fault or failure on the part of its operators. But it is significant that in the years to come far higher standards of duty were exacted from its employees in the marine stations.

[18] The phenomenon known as 'Swatow white fog' is not mentioned at all in the local sailing directions. It is of comparatively rare occurrence; according to the local pilots and masters, a ship might be running into Swatow regularly every few weeks, and experience the white fog, perhaps, once in three years.

[19] Alfred Hogg had given testimony to this effect at the American Inquiry—'If we had had the glasses, we might have seen the berg before'. Several weeks later the Captain of H.M.S. *Sirius*, who had had much experience of ice, informed the Board of Trade that, 'It was the unanimous opinion of officers and other observers, that bergs could be picked up very much quicker with glasses than with either the searchlight or the naked eye'. He was strongly of opinion that glasses were the most efficient means of picking up icebergs on a clear dark night, and with a clear sky they should be sighted at a considerable distance (M 20837).

[20] The superior manoeuvrability of the Cunard *Mauretania* was the means of saving her just in time when, on the night of May 20th, 1914, her look-out sighted an iceberg immediately ahead—the wheel was thereupon whipped over hard-a-port, and the vessel slipped by without touching the berg (*Globe*, May 23rd, 1914).

[21] Bisset, pp. 298–9.

[22] Joseph Conrad, *Some Reflexions . . . on the Loss of the 'Titanic'* (1919), pp. 17th, 19.

[23] *Syren and Shipping*, April 24th, 1912.

[24] *Some Reflexions . . . on the Loss of the 'Titanic'*, pp. 25–6.

[25] *Syren and Shipping*, April 17th, 1912.

Index